ON THE

WATERFRONT

ON THE WATERFRONT

THE PULITZER PRIZE–WINNING ARTICLES THAT INSPIRED THE CLASSIC MOVIE AND TRANSFORMED THE NEW YORK HARBOR

MALCOLM JOHNSON

Foreword by
HAYNES JOHNSON

Introduction and additional articles by
BUDD SCHULBERG

CHAMBERLAIN BROS.
A MEMBER OF PENGUIN GROUP (USA) INC.
NEW YORK

CHAMBERLAIN BROS.
Published by the Penguin Group
Penguin Group (USA) Inc., 375 Hudson Street, New York, New York 10014, USA
Penguin Group (Canada), 10 Alcorn Avenue, Toronto, Ontario M4V 3B2, Canada (a division of Pearson Penguin Canada Inc.)
Penguin Books Ltd, 80 Strand, London WC2R 0RL, England
Penguin Ireland, 25 St Stephen's Green, Dublin 2, Ireland
(a division of Penguin Books Ltd)
Penguin Group (Australia), 250 Camberwell Road, Camberwell,
Victoria 3124, Australia (a division of Pearson Australia Group Pty Ltd)
Penguin Books India Pvt Ltd, 11 Community Centre, Panchsheel Park, New Delhi–110 017, India
Penguin Group (NZ), Cnr Airborne and Rosedale Roads, Albany, Auckland 1310,
New Zealand (a division of Pearson New Zealand Ltd)
Penguin Books (South Africa) (Pty) Ltd, 24 Sturdee Avenue, Rosebank,
Johannesburg 2196, South Africa

Penguin Books Ltd, Registered Offices: 80 Strand, London WC2R 0RL, England

Chamberlain Bros.
a member of Penguin Group (USA) Inc.
375 Hudson Street, New York, NY 10014

Library of Congress Cataloging-in-Publication Data
Johnson, Malcolm M. (Malcolm Malone), 1904–1976.
On the waterfront : the Pulitzer Prize–winning articles that inspired the classic movie and transformed the New York Harbor / by Malcolm Johnson ; introduction and additional articles by Budd Schulberg ; foreword by Haynes Johnson.
p. cm.
ISBN 1-59609-013-8
1. Stevedores—New York (State)—New York. 2. Organized crime—New York (State)—New York. 3. New York Harbor (N.Y. and N.J.). 4. On the waterfront (Motion picture).
I. Schulberg, Budd. II. Title.
HD 8039.L82U65 2005 2004063403
364.1'06'09747109044—dc22

Printed in the United States of America

10 9 8 7 6 5 4 3 2 1

Book design by Jaime Putorti

Contents

Foreword

By Haynes Johnson

It started as a routine assignment.

A hiring boss on New York City's Cunard Line Pier 92, a young brawler named Thomas Collentine, had been shot and killed by an unidentified gunman as he left home for work. Later that morning, in the City Room of *The New York Sun*, the top editor, Edmund P. Bartnett, summoned reporter Malcolm Johnson to his desk. "Lots of unrest down there," Bartnett said, handing over a brief news account of yet another waterfront murder to Johnson. "Why don't you take a look? Maybe you can get a story out of it."

So "Mike" Johnson, *The Sun*'s star reporter, began an assignment that many months later led to a startling exposé of what he called an "outlaw frontier" where organized criminals had a stranglehold on the greatest, and busiest, port in the world. There, against the backdrop of New York's magnificent skyscrapers and in the heart of America's financial and cultural centers, these criminal gangs enforced their reign of terror through unchecked thievery, control of the fantastically lucrative narcotics traffic, smuggling, shakedowns, kickbacks, bribery, extortion, and murder. They, in turn, were allied to a vast crime cartel he called the syndicate, now known as the Mafia, that Johnson said controlled organized crime in America. He was the first to reveal the existence of that "underworld syndicate," with national and international connections, which "operates in every major city and also has big interests abroad . . . in Italy, South America, and Mexico." As he reported, the waterfront gangs operated "with apparent immunity from the law," and their control of the piers was absolute. "Their greatest weapon is terror," he wrote, "invoked by their strong-arm squads and their gunmen. Their power is such that they are able to levy tribute on every pound of cargo arriving at this port."

At that time, more than seven trillion dollars in waterborne commerce passed annually through the Port of New York. This represented nearly twice as much traffic as all other Atlantic ports combined, and a fifth of the tonnage of all exports and imports of the United States. The waterfront rackets were adding hundreds of millions of dollars a year to shipping costs as a result of higher freight handling charges. In the end, consumers throughout the United States bore these costs in the higher prices they paid for goods.

A key to these rackets was mob control of the powerful international longshoremen's union. "Through the union," he explained, "mobsters are able to control all key jobs on the piers and rackets operate without interference. In some instances, known criminals have official positions in the union locals. In others, they have strong alliances and can dictate policy. By dominating the locals, the criminals succeed in placing their own men—or men approved by them—in jobs controlling the hiring of stevedores and the checking of cargo. . . . The waterfront, therefore, has become a veritable haven for ex-convicts, many of whom are in key jobs. In fact, rank-and-file longshoremen, themselves victims of the racketeers, complain bitterly that an honest man has difficulty in improving his lot on the waterfront; the preference is given to ex-convicts."

Not only was there a preference for ex-convicts; the union even recruited men for waterfront jobs while they were still in prison.

All this was only part of the story Mike Johnson told. The shocking conditions he described had been festering for decades; they could not flourish without political protection from on high, the connivance of public officials, and the forbearance of shipping executives either too frightened to protest or too selfish to challenge a corrupt system by which they profited.

The series of twenty-four front-page articles that he entitled "Crime on the Waterfront" caused sensation after sensation when they appeared in *The Sun* in November and December of 1948. As for his revelation about an underworld syndicate, he said it was "composed of master criminals and racket bosses" in "every major city in this country," and it "controls virtually every phase of organized crime: the narcotic traffic, gambling, vice, labor and industrial racketeering. In addition to its underworld operations, the syndicate members have tremendous investments in numerous legitimate enterprises. They own hotels, restaurants, nightclubs, banks, apartment buildings. They also own, all too often, judges and policemen and other officials sworn to uphold the law."

Heading this illegal global enterprise were such criminal leaders as Charles (Lucky) Luciano, Frank Costello, Albert Anastasia, Joe Adonis, and Meyer Lansky, all of whom Johnson named in print. Three years later, their names and their criminal enterprises became familiar to Americans through the televised congressional committee hearings into organized crime, chaired by Estes Kefauver, which cited Johnson's articles as an impetus for launching the investigation. And still later, of course, these criminals became familiar as prototypical characters in the *Godfather* films, for instance, and such television series as *The Sopranos*.

Such are the consequences flowing from that "routine assignment" so long ago. There were also a number of reforms, including the creation of a bipartisan Port Authority Commission that oversees hiring along the New York/New Jersey waterfront to this day; the banning of the vicious "shape-up" system that had life-and-death power over workers economically and left them at the mercy of unscrupulous mobsters who extracted kickbacks in exchange for employment; the expulsion of the International Longshoremen's Association (ILA) from the AFL-CIO, the first union to be banished from the national trade council for racketeering; the imprisonment of the union president on charges stemming from the newspaper exposé; the jailing, and sometimes execution, of other waterfront criminals featured in the series; congressional and state legislative hearings; the awarding of the Pulitzer Prize to Johnson for his articles; the awarding of the New York County Grand Jury Association's Gold Medal, given to only four others in the thirty-nine-year history of the association, and the first ever to a newsman; and the making of the movie *On the Waterfront*, which the articles inspired.

For years afterward, as John Hohenberg, secretary of the Pulitzer Prize Advisory Board, wrote in *The Pulitzer Prize Story*, "his stories in *The Sun* served as primary source material for new investigations, for novels, radio and TV shows and movies. It is difficult to trace the results that have flowed specifically from the series, but there is no doubt of the overall effect. In the city, state, and nation the rule of murder and mayhem on the New York waterfront became common knowledge—and a common shame." He added: "There have been many investigations since Johnson's exposé. . . . But nothing has approached the fearlessness and candor of that first series."

As I write now, in the spring of 2004, more than half a century has passed since the "Crime on the Waterfront" articles first appeared, and it has been exactly fifty years since *On the Waterfront* had its premiere. Next spring marks another half-century milestone in this saga, when the movie, which never would have been made without the talent and tenacity of its screenwriter, Budd Schulberg, won eight Academy Awards. It is now ranked among the greatest of American films.

I suppose these are reasons enough to recall this journalistic, political, and ultimately cultural history and attempt to place it in perspective of today's America. But I have other, more personal reasons for doing so, for I am not a dispassionate, uninvolved chronicler of this story. It affected my life at the time, and continues to affect my work and the way I see things all these years later.

You see, Malcolm Johnson was my father, and the waterfront

This photograph of the New York docks taken at the turn of the century shows the increasing traffic and business that used to deposit millions of immigrants on the shores of Manhattan Island.

story had a great impact on his life and our family. I was in high school then, and I remember the days and nights, for month after month, when my father was developing material for the series. I remember, too, him telling me often that he thought they would never be published. Even before they eventually were, we had frightening evidence of how our lives were going to be affected.

As news of his assignment got out, our telephone at home began ringing. In a stream of anonymous, threatening calls, strangers warned my father, or my mother if she happened to answer the phone, to stop the investigation or he—or we—would be killed. The calls terrified my mother and obviously worried my father. But that didn't stop him. He changed our phone number to an unlisted one, which remained unlisted for the rest of my mother and father's lives, and went on digging for the story behind the story.

That isn't my only intensely disturbing memory of that time. From the moment the stories began running, the union president, Joseph P. Ryan (who later went to prison on corruption charges), started a long campaign in which he repeatedly accused my father of being a communist, of relying on procommunist sources for his articles, and of being taken in by communist-line reformers.

This was during the most fearsome period of the communist hysteria spawned by the cold war, a time marked by charges of spies and traitors and threat of nuclear incineration. In fact, the waterfront articles competed for front-page space with the trial of Alger Hiss, the most famous espionage case in American history, taking place at the same time in the Criminal Courts Building a few blocks from *The Sun*. In the McCarthyism years that followed, Ryan renewed his communist charges against my father. He then tried to get him fired and the movie stopped, which was struggling to get made, by labeling it as an un-American, antiunion screed inspired by communists. Ryan cited not only my father as a communist but Budd Schulberg as well. But more about that later.

For now, let me say I hope this background will explain why I take great pride in seeing my father's original work, and that of Budd Schulberg's, presented to a new audience in an America that is vastly different today. On reflection, though, perhaps our New Millennium America is not so different after all, for as I write we find ourselves in the grip of a new wave of fear, this time over terrorism instead of communism, and certainly the problems of political corruption and organized crime are with us still.

My intention here is to describe how the waterfront articles—and the movie—came to be, and to introduce readers to my father and some of the other principal players in the story. First, my father.

THE REPORTER

"Mike," as I was taught to call him, instead of the more familiar "Dad," was forty-three years old when he strolled across the City Room of *The Sun*, overlooking Broadway and City Hall in downtown Manhattan, that morning in 1948, to receive Bartnett's suggestion he look into unrest on the waterfront. He was short (five foot seven), stocky, with dark complexion, deep brown eyes, and black hair. As one of his *Sun* colleagues wrote of him: "His face, with prominent nose, is most mobile. He smiles all over it, but in moments of concentration he scowls terrifyingly."

He had an unassuming manner, with a gift for making friends, and was liked for his modest ways and self-deprecating sense of humor. He was, in fact, known among his colleagues as "Modest Mike." This was deceptive, for as *Time* magazine wrote of him after he won the Pulitzer, "his drawl and easygoing manner hide a bulldog tenacity." Perhaps those disarming traits stemmed from his Southern upbringing. While he was as passionate a New Yorker as anyone I've known, his roots—and accent—came from his native Georgia, where he was born in the foothills of the Blue Ridge Mountains, in the small town of Gainesville.

Mike's father was a lawyer. Before embarking on his practice, he

Haynes and Malcolm Johnson circa 1948. Taken at the Johnson summer home in Killingworth, Connecticut. Reprinted with permission of Haynes Johnson.

had been a teacher, a high school principal, and a district superintendent of schools. He was a scholarly man, and a deacon of his church, but he was somewhat reserved and distant. Mike worshipped him but never felt like he really knew him; that feeling was compounded when his father died during the great influenza epidemic just prior to the armistice at the end of World War I in 1918. Hence, Mike's wish that I call him by his nickname, to make us closer. Mike was only thirteen when his forty-three-year-old father died, leaving Mike the eldest of six surviving children. His mother, described in one written account as "a woman of character and courage," had been a teacher and assistant principal before marriage, but to keep the family together she took in boarders, and she managed to see all of her children through college—no small feat for a widow in a small Southern town with limited financial resources.

Both of Mike's parents bequeathed to him a strong sense of independence and what I can only describe as a passion against injustice. His father, for example, had demonstrated admirable courage in 1914 when he was one of the lawyers who defended Leo Frank, the Jewish manager of an Atlanta pencil factory who was unjustly charged with the murder of thirteen-year-old Mary Phagan. It was a notorious case that attracted international attention, stirring up deep religious and racial prejudices in the South at the time, leading to the rebirth of the murderous Ku Klux Klan and the eventual lynching of Frank himself. Against such a backdrop, Mike's father made a number of speeches denouncing the Klan, describing it in one address as "nothing but the shell of a rotten un-American organization." Not long before his own death in 1976, Mike recalled his father's attacks on the Klan admiringly, telling me proudly how his father "denounced it publicly, and it took a lot of courage, didn't it? After all, that was more than sixty years ago."

Mike was so strongly influenced by that example that when he became a young reporter in Macon, Georgia, while in college there, he exposed the depredations, including lynchings, of the Klan in rural Toombs County. Those articles attracted state and national attention, including publication in Joseph Pulitzer's famous *New York World*. One man, mistaken for an informant, was beaten and left for dead. The Klan threatened to kill Mike, and burn down his newspaper, *The Macon Telegraph*. The governor of Georgia offered protection following the threat on his life.

This was in 1926; Mike was barely twenty-two years old. Two years later, his editor, Mark Ethridge, subsequently managing editor of *The Washington Post* and later publisher of *The Louisville Courier-Journal*, sent him to *The Sun*, where, on Ethridge's recommendation, he became the first *Sun* reporter to be hired "sight unseen." The idea was for him to return to Macon as managing editor after a year or two in New York. He never looked back.

Mike gloried in being a reporter in the New York of the twenties, thirties, and forties, where he worked on most of the major stories of the time. He always resisted being "typed," and he sought, and received, the widest range of assignments possible, first as a reporter, then as a critic, a Broadway columnist, and, finally, as a war correspondent in the Pacific. There he covered, among other engagements, the first carrier raids against Tokyo, the invasions of Iwo Jima and Okinawa, the bombardment of the Japanese homeland by Nimitz's and Halsey's battleships, the surrender of Japan aboard the USS *Missouri* in Tokyo Bay, the landing with the Marines on Japanese soil, and the horrific scenes at Hiroshima, witnessed with the first group of correspondents to enter the city following the dropping of the atomic bomb.

Mike's politics were typical of that Great Depression/World War II era; he was a passionate supporter of FDR and the New Deal, ardently pro-union, and was one of the New York newspapermen who met in Heywood Broun's apartment in the early thirties to found the Newspaper Guild.

When he started his waterfront investigations, as *Time* reported, "he was neither a crime specialist nor an I-cover-the-waterfront expert. He was a general assignment man who had served *The Sun* for twenty years, on everything from the burning of the *Morro Castle* to the storming of Okinawa. In a 1946 series on hijacking, he had picked up some waterfront contacts. Using them, he started his digging into waterfront crime."

Let me add one more assessment that I believe captures the essence of his character; it comes from Murray Kempton, the columnist, writing several years later upon the premiere of *On the Waterfront*:

> Malcolm Johnson came to New York from Georgia a long time ago. He became, by slow application, a great newspaper reporter in the old-fashioned sense: there does not seem to be a new-fashioned one. He was the star man of the *New York Sun*; it gave him roving assignments; during the war he was in the Pacific. He came back to city stories, and then in 1948, in middle age, he discovered a passion. *The Sun* had assigned him to write a series on what was wrong with the Port of New York. He gave it a year's patience. When he had finished, he had the first great series on waterfront racketeering. . . . The waterfront was corrupt and contented, and Mike Johnson could not even find an employer who would speak on the record about the state of things. There was passion in his pieces; their very indignation was old-fashioned, because Mike Johnson is blessedly impervious to the corrosion of cynicism. To its credit, *The Sun* gave them a tremendous ride. A lot has been said and written about the New York waterfront since then; it has all been supplementary.

THE STORY

Armed with the contacts Mike developed in writing his series on truck hijacking, he began looking into waterfront operations. But after probing for six weeks, he had gotten nowhere. Nobody was talking, not even the police. The longshoremen—the people he cared about most—were suspicious of reporters, and they kept silent both out of fear and reluctance to "rat" on superiors. They adopted what they referred to among themselves as a "D 'n' D" attitude—"deaf and dumb"—when meeting outsiders.

Mike was so discouraged he thought of admitting defeat and chucking the assignment. But he kept on digging. Then came two critical breaks. The first was a call from a former FBI man Mike knew who had taken a job with a transportation firm engaged in business on the waterfront. Through the grapevine, the man had heard about Mike's making inquiries, so he put Mike in touch with an informer who told a horrifying tale of crime, corruption—and murder.

It was then that Mike got his second break: he met William J. Keating, a young, idealistic assistant district attorney with the Homicide Bureau. A year earlier, Keating had successfully prosecuted a notorious killer, John M. (Cockeye) Dunn, for the murder of union dock hiring boss Anthony Hintz, whose slaying closely resembled that of Thomas Collentine. Keating was obsessed with the rampant criminality he was seeing on the waterfront, and he was compiling a devastating file on the various rackets as well as the alliance between the gangsters and politicians and industrialists. But Keating, too, was frustrated by his failure to get authorities to act on this information, or even for the public to pay attention.

Years later, in his memoir, *The Man Who Rocked the Boat*, Keating described how his meeting with Mike changed all that.

"Morty Davis, criminal courts reporter for *The New York Sun*, said that his city editor had assigned the paper's ace, Malcolm Johnson, to do a piece or two on the Collentine case," Keating recalled. "He asked me to meet Johnson. I did so, and explained to Johnson that, under office regulations, I was forbidden to discuss a case in progress. But there were other possibilities.

" 'You remember the Dunn case?' I said.

" 'Sure,' said Mike.

" 'Well, the Dunn mob was more important. . . . There is no reason at all why you can't go through the Dunn case file. You'll be the first newspaperman to do it, and I'm sure you'll pick up a lot of interesting material. With that as background you ought to be able to do a pretty good job on the Collentine story. Actually, apart from some inside angles which would be libelous if printed, we don't know much more about the Collentine murder than you've already covered in your newspaper.' "

Mike, as Keating remembered, became so interested in the material that he proposed to his editors that he do a series on waterfront crime. Keating introduced him to some of the longshoremen he knew, and Mike met many more on his own. "He explored the waterfront jungle as no other newspaperman had ever bothered to do," Keating wrote. "He interviewed workers, union officials, gangsters, politicians, industrialists. He worked all spring and all summer and wrote his 'Crime on the Waterfront' series, which named names, covered the rackets thoroughly, won a Pulitzer Prize, and made the Port of New York a national scandal of such proportions that New York government could no longer ignore it."

From that raw material, Mike tenaciously began adding his own until he had documented a longshore empire of gangsterism rife with systematic theft and murder that was, as *The New York Times* later described it, "costing millions of dollars a year in lost trade and perpetuating a reign of fear among workers." He interviewed hundreds of longshoremen, union officials, shipping officials, steamship executives, trucking officials, policemen, and private investigators. He conferred with the mayor of New York, the district attorney, many other public officials, engaged the president of the International Longshoremen's Association in public debate, and studied invaluable books and pamphlets on waterfront concerns, some dating back to the late nineteenth century. He haunted saloons along the waterfront, met criminal "stool pigeons" in their hideaways, attended union meetings, scrutinized the union's constitution, scanned the police records of dozens of waterfront gangsters, questioned murder witnesses, and, as he later wrote, "listened for hours to the complaints of the men who are really hurt by crime in labor—the rank-and-file union members."

In his 1950 book *Crime on the Labor Front*, an expansion of his waterfront articles, he drily noted that "some of my informants are now in prison; several who figured in my inquiry have since died in the electric chair; many more were shot to death in the normal course of labor-crime events."

All told, he wrote more than two hundred newspaper articles about the waterfront: the initial twenty-four-part "Crime on the Waterfront" was followed by another front-page series of ten articles, "Crime on the Waterfront: The Cause and the Remedy." These were followed by another, lengthy series of eight articles in which he engaged Joe Ryan, the ILA president, in a strong exchange: "Ryan Answers Johnson's Crime on the Waterfront (and Johnson Replies)."

All these years later, it's hard to recapture the impact of those articles, but Bill Keating's memoir describes it memorably, and revealingly.

"As the Johnson series continued to unfold in *The Sun*," Keating wrote, "creating sensation after sensation, unease spread in our office. The usually equable [District Attorney Frank] Hogan was described as being 'sore as hell.' The news was brought by George Monaghan [Hogan's top prosecutor, Keating's immediate supervisor, and later NYC police commissioner].

" 'He's fit to be tied,' said George. 'He wants to know if you have anything to do with those articles. Is Johnson getting any information from our files?'

" 'All he got from our files was the Dunn case. What's all the excitement?'

" 'Well, for crying out loud, Bill, the guy's series is all about racketeering, crime on the waterfront, unsolved murders and that sort of thing. It's an indirect criticism of the DA. The implication is that the DA ought to be doing something about it.' "

As Keating observed, "The outcome was happy, however. Mike Johnson sought and was granted an interview with Hogan . . . and his statements to Mike were undoubtedly the most forthright ever made about the waterfront by a public official of his standing. He blasted the shipowners and urged state laws illegalizing the shape-up, which he denounced as the root of a corrupt and outmoded employment system."

By that point, the waterfront articles had sparked a strong public reaction—and official action. Keating continues:

> Wherever you turned the forces of law and order could be seen making progress. The Police Department announced a drastic shake-up among its waterfront forces, and this with the activities of the mayor and the Investigations Commissioner, the sensationally hard-hitting statements of District Attorney Hogan and the imminent electrocution of [three waterfront gangsters featured in the articles] combined to lull the public into its accustomed and unwarranted sense of security. It could not be denied, however, that Mike Johnson had torn the shroud of mystery from the waterfront, had revealed the ILA as the fraud that it was, had embarrassed stevedoring and shipping tycoons by exposing their employment of murderers as foremen, had bolstered the morale of the longshoremen and had organized formidable public support for any law enforcement official who might have dared to supplement gestures with real action.
>
> None dared.

THE GREAT HUE AND CRY

No sooner had the initial series began appearing than *The Sun* was deluged with letters and phone calls, many offering new leads. Some were useful in subsequent stories. Among the letters was one from a Jesuit priest at the St. Francis Xavier Labor School, in Manhattan, which had long devoted special attention to needed waterfront reforms. Again, *Sun* editor Edmund Bartnett played a critical role in what was to follow. After reading the letter from the Reverend John M. Corridan, Bartnett passed it to Mike, with the advice: "You'd better go around and see this man; he seems to know what he's talking about."

Thus began a critically important connection between Mike and the man he later described in print as "the Waterfront Priest."

As Corridan's biographer, Allen Raymond, wrote in *Waterfront Priest,* "Corridan and Johnson met. Thereafter Father Corridan became an assiduous tipster for the star reporter. Together they set off a great hue and cry against the waterfront racketeers."

Corridan, the eldest of five sons born of Irish immigrants, was raised in poverty after his policeman father died when Corridan was nine years old. He grew up to be a brilliant and tireless crusader for social justice, especially on the waterfront, where many of the suffering longshoremen viewed him as their friend and had the greatest respect for his judgment. He also impressed them with his courage and his willingness to challenge the gangster control of the docks.

As Mike wrote of Corridan: "He can teach the longshoremen the minutest detail of parliamentary procedure; he can name the gangsters in control of every dock on the west side, and cite their criminal record; he can point to the mobs' political contacts in City Hall, and he can explain the most intricate type of waterfront graft which might very well involve stevedores, loaders, checkers, watchmen, policemen, and city officials."

Corridan supplied Mike with new material, helped him in his

Reverend John M. Corridan, S.J., the associate director of the St. Francis Xavier Labor School, and adviser to the strikers, was widely recognized by the local press as an expert on labor relations. Corridan went on record, with Malcolm Johnson and other local reporters, saying that the wildcat strike was largely a revolt against Joseph P. Ryan and the racketeers and mobsters along the waterfront. The reverend also predicted that even if the strikers went back to work, "an explosion is brewing on the waterfront which will make this strike seem like a picnic."

follow-up articles, and was so impressed with public reaction to his waterfront stories that he became an ardent worker in mobilizing public opinion for reform. As Raymond reported, "[T]he longshoremen who were his friends were so impressed by the effect of Johnson's work that they turned to Corridan to help them to get out their own publicity."

In due course, Corridan's own major role on the waterfront was made known to the public through Karl Malden's depiction of him as "the Waterfront Priest" in Budd Schulberg's *On the Waterfront* script.

THE MOVIE

In June 1949, six weeks after winning the Pulitzer Prize, Mike sold the screen rights to "Crime on the Waterfront" to the Monticello Film Corporation, an independent production company in Hollywood. Robert Siodmak, a director of thrillers, was named to direct what was billed as a "semi-documentary" movie to be filmed on location in New York. It wasn't the only film offer; I remember Mike receiving calls from, among others, Sam Goldwyn, and Ida Lupino, the actress then producing films in her own right. This began a long, tortuous effort to make the movie.

Then, early in January 1950, *The Sun* folded. As its star reporter, Mike wrote his own paper's obituary, describing some of the highlights of its 116-year history, and then he began looking for another job. By the end of the month, he signed a two-year contract with Hearst ("GET HIM AT ANY PRICE," William Randolph Hearst had wired his editors from his San Simeon estate), his work to be distributed through King Features and Hearst's International News Service (INS).

That spring, after completing his waterfront book, Mike began working for Hearst. By then, the producers in Hollywood had tried out several screenwriters to adapt his material as a movie. None of them proved satisfactory, however. Toward the end of 1950, the producers commissioned Budd Schulberg, whose novel about the final days of F. Scott Fitzgerald in Hollywood, *The Disenchanted*, had just been published to much acclaim. Mike was delighted. Schulberg was a distinguished writer with impeccable film credentials. His father was the major producer, B. P. Schulberg, and Budd had a string of well-received film credits. And his first novel, *What Makes Sammy Run?*, had become a classic in the early forties.

Schulberg was consumed by the waterfront project until his "final draft" was completed on April 14, 1951 (it was far from final, as it turned out), for the script of *Crime on the Waterfront*, as the movie was then titled, using the same name as the newspaper series. This drew mention in the press. At that point, the frightening effects of McCarthyism took hold. Some months before, in testimony before the House Un-American Activities Committee (HUAC), another Hollywood writer had named Schulberg as having been a Communist Party member after his graduation from Dartmouth at the end of the thirties. That revelation, coupled with news of Schulberg's work on the movie, led Joe Ryan to write a classic guilt-by-association letter to William Randolph Hearst, Jr., three days after stories were published about Schulberg's final script having been completed.

In his letter, Ryan exposed Schulberg's past communist connection, and he renewed his accusation that my father also was a communist. Hearst, then overseeing his father's editorial empire in New York, was addressed as "Friend Bill." The letter began by saying that the script for an earlier version of the waterfront movie, which (falsely) had been "rejected by several of the large motion picture firms," was written "by Budd Schulberg, who was, or had been a member of the Communist Party." He added: "I understand now that the Monticello Motion Picture Corp. is contemplating producing this picture in the near future, and this Budd Schulberg has been mentioned recently by a motion picture artist, Richard Collins, as definitely a member of the Communist Party."

Then Ryan wrote: "Knowing of the long fight that your father and yourself have waged against communism, in every form, I felt that I should call to your attention that Malcolm Johnson is employed by International News Service and while I do not expect him to change his identity, I believe he should be in accord with the policies of his employer."

Hearst immediately forwarded Ryan's letter to Seymour Berkson, the chief executive of INS, with a penciled notation about Ryan that read: "I know and rather like him personally. Very anti-commie."

Mike replied: "In general, I will say that this letter is typical of Ryan's tactics. Ever since my exposé of the New York waterfront and of his union in particular he has tried to smear me as a Communist or Communist sympathizer. He even tried it while I was on *The Sun*. But whatever else could be said of the old *Sun*, it could not be accused of being pro-Communist or of employing pro-commie writers. The truth is that Ryan is understandably sore because I have attacked him and his union and will continue to do so, whether I work for INS or not. In print, over radio and television and in lectures and public speeches I have accused Ryan of protecting racketeers, and I have proved it. . . . Ryan is anti-Communist and as far as I am concerned that's the only good thing you can say about him. He has used his anti-communism as a blanket defense of everything rotten in his racket union. He would have you believe that anyone who criticizes the union or his leadership is, per se, a Communist, Communist sympathizer, or tool of the Communists."

Another year passed. Ryan continued his accusations of communist influence, and added threats of a union boycott of the film; the fever of McCarthyism raged; the film company had difficulties raising money to produce the movie: Budd Schulberg's script was rejected by Hollywood moguls as "communistic." At that point, Schulberg took the plunge. He bought the film rights to Mike's copyrighted "Crime on the Waterfront" articles and his book *Crime on the Labor Front*, rights which had reverted back to Mike when the movie wasn't made. It was now Schulberg's story.

For two years Schulberg already had been doing extensive first-hand, original research on the waterfront, working closely with men such as Father Corridan. When Schulberg began his research for the film script back in 1950, as he wrote in an introduction to Father's Corridan's biography, "New York harbor, I was beginning to discover, was a world to itself, with its own heroes, villains, and taboos. Malcolm Johnson . . . had described our greatest harbor as a lawless frontier beyond the jurisdiction of police officer, jurist or legislator. It was Johnson's bristling account that first opened my eyes to the story of crime and industrial-political corruption on the docks. But how could an outsider begin to penetrate this jungle? Malcolm Johnson's advice was, 'Start with Father Corridan. Go down to Xavier's and see Father John. He really knows the score.'"

Schulberg did just that. Then, with enormous perseverance, and through his alliance with director Elia Kazan, who assembled a great cast headed by Marlon Brando, Lee J. Cobb, Karl Malden, Rod Steiger, and Eva Marie Saint, Schulberg worked for yet another two years, producing at least seven more scripts that ultimately transformed the original raw journalism into a lasting work of art.

As they say, the rest is history.

AN AFTERWORD

I find the experience of exhuming these old memories somehow unsatisfying and incomplete. I say that because what matters most to me now about Mike's life is something more personal than a chronicle of his professional achievements.

Looking back, I find an old-fashioned quality that I never associated with him in life. I suspect he was more representative of an innocent, vanished America than I realized, especially of the South at the time of his upbringing there. Not that the South was without great problems: race relations probably reached their lowest point then, with the Klan openly terrorizing communities and committing atrocities, and poverty, ill-health, and ignorance still afflicted the region. Yet I think it's fair to say that most people had a sense of optimism about the future, that most parents implicitly believed their children's lives would be better than theirs, that there were no problems that couldn't be solved by common purpose and effort. I smiled when I discovered the old clipping from *The Macon Telegraph*, with its picture of young Mike, and the headline:

MALCOLM JOHNSON
OFF TO NEW YORK
TO TAKE POSITION

How perfect: local boy on the way to the big time. He looked so solemn, so earnest. That isn't how I remember him: he had a marvelous sense of the absurd, and I think of him most as teasing and smiling.

When he left Macon for New York, at the ancient age of twenty-three, the paper reported: "Mr. Johnson had a wide circle of friends in Middle Georgia." Years later, when he went to the Pacific as a correspondent for *The Sun* during World War II, that paper reported: "His friends at *The Sun* and in New York include practically everyone who has ever met him."

I believe that was true, literally.

Mike could be serious, though, and seethe with indignation at injustice and cruelty. His best work—his writings about the depredations of the Klan in Georgia in the twenties, and the mob reign of terror on the New York waterfront in the forties—were outgrowths of these feelings. But in these, too, it seems to me now, he was expressing common values of his time and place. Mike just happened to have the gift of expression, and he probably was better able than most people at getting his emotions down on paper.

On the eve of the invasion of Okinawa, Easter Sunday, 1945, while aboard a battleship offshore, he wrote me an extraordinary letter during the preinvasion bombardment. He was to land at dawn the next morning, and, as he said, at risk "of embarrassment to us both," he had some things he wanted to say. I was thirteen at the time—the same age Mike had been when his own father died—and those facts were obviously on his mind.

"I firmly believe that when it comes to setting a standard of values in life—a code of ethics or whatever you want to call it—that there are certain things each man must discover for himself," he said. "For myself, I believe I have made an important discovery. I believe that the most important thing in life, as far as I am personally concerned, is maintaining one's personal honor and integrity. As a nation that is what we are fighting for now: national honor and integrity. But it goes deeper than that. I am talking now about the individual."

He apologized for preaching, and hoped he didn't sound sanctimonious. Nor was he suggesting I adopt his own standard of values: "You must find and adopt your own and for all I know they will be much higher than mine. I hope they will be." Then he added: "In a few years you will be grown and setting out for yourself. I don't care what you do, Haynesy, so long as it is honorable and you do your job—whatever it is—to the best of your ability. My own father once told me something that I never forgot. I pass it on to you. He said: 'Do whatever you do to the best of your ability but no matter how good you may think you are, remember there is always somebody else who can do it as well and probably better.' I think that is a good thing to remember. It keeps us from getting too conceited. Humility is a very desirable virtue."

My mother put that letter away, with the others from the war, and I didn't see it again until after Mike died. He had never mentioned it to me again; I knew he was self-conscious about it. But then he would have been self-conscious about this entire foreword.

Way too long, I can hear him saying; waste of space and effort and all the rest.

I'll take the blame for that, Mike, and not apologize for the material, either.

Haynes Johnson, a best-selling author, journalist, and television commentator, won the Pulitzer Prize in 1966 for his coverage of the civil rights struggle in Selma, Alabama. That award marked the first, and still the only, time in the history of the Pulitzers that a father and son won the prizes for reporting.

Introduction

by Budd Schulberg

It's been more than half a century since I first read the opening blast of Malcolm Johnson's explosive exposé "Crime on the Waterfront."

Greed, corruption, and cold-blooded murder had been going on for generations, but a complacent city paid it no mind until this pioneering and fearless reporter for the now defunct *New York Sun* laid it out for all to see.

The greatest harbor in America, all nine hundred piers and nine hundred million dollars of it, from Brooklyn to the Jersey shore, was revealed as an outlaw frontier run by labor racketeers who used the union—the International Longshoremen's Association—as a front for every type of criminal activity: systematic pilferage, shakedowns and extortions, kickbacks from the daily wages of the dockworkers who had to shape up for their jobs every four hours. As five hundred men or more formed themselves into a docile horseshoe, one in every five or six was singled out by a dock boss whose main qualifications were the length of time he had spent in Sing Sing or Dannemora, and his readiness to do violence to anyone who dared question the system.

The Johnson *j'accuse* ("series" is far too mild a word for it) ran day after day, and I read it with mounting horror and even a sense of guilt. These crimes were shrugged off as business as usual, accepted and even encouraged by the supposedly respectable New York Shipping Association. The sprawling labor union, the ILA, which should have protected the men, was headed by its president-for-life, Joe Ryan, who hobnobbed with the top city officials and churchmen on

This photo showing the Hudson River with the midtown skyscrapers towering above, taken in the thirties, is a record of the West Side piers at their peak. Photograph copyright © Bettmann/CORBIS.

one side while playing footsie with the Mafia and the Irish mob on the other.

I wondered if Malcolm Johnson wasn't taking his life in his hands by laying it out in big bloodred letters, name by name and pier by pier. Mickey Bowers's aptly named "Pistol Local" had the luxury liners, Cunard and the French and German floating palaces, in its pocket, as well as everything above Forty-second Street on the West Side of Manhattan. Westside South belonged to John (Cockeye) Dunn and Eddie McGrath, who whacked anybody who crossed them—more than thirty and counting. Lower Manhattan was Socks Lanza territory, and the East River and Brooklyn were the hunting grounds of Albert Anastasia of Murder, Incorporated (Murder, Inc.), fame. Over in Hoboken was Charlie Yanowsky (Charlie the Jew), who was getting too big for his britches and would soon be on his way to the bottom of the river.

The boys had it nicely worked out, Johnson told us, the great harbor carved up among them like a big fat turkey, with so much loot pouring in to them in so many ways that there was enough for everybody. Just don't overstep the syndicate boundaries.

I couldn't wait for the next installment, and the next, explaining how rampant crime could flourish because law enforcement on the docks was virtually nonexistent. Stone-cold killers like Cockeye Dunn had friends in high places. Congressmen and Army brass, no less. Mike Johnson was a welcome throwback to the great muckrakers of the past, from Ida Tarbell to Lincoln Steffens and Upton Sinclair, spokesmen for the underdogs. Johnson's was a lone voice for the defenseless longshoremen, whose union had sold them out to the overdogs who kept them needy and hungry, driven to fighting each other for a half day's starvation wage.

At last, someone was turning a spotlight on the outmoded system of the shape-up, a humiliating mode of hiring that had been outlawed from the docks of London at the end of the nineteenth century, and from every European port as well. Dockworkers who spoke out against the shape-up had their legs broken, or worse, while the powerful Joe Ryan defended it as a system "the men themselves preferred." Bottom line: Who were they to deny their mobbed-up president, if they wanted to stay in one piece?

Johnson followed his twenty-four-article barrage with a second set, outlining the reforms that cried out for the doing. He would go on to win a Pulitzer Prize for his efforts, finally bestirring the establishment to take notice. The televised Kefauver investigation brought it into our living rooms. An assistant district attorney was moved to prosecute Cockeye Dunn for the murder of Anthony Hintz, a hiring boss who had refused to play ball. Talk about one man making a difference—Malcolm Johnson was the waterfront's Paul Revere.

My pores had always been open to the kind of labor exploitation that Johnson revealed. At Dartmouth, I had almost been "separated from the college" (as our president, Ernest Martin Hopkins, put it so gently) for championing the cause of the embattled marble workers in the nearby quarries. I responded to Johnson's singling out of a humble Hell's Kitchen Catholic priest who was looking for trouble he could have avoided. That was Father John Corridan, of the St. Francis Xavier Labor School, an unlikely champion of the restive rank and file. Denouncing the shape-up, he was calling for urgent reforms: setting up hiring halls on the orderly Seattle model, conducting an official waterfront investigation, and establishing a bistate oversight commission to bring some order to the criminal chaos.

When all this was coming down, I was on my farm in Pennsylvania, working on a novel (*The Disenchanted*) that had been triggered by an ill-fated film writing journey to the Dartmouth Winter Carnival I had taken with F. Scott Fitzgerald ten years earlier. But I clipped the Johnson material for my files, with no idea how I might ever use it.

That all changed when young Joe Curtis, Columbia honcho Harry Cohn's nephew, came to my Buck's County, Pennsylvania, farm with the veteran German director, Robert Siodmak, best known for his effective helming of Ernest Hemingway's *The Killers*. They had optioned the rights to Johnson's series, and were hoping I would do the screenplay. I explained that I had left Hollywood—or it had left me—after my first novel, *What Makes Sammy Run?*, was attacked as the work of a "traitor" by the Hollywood establishment.

Quieting my anxieties, Curtis and Siodmak assured me that I could do the job entirely on my own in the East. An added inducement was that my father, B.P., could be one of the producers. After having run the West Coast Paramount Studio for many years, he had fallen from his top perch, and had kept on falling, until now all those millions were gone and he was living in my guesthouse working on his memoirs.

When I decided to take a year off from novel writing and devote myself to the waterfront, my first move was to look up Malcolm Johnson. Not at all the fiery "commie" the self-righteous Joe Ryan had tried to brand him, I found a quiet, likable, no-nonsense, extremely supportive man who welcomed the film, if it could be done honestly and without pulling any punches. I assured him I'd do my best to maintain the spirit and daring content of his waterfront crime exposé.

With his "Go see Corridan—Father John, he really knows the score" ringing in my ears, that's exactly what I did. My response to Father John is spelled out in a number of pieces I did for *The New York Times*, the liberal Catholic magazine *Commonweal*, *The Saturday Evening Post*, and in my introduction to Corridan's own book, *Waterfront Priest*. Thanks to Mike Johnson, once I caught the fever, I couldn't stop writing about Father John, or "Father Pete" as his followers called him. Indeed, when he died some thirty years later I was still so devoted to him that I was asked to deliver the eulogy at the funeral mass conducted at the Fordham University Chapel.

Getting involved with Corridan and the gutsy "stand-up guys" who gathered around him in the basement of St. Xavier's, I had the feeling of having fallen down a rabbit's hole into a tough new world that couldn't have been further from my own. But I felt an affinity with these men. When Father Pete began to trust me, which took some time, he assigned a little gadfly called Brownie to be my guide. With his bashed-in nose, Brownie looked like an old bantam-weight fighter. For daring to stand up to them, the goons had thrown him through a skylight, and, another time, off the end of a pier. "I was lucky it was winter," he laughed. "I was out cold but the ice in the river woke me up. In the summer I woulda drowned."

I found myself writing down one Brownie quote after another, and, in time, they would find their way into the screenplay. Indeed, Brownie became "Kayo Dugan," one of the principal characters in the film. I was able to bond with Brownie and his fellow "insoigents" because, to my surprise, we had so many interests in common. Dockworkers were ardent boxing fans, and at the time I was co-managing a promising heavyweight, Archie McBride, who had been training in my barn and was now fighting main events in the Garden. And when I noticed the flocks of racing pigeons flying in great training circles over the waterfront rooftops, I told Brownie that I had raced pigeons growing up in Hollywood; and, in fact, had been secretary of the Southern California Racing Pigeon Association. And in the waterfront bars where Brownie and his pals hung out, they liked to quench their "thoist" with Guckenheimer Whiskey with beer chasers, which I found quite agreeable, too.

Brownie would point out the good guys and the bad guys, warning me to just shut up and listen. It was exciting for me to find myself lifting boilermakers with the people I had read about in Johnson's exposé. In time, I got the screenplay together, originally using Johnson's title, "Crime on the Waterfront." Of course, along with Brownie, Father Corridan (Father Barry) became a major character in it. Even Edie, the innocent Catholic girl played so memorably in the film by Eva Marie Saint, was modeled on the daughters of dockworkers I met in the course of my adventure.

Once Robert Siodmak and Father Corridan had approved it, out it went to tough Columbia honcho Harry Cohn, who turned it down, with an assist from Joe Ryan. He told Cohn it was the work of a "commie"—me—based on the original series by another "commie," Malcolm Johnson. Ryan was a master at dismissing every valid criticism of his rotten regime as the evil doings of the "Reds."

We were dead in the water, but when Joe Curtis's option on the material ran out I acquired the rights from Johnson. I had no idea who I could find to back the project, but I was now too attached to it—and to Father Corridan and his band of dock-walloping angels—to let it go.

Time passed, and I had put the waterfront on a back burner and turned back to writing fiction when out of the blue came a call from director Elia Kazan, whom I had never met but whose work as a gifted social realist I admired. At the time, a lot of people I didn't know were calling me because *The Disenchanted* had been published, and praise from James M. Cain on the front page of the *New York Times Book Review* had sent it to the top of its best-seller list. Kazan said he'd like to come out to meet me, he had something on his mind. At the farm, he asked me if I'd like to do a film with him, set entirely on the East Coast, based on some pressing social issue. That was his only criteria. There was no mention of making a film to justify his HUAC testimony, as has been charged by all those second-guessers. First, we considered doing the "Trenton Six," about the black teenagers who had been indicted for murder in what seemed a rush to judgment along the lines of the celebrated Scotsboro Boys case back in the thirties.

I checked it out in Trenton, and thought there could be a Dreiserian novel in it, but at a second meeting with Kazan I pushed harder for my waterfront script. That's when he told me for the first time that he had been working on his own waterfront project with Arthur Miller, "The Hook." "So now read mine," I suggested, and Kazan did, that very day. He liked a lot of it but had some serious suggestions for improvement. I was ready to go back to work.

Father Corridan and the boys were delighted that our project got a second chance, especially with a director of Kazan's reputation at the helm. Meanwhile, events on the docks had been heating up. The AFL-CIO had finally expelled the ILA, and the rebel group at Xavier was growing, with men coming in from all over the harbor.

Now sold on my devotion to their cause, Father Corridan urged me to do what I could to bring their struggle to public attention. Despite Johnson's breakthrough work in the late forties, the public was still almost totally unaware of what the honest longshoremen were up against. Even the august *New York Times* was ignoring the issue. "Our guys are getting killed down here but you'd never know it from reading the *Times*," Corridan said.

So I went to the *Times* managing editor, Turner Catledge, and told him of Corridan's accusation. Catledge took it well, and invited me to write our side of it. When I wrote "Joe Docks: Forgotten Man on the Waterfront," for the *Sunday Times Magazine*, I felt I was running with the baton that Mike Johnson had handed me. "Joe Docks" described the shape-up in all its brutal inhumanity, as well as the desperate lives of the men caught in its trap. Thanks to Johnson, Corridan, and Brownie, I had been moved to go down to watch the shape-up for myself, and to follow the rejected men back to the bar where they took refuge and drank their beers in bitter frustration. The article was so well received that I went on writing articles for the *Times* and other periodicals, at the same time taking notes for the revised screenplay and discussing its progress with Kazan.

When I finally finished the screenplay, to Kazan's enthusiastic approval, we took it out to Darryl Zanuck, the cocky little boss of 20th Century-Fox. All the way out on the Santa Fe Super Chief, Kazan kept telling me how much Zanuck was going to love it. And when I said I wouldn't be too sure about that, he thought I was being a nervous Nellie. But I knew my Hollywood. After all, it's my hometown. When we finally got in to see Zanuck, having waited all day, he promptly threw it back in our teeth, stabbing me in the heart when he said, "All you've got is a lot of sweaty longshoremen. Exactly what the American public doesn't want to see." When every other major studio turned us down, it looked as if we were dead in the water again. Harry Cohn, the all-seeing *macher* of Columbia, had now rejected it twice, first my script for Joe Curtis, and now my revised version for Kazan. If you add Arthur Miller's script to the list, *The Waterfront* was three strikes and you're out.

I was ready to go back to my farm to write the screenplay as a novel. Kazan won my heart, though, by saying he was so determined to make it that he was ready to get a handheld camera, get actors from the Actors Studio to work for scale, and shoot it himself on the docks. But freebooter Sam Spiegel, providentially across the corridor from us at the Beverly Hills Hotel, came to our rescue. He had a dismal flop on his hands, *Melba*, a movie about the old opera star Dame Nellie Melba that he literally couldn't give away. In his desperation, he told Kazan that if he could shoot my script on a B budget, in thirty-five days, he thought he could raise the money from United Artists. By this time, Marlon Brando, our first choice, had also turned it down, and we had Frank Sinatra in tow. He had just scored in *From Here to Eternity*, and he had grown up in Hoboken, where we planned to shoot the film. It seemed an ideal fit. Spiegel set it up at UA for $800,000, but he was still determined to *schmeikel* Brando back into it. And that's exactly what he did. You could hear Sinatra screaming from one coast to the other, with good cause. But, somehow, Spiegel, a devious genius, worked out a settlement, and with Brando back in the fold Sam managed to finagle the script away from UA and back to Cohn, who signed on, reluctantly, because, with Brando on board, he had little to lose on such a low budget.

So Kazan and I, and Father Corridan and Brownie and all those stand-up guys, were finally in business. I wonder if there's ever been a film so closely identified with a cause. It was, in many ways, a documentary. There was the shape-up battle for the metal work tabs; the meetings in the church basement; the beating of the men by ILA goons; the establishment of a Waterfront Crime Commission hearing, with Corridan urging the men to break their Mafia-like D 'n' D (deaf and dumb) code in order to bring the ILA's crimes to public attention; the takeover of one racket-ridden pier by the rebels, as described in my *Times* piece, "How One Pier (#45) Got Rid of the Mob"; the unforgettable sermon Father Corridan gave on the docks, "Christ in the Shape-Up," which I laid in virtually word for word—there was hardly a scene in the film that I hadn't actually seen or heard of firsthand.

Kazan and I were hoping the film could be shown before the impending National Labor Relations Board election between the ILA and the insurgent union backed by the AFL. Corridan and the rebels felt it would definitely help their cause. We suspected that Spiegel wanted to release it after the election, since he wasn't as involved in the cause as we were and instead wanted to separate the film from the active struggle as much as possible.

When we opened, unheralded, at the Astor at eleven in the morning, our loyal little band was all there together; Kazan and I, Father Corridan, Brownie, and half a dozen fellow "insoigents." We were amazed to find a line around the block. But we reasoned that with twenty-five thousand working longshoremen and their families, all the related workers, and the mob and their families, we'd be doing business for at least a couple of days. None of us dreamed of what lay ahead. But the next morning's reviews were unqualified raves, even hailing it as a new kind of American film. It was beginning to dawn on us that we had touched a nerve. When our friends had asked us if we thought the public would like it, our stubborn answer had been: "We have no idea. All we know is *we* like it." Harry Cohn had walked out of the projection room without even saying good night. And after a screening for the cast, Marlon Brando summed it up for Karl Malden: "In and out. In and out." So when we won all those Oscars, including Marlon's first, we were still so

New York was one of the leading ports in the United States for more than a century. This drawing, from *Harper's Weekly* (July 14, 1877), shows the crowded, busy docks during the heyday of the sailing era.

teed off at the Hollywood bigs that we refused to attend their fancy Governors' Ball and instead we threw our own party at our favorite Chinese restaurant, the House of Chan, for the dockworkers who had helped us, five ex–heavyweight title contenders cast as the ILA goons, and the crew—a real blue-collar blowout that went on until dawn. Father Corridan was there. Even Kazan had a drink. And instead of champagne, a lot of Guckenheimer's and beer went down that night.

It's been an amazing ride. Who could have guessed when Malcolm Johnson got the ball rolling in *The New York Sun* that it would keep on rolling for fifty years and more? When Father Corridan saw the movie, he said, "When the public sees what a shape-up is really like, they'll never be able to hold 'em again." When the shape-up was finally banned soon after, it meant more to us, honest to God, than all those Oscars. And when hiring halls were established and a bistate waterfront commission set in place, Johnson's and Corridan's and all of our hopes were finally being answered, even though there was still a long way to go. We're proud that our film filled such an urgent need. And it all began with the story behind the story, so fearlessly told by Malcolm Johnson, in whose groundbreaking steps I did my best to follow.

Brookside
October 21, 2004

PART ONE

CRIME ON THE WATERFRONT

NEW YORK, MONDAY, NOVEMBER 8, 1948

Mobsters, Linked to Vast International Crime Syndicate, Rule New York Piers by Terror, Reaping Untold Millions

OUTLAW FRONTIER

New York's great waterfront, representing an investment of approximately $900 million in port facilities, has been aptly described as an "outlaw frontier" where organized crime flourishes unchecked at a cost of untold millions of dollars annually to the port's shipping.

Here, in the world's busiest port, with its 906 piers, 100 ferry landings, 96 car-float landings and 57 ship building, drydock and repair plants, criminal gangs operate with apparent immunity from the law. These gangs are well organized and their control of the piers is absolute. Their greatest weapon is terror, invoked by their strong-arm squads and their gunmen. Their power is such that they are able to levy tribute on every pound of cargo arriving at this port. This is accomplished through highly lucrative rackets controlled by gangsters.

The fact that lawlessness and racketeering exist on New York's waterfront is nothing new. Indeed, that fact is part of this story. The point is that for many years little or nothing has been done to bring law and order and efficiency to the waterfront. As a result, the situation today probably is worse than ever before. Powerful forces are at work to coordinate all the rackets on the waterfront, with a view of taking an even larger bite out of the port's estimated annual revenue of more than $146 million.

MOBSTERS GROW BOLDER SINCE END OF WAR

An extensive investigation by *The New York Sun*, conducted with the cooperation of official and private agencies, indicates that since World War II the waterfront mobsters are stronger and bolder and more firmly entrenched than ever before. The situation is causing New York to lose shipping revenue as shippers move to other ports where such conditions do not prevail.

Thus New York's preeminence as a port, capable of handling almost twice as much traffic as all other Atlantic ports combined, is threatened. This is due to one factor alone: rackets on the New York waterfront are driving costs higher and higher, causing shippers to boycott this port whenever possible.

On that point spokesmen for trade agencies glumly agree. They also agree, as do official investigators, that the key to the control by the waterfront criminals is through the unions, particularly the powerful International Longshoremen's Association, AFL, headed by Joseph P. Ryan, who has a lifetime job at $20,000 a year.

Officials of this big union have been publicly accused again and again of associating with and protecting known gangsters and racketeers. The union has been described in official reports, notably that of the Citizens Water Front Committee, of being "notoriously graft- and racketeer-ridden." The committee also charged that the union leadership has been "unable, or unwilling, to take the lead in reorganizing the labor market, in wiping out the graft and rackets which sustain themselves through the shape-up," the antiquated system of hiring, condemned as far back as Mayor Mitchel's administration in 1916.

EX-CONVICTS HOLD KEY JOBS ON PIERS

Through the union, mobsters are able to control all key jobs on the piers and rackets operate without interference. In some instances, known criminals have official positions in the union locals. In others they have strong alliances and can dictate policy. By dominating the locals, the criminals succeed in placing their own men—or men approved by them—in jobs controlling the hiring of stevedores and the checking of cargo. It will be seen that this is vital to their purpose in maintaining complete control of the piers.

The waterfront, therefore, has become a veritable haven for ex-convicts, many of whom are in key jobs. In fact, rank-and-file longshoremen, themselves victims of the racketeers, complain bitterly that an honest man has difficulty in improving his lot on the waterfront; the preference is given to ex-convicts.

Control on the various piers shifts from time to time. The shift usually is accompanied by murder as one gang ousts another and takes over. And the prize for control is a big cut in the estimated $25 million paid annually for loading and discharging cargo.

The racketeers and gang bosses also reap handsome profits from systematic thievery at the piers. This has been estimated as high as $50 million a year in cargo losses. Another lucrative racket is the loading racket, a system by which the mobsters, controlling the so-called public loaders, collect a fee on every pound of cargo loaded on trucks at the piers. The truckmen forced to pay this loading fee pass the cost on to the consignee. In the end the public pays, as usual, in added costs for consumer goods.

SUN SERIES WILL IDENTIFY LEADERS

Nor do the rackets end there. The gangsters control and collect on every form of illegal activity on the waterfront. This includes extortion, kickbacks from the wages earned by the longshoremen, loan-sharking, gambling, duplicate hiring, smuggling, and various other criminal enterprises. These rackets and the manner in which they operate will be described in detail in succeeding articles in *The Sun*.

Succeeding articles also will identify the leaders and their principals in the waterfront gangs and the territories controlled by them. Hiring bosses with criminal records will be identified and racket unions exposed. It will be shown that the mobsters can exert powerful influence in high places, this influence extending to Washington.

In this connection, experienced investigators are convinced that New York's waterfront criminals operate with the knowledge and consent of a vast crime syndicate that has national and international connections. It is admittedly difficult to link the big crime syndicate with direct participation in the waterfront rackets, but no organized crime exists in the United States today without the consent of these higher-ups in the echelons of crime, who take their cut on all sources of underworld revenue.

CRIME SYNDICATE IS LOOSELY KNIT

The crime syndicate is described by these official investigators as a loosely knit organization with alliances and interests in every major city in this country, and with connections in Italy, South America, and Mexico. Composed of master criminals and racket bosses in the big cities, the syndicate controls virtually every phase of organized crime: the narcotic traffic, gambling, vice, labor, and industrial racketeering. In addition to its underworld operations, the syndicate members have tremendous investments in numerous legitimate enterprises. They own hotels, restaurants, nightclubs, banks, apartment houses, and office buildings. They also own, all too often, judges and policemen and other officials sworn to uphold the law.

"I know it sounds fantastic, but it's true," said one investigator. "The syndicate is like a big trade association in crime. It began back in Prohibition, and it is still strong today. It has big interests in New York, of course, and in Hollywood, Miami, Chicago, Detroit, and other key cities. Its chief source of revenue is from gambling. It owns big gambling houses, controls bookmaking. The take is beyond estimate."

On the subject of the syndicate an FBI agent said cautiously, "I can tell you this much: people who are in a position to know are convinced that such a syndicate has existed for years."

New York, Tuesday, November 9, 1948

Actors in Pier Drama Have Long Police Records—One, "Marked" for Death, Tells How a Mob Takes Over

MEET THE BOYS

The New York waterfront covers an area of some 770 miles, of which about 350 miles have been developed with piers and slips. These piers, almost without exception, are controlled by mobsters and labor racketeers. Each gang rules a territory and rules it with an iron hand, its power enforced by killers and strong-arm squads.

Meet, then, some of the boys: On the Hudson River piers, on Manhattan's West Side, a mob headed by Mickey Bowers, a convicted robber with a long criminal record, controls everything above Forty-second Street. The principal piers in this area are Piers 84, 86, 90, and 92, which the District Attorney's Office has described as "hot piers."

Between Forty-second and Fourteenth streets, including the Chelsea district, control of the piers is divided among several racket bosses. One of the reputed powers in this section is an old-time criminal named Tim O'Mara, or O'Meara, an alumnus of Owney Madden's big mob that flourished in Prohibition days. O'Mara's criminal record shows nine arrests between 1910 and 1924, and includes prison sentences for burglary and armed robbery.

The piers below Fourteenth Street, from Pier 51 down to the foot of Cedar Street, are dominated by a mob formerly headed by John M. Dunn, now held at Sing Sing under pending action by the Court of

Appeals on a motion for a new trial. Dunn's brother-in-law and early partner in crime, Edward McGrath, an ex-convict, is the present power behind the Dunn mob, according to official investigators.

The lower Manhattan piers are controlled by representatives of the old Socks Lanza gang, which long dominated the Fulton Fish Market. Lanza is in prison, but still maintains control, according to waterfront informants, through his lieutenants.

The East River piers and the tough South Brooklyn docks are controlled by the notorious Albert Anastasia, a gunman arrested five times for murder. He once spent eighteen months in the death house, until he won a new trial and acquittal.

ONCE NAMED AS LEADER IN MURDER, INC.

Anastasia, once named as a director in Murder, Inc., the organization of hired killers, continues to rule the Brooklyn waterfront, his bailiwick for years, as the representative of Joe Adonis, Brooklyn's boss racketeer, now ruling in absentia, directing his numerous operations from New Jersey. Adonis is pictured as one of the principals in the big crime syndicate that reputedly controls rackets on a national and international scale.

These racketeers on the waterfront control all activity on the piers: the loading of trucks, for which they charge fees running into millions of dollars annually; policy games, shylocking, bookmaking, kickbacks, and a clever system of duplicate hiring by which steamship and stevedoring companies are gypped on padded payrolls.

The domain ruled by Mickey Bowers on Manhattan's Upper West Side is operating so successfully that Bowers has organized his own company, the Allied Stevedoring Company, which engages in loading operations. Profits have been so high that the company now has about $60,000 worth of equipment.

Lieutenants in the Bowers gang are John Keefe and John Applegate, who, like Bowers, are ex-convicts, and a mystery man who has no record. This man is the president of the Allied Stevedoring Company, though his experience on the waterfront seems to be nonexistent. He is John T. Ward, thirty-nine. Bowers is secretary and Keefe is treasurer. Each of the officers draws a nominal salary of $100 a week. The company hires up to twenty-five "public loaders" a day. These are members of the International Longshoremen's Association and are paid the union scale for their work. They are under the jurisdiction of Local 824 of the ILA, of which Harold Bowers, a cousin of Mickey's, is the delegate.

HOW GANG OBTAINS CONTROL OF PIERS

And how does a gang obtain control of a rich waterfront section? It's easy if you are strong enough—and God help you if you are not. All you do is to move in and declare yourself in control. That's how the Bowers mob did it.

Listen to an informant, whom we'll call Joe, because that's not his name, and because Joe feels that he's marked for death for having crossed the Bowers mob. He says that one attempt has been made on his life, and that all he craves now is to get out of town. That's Joe, who looks meek and mild, but isn't.

"While I was in Sing Sing back in 1933, doing time for robbery, I met Johnny Applegate," said Joe. "Apple was in for burglary. We got to be friendly. Apple told me to look him up when I got out. Some months later I looked up Apple on the waterfront. He introduced me to a union delegate they called the Bandit, who got me a union membership book without me having to pay for it. I got steady work as a longshoreman, though I had never done a day's work on the waterfront in my life. I got to know all the ins and outs. How the rackets worked. You know."

At that time a mobster named Beadle was in control of the piers above Forty-second Street. Beadle, himself suspected of several killings, was murdered in December 1939. Then Richard Gregory, the union delegate known as the Bandit, was killed just a year later.

"After the Bandit was knocked off," said Joe, "there was a fight for power on the Upper West Side. Suddenly, a new mob walked in and took over. That was the Bowers mob, and I started paying dues to these boys. We got a membership book for $26, a cut rate. The official rate was $150. The mob never put no stamps in our books. I guess two thousand men paid off in this way. The collector was Harold Bowers, Mickey's cousin."

GANGSTERS POSSESS LONG POLICE RECORDS

The Bowers gang has been in control ever since. Bowers, a growing power on the waterfront, has been arrested fourteen times, his record dating back to 1920, when he got an indeterminate prison sentence in New Jersey for violating the highway law. In 1924, he got another sentence, up to three years for grand larceny, and in 1930 he was sent away for ten years in New Jersey for a payroll robbery. He was released on parole in 1937, and, two years later, arrested for bank robbery and discharged.

Bowers's lieutenants, Keefe and Applegate, also have lengthy records. Keefe has been arrested eight times and convicted twice. In 1925, he was sent to Elmira Reformatory for assault. In 1928, he was sentenced to twelve years in the New Jersey State Prison for assault and battery and robbery.

Applegate, arrested five times, was sentenced in 1933 to two and a half to ten years in Sing Sing for burglary, and paroled in 1936.

Ward, the husky, six-foot president of Bowers's company, Allied Stevedoring, has no record and because of this he was recently described by Assistant District Attorney William J. Keating as "the luckiest man in New York."

When questioned as to how Ward happened to become president of Allied Stevedoring, in view of his complete lack of experience on the waterfront, Mickey Bowers glared at his questioner and retorted: "Hell, if you'd been up there and put up $2,000, we'd have made you president!"

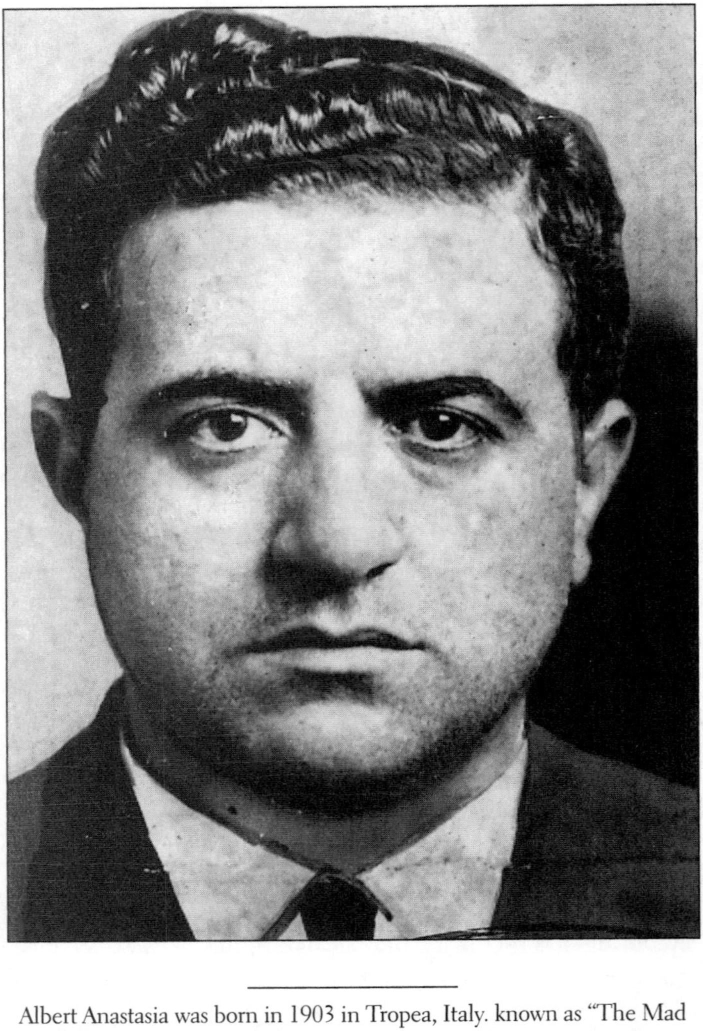

Albert Anastasia was born in 1903 in Tropea, Italy. known as "The Mad Hatter," and the "Lord High Executioner," he was the head of Murder, Inc. He was closley tied to lucky Luciano and Louis (Lepke) Buchalter. He was murdered in a New York City barbershop in 1957. Reproduced from the Collections of the Library of Congress.

WARD DESCRIBED HIMSELF AS BOOKIE

Curious about Ward, District Attorney Hogan's office early last summer picked him up on a vagrancy charge, though he owns a $15,000 home in Queens and had $350 in his pocket when arrested. He explained that he got the money booking horses.

When Ward was arraigned before Magistrate Leonard McGee on June 24, Assistant District Attorney Keating told the court:

"This man, the defendant, was picked up and arrested at my order in connection with the investigation of several homicides on the West Side, one of which involved the shooting and killing of a man named Whalen. This man has never been arrested before. He has been under investigation and he was picked up in the past and questioned in connection with bank robberies both by the FBI and city authorities. He has a reputation of being a knockdown man without ever having been arrested before, as a result of which he has the reputation of being the luckiest man in New York.

"He seems to be living in good circumstances. He has a $15,000 home with only a $4,000 mortgage on it. He gives no satisfactory explanation for the source of his income, except that he is president of the Allied Stevedoring Corporation, which is an organization including several notorious criminals and which operates as a front for the loading racket on the docks. He said he hasn't picked up his weekly check of $100 in four weeks but he says he has been booking horses."

ATTEMPTED TO BRIBE REPORTER FOR *SUN*

Keating continued: "He admits being closely associated for years, and at the present time, with such characters as Charlie Yanowsky, a Jersey racketeer who is now making attempts to get control of various International Longshoremen's Association charters, and also with Whitey Miller and Hugo Fried, who were mixed up in the gasoline stamp racket. Also Mickey Bowers and John Keefe, notorious bandits and hijackers."

Yanowsky, mentioned by Keating as an associate of Ward's, was murdered last July in New Jersey.

On being discharged for lack of evidence, Ward, who weighs 245 pounds and has a plump, babyish face, attempted to bribe a *New York Sun* reporter to keep his name out of the paper. "Go buy yourself a smoke," Ward said, handing the reporter a $10 bill. The reporter returned the money. Ward then tried to stuff the bill in the reporter's coat. The reporter again returned it, and Ward shrugged and walked away with his attorney.

So much for the Bowers gang. Activities of other waterfront gangs will be described in subsequent articles in this series.

NEW YORK, WEDNESDAY, NOVEMBER 10, 1948

Annual Cargo Losses From Organized Thefts Put at $50 Million

ENTIRE TRUCKLOADS VANISH

Still Shipping Lines Hesitate to File Complaints, But Engage FBI Veteran

---

THE BIGGEST RACKET

Organized thievery at the piers is by far the most lucrative of all the rackets controlled by criminals on the waterfront. Losses from cargo thefts run into millions of dollars annually. The exact total cannot be calculated, due to many intricate factors, but it has been estimated as high as $50 million a year.

Whole truckloads of cargo disappear from the piers without a trace. Hijackers take their toll from shipments en route to and from the piers. Casual pilferage by individual thieves, awaiting only opportunity, sends the loss totals higher, but this form of theft is negligible compared with the highly organized stealing by the gangs. And here again the key to the business is thorough control of the union labor by the mobsters in power on the piers. They dictate the hiring of union members and see to it that the "right men" get the important jobs. The right men in most instances are members of the mob, usually ex-convicts.

"To do it right some of the clerical help must be in on the racket," said one informant, an ex-convict who freely admitted having worked with the mob in various thefts. "It is a mob operation from beginning to end. You can go in for larceny on your own, but it's dangerous. The gang bosses don't like it. Have you ever noticed how many times some longshoremen get turned in for stealing a bottle or two of liquor or maybe a sack of potatoes to take home to their families? The mobs, working through the union, turn them in. They don't want any amateur thieves cutting in on them.

HOW MOBSTERS "FINGER" A LOAD

Organized thefts, the informant continued, are committed with the cooperation of checkers controlled by the gang.

"The crooked dock boss, in most cases a member of the mob, 'fingers' a load, taking his orders from a gang lieutenant," he explained. "He goes to the checker, points out a truckload of merchandise, and says: 'Danny said get this one.' The checker knows what to do. He measures the load, then gives the truck driver a receipt. Only it's a phony receipt, signed 'Joe Blow.' Understand? Then he makes out a legitimate receipt, but the trucker doesn't get this. All his other papers are legitimate and stamped. Up to now, everything has been legitimate except that phony receipt."

Finally, somewhere along the line, the legitimate papers are recovered and destroyed before the consignment is loaded on the ship.

"The stuff, of course, never is loaded on the ship," the informant explained. "It is taken away at the convenience of the mob. They'll send a truck down for it. The driver has papers. They look okay. He tells the dock boss he's there for a load of textiles, or whatever it is. The dock boss points it out to him, and he loads it up, checks at the gate with the checker, and goes on his way. That's all there is to it. This consignment is supposed to be bound for South America, say. It is weeks before the loss is discovered. It's never delivered in South America.

"Months later an insurance investigator comes around. He has that phony checker's receipt. He inquires about that cargo. Nobody ever heard of it. It never got to the pier. He says it must have, for here's the receipt. Where's Joe Blow, the checker? That gets a laugh, and they tell him there's nobody around there by that name, and never was. The stuff never got to the pier. They keep telling him that, and he goes away. He knows better, but he can't prove anything. The stuff is never traced. It's listed as a nondelivery."

BUREAU ORGANIZED TO REDUCE LOSSES

That's one way of doing it, according to this informant. There are other ways, and they are all practiced.

The thievery is so prevalent and costly that a bureau was organized by the leading steamship lines in an effort to reduce the losses. It is called the Security Bureau, Inc., and is headed by Edward E. Conroy, a gray-haired veteran of the FBI. Conroy devotes his full time to investigating thefts and devising means of reducing them.

In a recent bulletin, Conroy reported that some maritime cargo claim agents estimated that as many as ninety-nine out of a hundred cases of nondelivery are due to theft and pilfering. As a result of further information from experts in the marine insurance field, the Security Bureau recommended that the nondelivery losses should be reported on the theft forms, unless there was reason to believe that the loss was due to some cause other than theft, such as misdelivery, "sling losses," or the dropping of cargo overboard during loading or unloading operations, or the obliteration of names and addresses of consignees.

Until the Security Bureau corrected the situation about a year ago, through a campaign of education, the steamship lines often were reluctant to prosecute thieves, even when they were found in possession of stolen goods. The apathy on the part of the companies, it was explained, was due to fear of suits for false arrest. It also may have been due, in part—though the Security Bureau has never said so—to a fear of reprisals from the gangs in control at the piers.

"Almost invariably," said one bureau bulletin, "police officials have complained that they have been handicapped by lack of cooperation on the part of transportation companies. They state specifically that representatives of these companies often refuse to swear complaints against thieves found in possession of stolen property and that, as a result, the police are powerless to have warrants issued for the arrest of those thieves.

"When officials of steamship companies have been confronted with this criticism of the police, they have often contended that the situation was due to the fact that they were fearful of civil suits for false arrest. When these officials have cited specific cases, it has been found that they had little actual basis for this fear. It has been determined generally that the attitude was due to a lack of knowledge of legal procedure."

LAW OF THE JUNGLE PREVAILS ON DOCKS

Accordingly, Conroy issued digests of laws pertaining to larceny, false arrest, malicious prosecution, libel, and slander. The result, he says, has been encouraging. Shipping lines now are less reluctant to make complaints, and he urges vigorous prosecution whenever possible.

Due to so many factors involved, including the fact that known criminals infest the waterfront, the Security Bureau doesn't hope to eliminate cargo thefts entirely. It does hope to provide greater safeguards against this hazard and thus to keep the thefts, generally regarded as a "necessary evil," to a minimum.

But here again the law is pitted against powerful, highly organized forces: crooked truck men working in collusion with thieves; and graft and racketeering in the International Longshoremen's Association, the AFL union in control on the waterfront, and whose locals, in many instances, are dominated by criminals.

In short, law on the waterfront is essentially the law of the jungle.

It's every man for himself. This attitude is reflected by some steamship and stevedoring officials. They deplore the situation but hesitate to take any positive steps to correct it. With them, it's a matter of self-preservation, of survival.

SITUATION IS CALLED "A HELL OF A NOTE"

An official of a big stevedoring company summed it up this way:

"Sure, I'd like to see this situation cleaned up. It's a hell of a note. Crime and racketeering are driving business away from this port every day. But I'm in business to make money and for no other reason. I want to stay in business. I can't afford to stick my neck out. I'm no reformer. I can't be jumping into something that doesn't directly concern me. That goes for the loading racket and the thievery, too.

"Take the matter of thievery. That's up to the insurance companies and the steamship lines. If I went to my stevedores inquiring about cargo thefts and protesting, you know what would happen? The boss stevedore would look at me and say, 'What the hell business is that of yours? You didn't lose anything, did you? It wasn't your stuff stolen.' And that's as far as I'd get with that."

In connection with the truckers, the Security Bureau reported recently that its campaign to reduce thefts had run up against stubbornness on the part of truck drivers asked to give their names when delivering cargo for the piers. Many drivers refused, and their attitude was described by the bureau as a threat to security and an obstruction to pilferage investigation. It was found, the bureau said, that 599 out of 1,379 drivers checked at three piers had refused to reveal their identities. They would offer no explanation for this refusal, other than that it was nobody's business.

Failure of the drivers to be identified makes the investigation of thefts more difficult, since it is manifestly hard to trace lost merchandise handled by unknown truckers. According to the bureau, drivers generally do not sign their names when delivering cargo to the piers, though drivers picking up shipments must sign receipts.

At the bureau's request, trucking associations urged their members to instruct drivers to give or sign their names when asked by an authorized agent. Since then, the situation has been corrected to some extent.

NEW YORK, THURSDAY, NOVEMBER 11, 1948

Truckers Being Forced by Threats to Pay Toll to Loading Racketeers

OTHER PORTS CAPTURE TRADE

System That Started on Docks Has Spread to Terminals and Inland Markets

---

THE LOADING RACKET

Next to organized thievery, described in the preceding article, the most lucrative racket on the waterfront is the loading racket.

It is a system, long in existence, by which gangsters and their union henchmen collect a fee on every pound of cargo trucked from the piers by compelling truckmen to pay so-called public loaders to load the trucks. The truckmen pass the charges on to the consignees, so that in the end the public pays, as usual, in higher costs of consumer goods. These costs run to millions of dollars annually.

The loading racket originated in the waterfront shortly after the First World War. In recent years, the system has spread to inland platform terminals and markets. Efforts have been made, with varying degrees of success, to impose these racket fees wherever a truck backs up for loading. According to maritime experts, the system obtains in no other port in the United States—another factor cited as driving business away from the Port of New York.

CHEAPER FOR TRUCKER TO PAY RACKET FEE

The racket has become so commonplace, so generally accepted as another of the "necessary evils" plaguing the New York waterfront, that it has assumed an air of legitimacy. The so-called public loaders, members of the International Longshoremen's Association, AFL, are controlled by the racket bosses. The loaders are paid union scale for their labor, and the racket bosses collect the fees, which range from five cents to eleven cents a hundred pounds on incoming cargo trucked from the piers.

The loading racket has become so prevalent, so rigidly enforced, that no truckman dares attempt to load his trucks with his own men, without the consent, at a price, of the racketeers. Not only that, he dares not complain against the use of the public loaders. He uses the public loaders because he knows that if he refuses, his trucks will not be loaded. Indeed, his trucks may be tied up at the piers for many hours, if they are permitted on the pier at all. The trucker finds it cheaper to pay the racket fee.

The racketeers have many ways of compelling the use of their loaders. The recalcitrant truckman may find that he can get no checker to check the freight; thus his truck stands idle and is not loaded. Threats of violence have been common through the years, and the racket has flourished mainly through coercion. Truckmen have become so intimidated, so resigned to this racket, that they don't even complain anymore. And without complaints, the law cannot prosecute.

In some instances, the racket bosses in control at the piers are so brazen that they use as loaders men paid by the stevedoring or steamship companies. Thus, at no labor costs to them, the gangsters collect and keep the fat loading fees, their laborers drawn from the payrolls of the companies. There are cases, too, where the racketeers impose loading fees where no service is rendered. They permit the truckman and his helpers, paid by the trucking companies, to load the trucks, but they collect the loading fees.

In the early days, the loading charges averaged about three cents a hundred pounds. The rate has risen steadily through the years, to the minimum of five cents a hundred. Despite efforts in that direction, shippers complain that there are no uniform rate schedules. The gangster boss charges whatever he feels like charging, whatever he thinks the traffic will bear. And he collects, using strong-arm squads where necessary, through most truckmen today pay off without protest.

PROTEST WAS RAISED WAY BACK IN 1933

As far back as 1933, there was organized protest against the racket by the New York Merchants Association, now the Commerce and Industry Association of New York, and allied organizations, including the chambers of commerce of the state of New York, Brooklyn Chamber of Commerce, Shippers' Conference of Greater New York, Newark Chamber of Commerce, New Jersey Industrial Traffic League, and the Mineral Products Association.

"A group of men, so-called public loaders, infest the freight terminals and, principally through strong-arm methods, enforce an unnecessary tax, estimated at many millions of dollars, against a large volume of traffic destined to or moving through this port," these trade associations charged. "It is evident that the conditions complained of exist, because of intimidation, physical violence, and sabotage on the part of these loaders. This practice works a distinct hardship on legitimate business; it is diverting business from the Port of New York, and many claim it is a most reprehensible form of racketeering. This practice does not exist in any other competing city. . . ."

That was in 1933. The charges were true then, and they are true today. Nothing has been done to correct the evil. Truckmen still fear to make organized protest. Steamship lines say they can do nothing about it.

"It's a result of apathy on the part of everybody," commented Joseph A. Sinclair, secretary of the Commerce and Industry Association.

TRUCKERS WON'T PRESS CHARGES OF COERCION

Prosecution? Well, the District Attorney's Office, fully aware of the racket and its long history, patiently explains that there is nothing illegal in the use of public loaders, or their availability at the piers, as long as truckmen and others have free choice to use or not to use this labor. Coercion and intimidation are, of course, illegal, but to prove this there must be complainants. And the truckmen don't want to appear as complainants, for fear of reprisal.

But, privately, the truckmen and shippers alike have complained plenty. Here's what some receivers of freight have had to say:

"By the force of some unwritten law, applicable to loading and unloading practices, we are compelled to employ and pay the usual charges."

"On account of this system and high labor costs in New York, we are doing no shipping or receiving of goods in this port. The bulk of our work is now done through the Port of Philadelphia."

"We are much in sympathy with a campaign against this racket, but we are at the mercy of the loaders."

From truckmen: "We have experienced intimidation and delays to our trucking equipment, and also we have been compelled to pay these loaders without obtaining their services—in short, the labor was performed by our own employees. . . . In general, we have been intimidated and threatened with violence, and many delays were occasioned by these threats. To give all the details would make a book."

DRIVERS CHARGE LOADERS THREATENED VIOLENCE

Truck drivers have complained that the loaders and their gang bosses have threatened them with brickbats and revolvers; that union delegates, backing up the loading bosses, have threatened to throw the drivers into the river.

Such complaints are typical. But the complainants don't want to be identified. They want to stay in business. They want their trucks loaded without the expense and trouble of long delays with idle drivers and idle trucks. It's cheaper, they say, to pay and say nothing.

Then, too, there are some crooked truckmen who work in collusion with loading racketeers. They get a cut rate on loading charges, but charge consignees the full rate. Naturally they don't want to see the racket ended.

In sworn testimony before the United States Maritime Commission, steamship officials admitted that public loaders must be used, that this situation prevailed on the piers in the Port of New York, and that the steamship lines were powerless to do anything about it.

Shippers point out bitterly that such conditions, however, do not prevail at other ports and that consequently they are diverting shipping to these competing ports. It is a matter of growing concern to New York trade groups and to those interested in the further development of the Port of New York.

Further details on the loading racket will be described in subsequent articles.

NEW YORK, FRIDAY, NOVEMBER 12, 1948

Loading Racket Organized on Business Basis by Varick Enterprises

FEES TAKEN BY ARMED GOONS

Reluctant Truckmen Beaten Up—Paid Even Trebled Charges for Jobs Not Done

---

VARICK ENTERPRISES

The story of Varick Enterprises, Inc., is the story of the loading racket at its boldest and most efficient on the waterfront. Varick brought businesslike organization to a racket that has flourished for more than twenty years and which continues to yield millions of dollars annually to the gangsters in control of the piers.

Incorporated under the laws of the state of New York, Varick Enterprises served as a clearinghouse for the loading racket, the system by which the mobsters who rule the waterfront exact a fee on every pound of freight loaded on trucks at the piers. Varick at one time had as many as a thousand "accounts," or truckmen who were paying loading charges to the company. These fees were collected by squads of goons, who enforced their demands with blackjacks and guns. The truckmen paid, regardless of whether Varick's loaders performed any service or not. The evidence shows that in many instances no service was performed but that the organization was so strong that the loading charges were paid anyway. One official report to the district attorney concerning Varick states that a truckman who complained was "taken care of" by the boys. "He complains no more," the report concludes.

Varick prospered for years, but quietly folded after the District Attorney's Office began an investigation. Its principals, including certain union officials who acted as a "front" for the gangsters, scattered, but today still are involved in waterfront rackets, though not on such a pretentious scale. Though Varick no longer is in existence, it serves as a pattern by which similar organizations are conducted, in the opinion of investigators, under different names.

ORIGIN OF VARICK TRACED TO DRY ERA

The gangsters active in Varick Enterprises included John M. Dunn, the powerful waterfront criminal whose execution at Sing Sing for murder was stayed after he had appealed for a new trial, and his brother-in-law, Ed McGrath, though they remained pretty much in the background when Varick was at the height of its power. Dunn was just rising to authority and had not yet assumed leadership of the so-called Village mob, which controlled the piers below Fourteenth Street. The leader during this period was one George Daggert, who was killed in an automobile accident in 1940. Ed McGrath was driver of the car in which Daggert was killed. After Daggert's death, Dunn and McGrath assumed control of the mob.

The shady origin of Varick Enterprises goes back to Prohibition days. At that time, an accountant named Charlie M—— was working for various beer-running mobs. While doing this work, Charlie learned that some of the truckmen were keeping two sets of books, one set showing the actual condition of their companies, the other falsified for income tax purposes. He informed a certain union representative of this situation, and Varick Enterprises evolved as a medium by which the truckmen could be blackmailed as the price for silence on their income tax evasion.

When first set up, Varick was an unincorporated association with offices in Journal Square, Jersey City. It worked so successfully in

Jersey that it eventually was brought to New York, where it was incorporated on May 17, 1937, with the original union official, who is still prominent in union affairs, as one of its officers.

Charlie, the accountant, one of the founders of Varick, kept the records and accounts of the organization, which quickly obtained a stranglehold on the lucrative loading racket that provided a bigger and surer source of income than blackmail.

RELUCTANT TRUCKMEN WERE BEATEN UP

Varick was so well organized that those in control had sources of information as to every shipment of goods, whether by rail or water, arriving in the city. Early every morning, the boss loaders were dispatched to the various terminals, both rail and water. They would check on weights, names of truckers and consignees, compute the loading charges, and issue so-called loading tickets. Through these tickets, setting forth the amount of the charges, Varick made its collections. Payments were made by check or cash, turned in either at Varick's main offices, 99 Hudson Street, or at various collection agencies established in bars and grills and lunch counters along the waterfront. When payments were refused, truckmen were beaten up or threatened.

Investigation revealed that Varick worked closely with the unions, operating in conjunction with practically all of the AFL unions or locals whose membership had anything to do with the movement of goods. Through these unions, the gangsters could threaten reluctant shippers with stoppage of freight in transit if payments were refused.

These unions, of course, included the powerful International Longshoremen's Association, of which Joseph P. Ryan is president, with a lifetime job at $20,000 a year. Through this and allied unions, Varick was able to levy charges on freight arriving in New York and at some of the Jersey piers.

INVESTIGATORS REPORTED POLICEMEN ON PAYROLL

Investigators for the district attorney said there was evidence that policemen in large numbers were on Varick's payroll and were dominated by the racket group. Traffic regulations were unknown to the mob, which seemed to enjoy complete immunity, despite the fact that it folded quickly enough when the District Attorney's Office turned its investigators loose on it back in 1938. As a result, investigators today feel that official inquiry and the spotlight of publicity perhaps are potent weapons against the waterfront gangs, even where prosecution is not possible, due to the known reluctance of witnesses to appear as complainants.

In addition to its offices in Hudson Street, Varick Enterprises also operated from Fourteenth Street and Eighth Avenue, the headquarters of various union locals. Here, John Dunn made his headquarters, controlling delegates and union organizers, while Charlie, the accountant, kept the records at the main offices.

Some idea of the extent of Varick's "take" from the loading racket was obtained when investigators one day observed Charlie meet a Varick official at a cigar store in the Lawyers Trust Building at Fourteenth Street and Eighth Avenue. The time was 6 P.M., and the appointment was made by Charlie by phone. When they met, Charlie was seen to pass several large rolls of currency to the Varick official—the one who doubled as a union officer. The rolls were so large that the Varick official had trouble getting them into his two coat pockets. Subsequently, from Charlie's own statement to investigators, it was established that this money represented the proceeds of one day's loading "collections" by the Varick squads.

It was learned also that the racket group frequently made large deposits in banks and in safe-deposit boxes in the Empire State branch of the Manufacturers Trust Company.

The racketeers, then as now, charged as loading fees whatever they felt like charging, though the basic loading rate in the early days was three cents a hundred pounds. Today the minimum rate is five cents a hundred, and goes as high as eleven cents for certain products. But the fees differ at the various piers, depending, apparently, on what gang happens to be in control and the mood of the boss loader at the moment. And the complaint still is made, privately, that the racketeers exact these fees regardless of whether their loaders actually do any work for the truckman.

WEIGHT OF CARGO EVEN IS TREBLED

The system of collection is the same as that practiced so successfully by Varick Enterprises, through the issuance of loading tickets. These tickets vary in appearance. Some are labeled "Union Loading Ticket," others merely "Loading Ticket," and bear the penciled notation of the amount of the charge and the scrawled signature of the boss loader, who works under orders from the mob. Actually, of course, the tickets have no official connection with any union, despite the fact that the public loaders are union men and are paid union scale.

Complaints from receivers of freight to the Commerce and Industry Association of New York show how widely the loading fees vary and how the consignees frequently are charged double and treble the actual weight of their cargo. One company complained that its shipment totaled 10,000 pounds, but that it was forced to pay for 20,000 pounds. Another paid for 20,000 pounds when the actual weight was 14,000 and the charge was nine cents a hundred. Another paid for 30,000 pounds when the weight was only 10,000.

One shipper stated that he was charged twenty dollars at a Manhattan pier, thirty-five dollars at a Brooklyn pier, and ten dollars at a Jersey pier for three shipments of the same weight.

Theoretically, the loading racket covers only the loading of trucks at piers and freight terminals, but, since the end of World War II, when the gangs reassumed control on the waterfront, widespread ef-

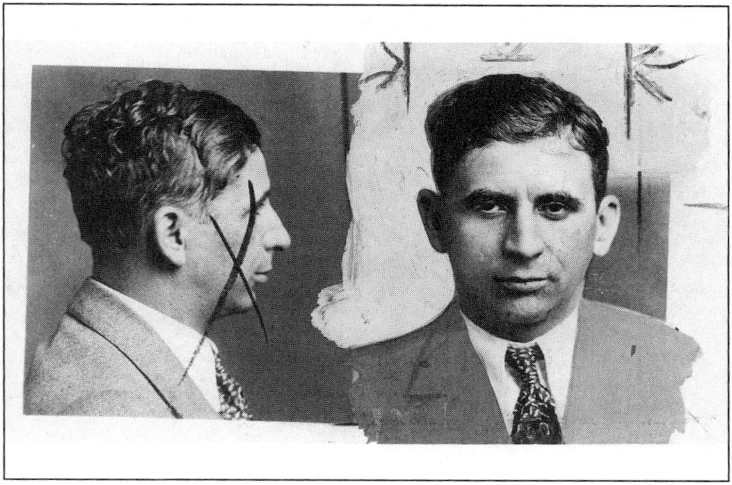

Meyer Lansky was born Maier Suchowljansky, in Grodno, Russia, to Jewish parents, in 1902. He established strong ties with Bugsy Siegel and Lucky Luciano in the 1920s. He was involved in bootlegging and the protection racket in the twenties, and established gambling operations in Florida, New Orleans, and Cuba in the thirties. By the 1960s, Lansky was involved in drug smuggling, pornography, prostitution, and extortion. He had the reputation of staying under the radar of the law, and being the most financially successful of all the national syndicate members. Upon his death, in 1983, it was estimated that he worth more than $400 million. Reproduced from the Collections of the Library of Congress.

forts have been made to extend the racket to the unloading of trucks as well. Here, the racketeers have been balked to some extent by the powerful Teamsters Union, which has always assumed jurisdiction of the unloading, though of late many shippers have complained of being forced to pay for unloading as well as loading.

NEW YORK, MONDAY, NOVEMBER 15, 1948

Telephone Wiretapping Reveals How Loading Mob Ran Racket

SOME SAMPLE CONVERSATIONS

Suspected Leader of Outfit Was Once Chief Gunman for Siegel-Lansky Gang

---

CONVERSATION PIECE

Wiretappers got an earful when they tapped the telephones used by a waterfront loading racket gang with offices on Warren Street. The suspected leader of this particular outfit was once a gunman lieutenant in the big mob headed by the late Bugsy Siegel, who was slain in Hollywood, and Meyer Lansky, a sort of mystery man of the underworld, listed by the late police commissioner Valentine as one of New York's ten public enemies.

Though a product of New York, closely allied with Lepke [Louis Buchalter], the big-shot industrial racketeer, the Siegel-Lansky gang, sometimes known as the Bug and Meyer mob, established its richest territory in Philadelphia, where it controlled the principal rackets, thus escaping the competition of Lepke and others in New York. Lansky is often pictured as one of the suspected principals in the super–crime syndicate, which has national and international connections and which controls major underworld enterprises throughout the United States. Lansky, however, like some others believed to be in this big syndicate, has always managed to escape serious difficulty with the law. He has a record of six or more arrests, but no convictions, though he has been known as an underworld figure for many years.

Whether there is any direct link between Lansky and this particular loading racket gang is not known, though it will be shown later that there were direct connections between Lansky and John M. Dunn, the waterfront mobster, whose execution at Sing Sing for murder has been stayed after he appealed for a new trial. In any event, recorded telephone conversations between office workers and outsiders dealing with this gang clearly show the method of intimidation employed by the loading racketeers to force truckmen to pay their loading charges, regardless of whether the so-called public loaders were used to load their trucks or whether the truckmen did the work themselves. They also indicate the extensive advance information obtained by the gang with respect to incoming freight arriving by rail or water.

CAST OF CHARACTERS IN TELEPHONE TALKS

Principals in this little telephonic drama include one Charlie, who acted as a front for the mob; his son, Larry, who worked in the office; Izzy, another worker, and various men employed on the piers. Here is a conversation between Charlie, from his office, and an outside member of the gang:

OUT: "Hello, Charlie."
IN: "When were you done?"
OUT: "About ten o'clock. They tied up Pete and Sam last night."
IN: "They should have tied up the other bum."
OUT: "I got the blame off Sam; he said I did it."
IN: "What was it all about?"
OUT: "You know."
IN: "I told him and his partner right to the point that the union knows everything and that they should know the score."
OUT: "Yeah, I spoke to Izzy and Joe."
ON: "This is only the beginning. He is going to be belted around like the rest."

OUT: "That's the way."
IN: "Those bums know the score."
OUT: "They oughta be smart, then."

After some conversation about a trip, they hung up.

ONE "GUY" CAUSES "BUNCH OF TROUBLE"

The next conversation overheard was between Larry and an outsider named Logan, presumably a boss loader.

IN: "Hello."
OUT: "Is this Izzy?"
IN: "No, this is Larry."
OUT: "This is Logan. Come down to Pier 18 right away. I have a fellow who is a bunch of trouble."
IN: "I can't come now. What the hell is wrong down there?"
OUT: "This guy here, he doesn't want to pay the price. Wants a receipt for everything. Just causing a bunch of trouble."
IN: "Make out the tickets and give them to him."
OUT: "He wants a union ticket."
IN: "Haven't you got any tickets on you?"
OUT: "No."
IN: "Go over and get some from Gene at 17."
OUT: "I asked Gene for some this morning. He said no good. He said he gave two books to Izzy and that Izzy isn't cooperating, so he isn't giving any more."
IN: "What's that Izzy trying to do, be a big shot?"
OUT: "I don't know. He won't give me any tickets."
IN: "See if you can straighten it out."
OUT: "I can't. This guy wants to shortchange me, and he wants a ticket."

Larry hangs up, calls another number, and speaks to one Jamsie.

IN: "Jamsie, Larry. Logan just called and he hasn't got any tickets. Izzy messed this up good. He thinks he's a big shot. If he says one word to me this afternoon, I'll punch him in the nose. Look, Jamsie, I want you to do me a favor."

OUT: "What is it?"

IN: "Go over to Gene on 17 and ask him for a few books. Tell him they are for Larry and not for that bum Izzy. If he acts as if he doesn't want to give them, tell him I'll give him five for one at the end of the week."

OUT: "Okay."

Larry hangs up.

HEARS BY TELEPHONE THAT FEE IS RAISED

Incoming call:

IN: "Hello."

OUT: "Mr. M——, please."

IN: "Talking."

OUT: "This is Mr. Hall. You have been loading honey off the pier for me at five cents a hundred. Now I understand there's an increase—is that right?"

IN: "Yes. A penny a hundred since last month."

OUT: "Well, your man has been charging me on seven hundred pounds to a barrel, and the manifest from the ship shows they weigh from six hundred to six hundred fifty pounds."

IN: "Well, we don't want any hard feelings on your part, so I'll tell you what. How about charging you for six hundred a barrel?"

OUT: "That's okay."

IN: "Tell the loader I said that."

OUT: "Fine."

IN: "Good-bye."

Incoming call, Logan to Larry:

IN: "What do you want, Logan?"
OUT: "I got some trouble. I wanted to give a fellow down here one of our men, but he doesn't want him. Says he has two men of his own doing the loading."
IN: "Who the hell does he think he is! That's what we are down there for."
OUT: "He refuses to sign the ticket. We had a pretty stiff argument."
IN: "Well, ask him to sign once more. If he doesn't, take the name of the outfit and the number of the truck and we'll take care of him."
OUT: "Okay."

LOADING FEE STANDS FOR BAD TOMATOES

Incoming call, Herman to Izzy:

OUT: "This is Herman. I got a ticket where you charged me $13.10. You have it marked 'In.' What is that?"
IN: "That's on that eight hundred and some odd Cuban tomatoes. We took them in at the dock."
OUT: "You did in the pig's neck. My men took them in. Your men weren't even on the pier."
IN (*very angry voice*): "I said we took them off. That's that. My man said he and a few others of my men took them off."
OUT: "Well your men weren't even there, and the Board of Health condemned more than four hundred of the tomatoes."
IN: "I can't help that. That's your headache."

OUT: "I suppose you'll even want to charge me for the bad tomatoes."

IN: "If we load them, why not?"

OUT: "But you didn't load anything. I'm going to find out about this, don't worry."

IN: "Go ahead."

MOB FINDS OUT WIRES WERE TAPPED

While Larry's father was in Florida for the winter season, the mob got wise to the fact that the wires were tapped, as indicated in the following conversation between the father, calling from Florida, and the son:

IN: "Joe L—— is leaving tonight or tomorrow. Meet him. He has a message that Izzy gave him to give you."

OUT: "What time is he leaving? How is he coming, by train or plane?"

IN: "I can't tell you now."

OUT: "What's the matter with you? If there is someone near the phone, chase them. What's the message Izzy gave to Joe? What is it?"

IN: "I can't tell you."

OUT: "Why didn't you write or send a telegram, if it's that important."

IN: "I didn't want to do that. You know."

OUT: "Why the hell can't you tell me now? If it's that important, empty the office and tell me."

IN: "I can't tell you."

OUT (*very angry*): "What the hell is the matter with you? Do you think the phone is tapped or something?"

IN: "I think the phone is tapped."

OUT: "Are you sure?"

IN: "I'm almost positive."

OUT: "Well, all right, then. I will see Joe and get the message from him. What makes you think the phone is tapped?"

IN: "I'm pretty sure. I can't say much. These guys that are doing that on the wire are nobody's fools. Joe will tell you everything when he sees you."

OUT: "Okay. So long."

Shortly after this conversation, the gang moved from the office on Warren Street.

NEW YORK, TUESDAY, NOVEMBER 16, 1948

Armed Criminals Attend Business Meeting at Hotel New Yorker After Truckers Appeal for Uniform Rates

A MEETING CALLED

In the fall of 1942, an important meeting took place at the Hotel New Yorker. Among those present were some of New York's best-known criminals, most of them heavily armed. They came as representatives of the so-called public loaders who operate the loading racket on the New York waterfront, the system by which racketeers levy charges on every pound of freight loaded on trucks at the piers and waterfront warehouses.

Present also was Joseph P. Ryan, president of the International Longshoremen's Association, the AFL union that controls waterfront labor. The meeting was arranged at the behest of truckmen, who were in a rebellious mood over the loading racket. Goaded by consignees who paid the loading charges exacted, the truckmen had appealed to Joe Ryan to help clean up the situation.

"We had a bellyful of it," the spokesman for the trucking industry explained. "There was no uniformity as to loading rates. The loaders were charging all the traffic would bear. There was no system, no regulation, no control of any kind."

The trucking industry appealed to Ryan in the hope that through his official position he could make the leading racketeers be "reasonable," though both the truckmen and the loaders were well aware that Ryan could not speak for the loaders. The loading racket is conducted by the gangs in control of the piers. Officially, the union's only interest or connection with it is to see that the men employed as loaders are union men, members of the ILA, and are paid the union scale.

HAD REACHED LIMIT REGARDLESS OF GUNS

So Ryan got the loaders together.

"We declared ourselves," said the spokesman for the truckers. "We told them we had gone as far as we could and we would go no further, regardless of their guns."

The loaders named a committee that met with a committee of truckmen. Eventually, for the first time in twenty years, a schedule of loading rates was devised, and a Truck Loading Authority was set up, with Ryan and Joseph M. Adelizzi as cochairmen, representing the ILA and the carriers, respectively, and with Hugh E. Sheridan, who is highly respected in the trucking industry, as arbitrator.

This rate schedule went into effect on February 1, 1943, and the contract, if it can be called that, was entitled "Official Loading Charges for Import Water Borne Traffic in the Port of New York." The agreement provided for the establishment of the Truck Loading Authority, consisting of six persons, three to be named by the employers and three by the union. "This Authority," stated the agreement, "shall have the power to administer and police the terms and rates set forth herein and to hear and rule upon any dispute arising therefrom. The decisions of the Authority shall be final and binding on all parties heretofore described." In the event of disagreement by the Authority, the dispute would be submitted to Sheridan as arbitrator, whose decision would be final and binding.

PROVISION MADE FOR HOLIDAY RATES

There were provisions for holiday rates, overtime, and the all-important loading rates. With respect to the latter, the agreement stated: "The rates named herein, no more or less, shall apply for loading of trucks at piers and waterfront warehouses in the Port of New York. Nothing contained herein shall be construed as giving the International Longshoremen's Association, Public Loaders Division, jurisdiction over the unloading of trucks. The charge for this work shall be agreed upon directly by the employer and loader."

This clause was inserted because the loading racketeers were attempting to extend their operations to the unloading as well as the loading of trucks at piers, a jurisdiction previously guarded by the locals of the Teamsters Union.

The rate schedule agreed on covered all manner of commodities, and ranged from four cents a hundred pounds to as high as ten cents a hundred on an item such as frozen beef, and with special rates by the package on various commodities.

These rates prevailed, on paper at least, for nearly four years; then they were revised upward. The higher schedule, with the loading fees ranging from five cents to eleven cents a hundred pounds, went into effect on December 15, 1946.

Early in 1947, the Motor Carrier Association of New York, in a bulletin to its members, urged compliance with this rate schedule, and advised them under no circumstances to pay rates in excess of the schedule.

The bulletin contained this significant passage, which gets at the root of past efforts to combat the loading racket: "In the past, efforts of this association to maintain and enforce rates which were agreed to by representatives of the trucking industry and public loaders, have been unsuccessful in part, due largely to the fact that some carriers made special arrangements with the loaders, no doubt in the hope that they would get preferred service, or that by paying on a package basis the charges on the shipment might be a shade less than on weight basis.

"In some instances, carriers pay rates demanded by loaders rather than have the trucks lay idle, which we try to adjust. When excessive rates are paid, all carriers, including the violating carriers, are

This forties aerial shot of the West Side piers shows the impact the shipping industry had on New York City. Passenger ships and steamers choked the piers with tourists and goods.

penalized because a general breakdown of rates eventually flows. . . . Do not enter into any special agreements with the public loaders. If loaders ask a rate in excess of those named in the schedule, refuse to pay and advise this office immediately, in order that we may arrange prompt compliance. Do not pay the excess rate, even though it is necessary to leave the freight at the pier."

"STABILIZING EFFECT" FAILED TO ENDURE

Well, what happened? Theoretically, this agreement still is in effect, but it is only in theory.

"It had a stabilizing effect for a time," said a spokesman for the trucking industry, "but it didn't last. The loaders agreed to it only because it gave them a semblance of respectability."

Receivers of freight tell a different story. They say the schedule never did much, as far as they were concerned. They were compelled to pay whatever the loaders demanded, and they still are. As it worked out, some truckmen got the benefit of the "official" rates, others did not. The truckmen, it must be remembered, pay the charges and pass them on to the consignees.

In this connection, the attitudes of some truckmen on the loading racket is interesting. Like so many rackets on the waterfront, they accept it as a "necessary evil." Frankly, some truckers say that the availability of this type of labor—the public loaders—is desirable. But they would like to see it regulated to eliminate the abuses. In a word, to eliminate the racketeering, the element of coercion by which the racket is able to exist.

NEW YORK, WEDNESDAY, NOVEMBER 17, 1948

Racketeers Tighten Grip on Piers by Taking Over Truck Unloading

ALREADY DOMINATED LOADING

Exports Shifted to Other Ports—Extra Costs Eventually Are Passed to Consumers

---

EXPANDING A RACKET

Within recent months, the waterfront racketeers have succeeded in tightening their stranglehold on the port's shipping by assuming jurisdiction over unloading as well as loading of freight trucked to and from the piers. It is a new development, an expansion of the long-established loading racket, and it enables the racketeers to collect additional millions of dollars annually by levying tribute from exporters as well as importers, their principal victims in the past.

This expansion adds still another hazard to shipping here and is diverting more and more business to other ports. As a concrete example, one of the greatest and best-known corporations in the United States, a company with affiliates throughout the world, now is sending a substantial amount of its export freight to such ports as Philadelphia and Baltimore rather than pay the unloading charges exacted by the gangs in control of the New York piers. The one company's exports run into millions of dollars a year.

To understand the full significance of this expansion on the part of the racketeers, it must be remembered that the so-called loading racket, which originated shortly after World War I, applied for many years only to import waterborne traffic; that is, to freight loaded on trucks at the piers for delivery to inland points.

True, there were instances of charges exacted and paid for unloading as well as for loading, but for the most part the gangs never were able to expand the racket on a wide scale. As stated in previous articles, they were balked to some extent by the truckmen themselves, through the Teamsters Union, which had guarded the unloading privileges.

HUNDREDS OF EXPORTERS LODGING COMPLAINTS

Now, however, the racketeers are succeeding with a vengeance in imposing unloading charges at piers throughout the port. In the last few months, hundreds of exporters have complained, saying that for the first time in their experience they are being subjected to unloading charges, paid by the truckmen and passed on to the exporters.

The complaints still are pouring in to trade groups at the rate of about 125 a month. Specific instances cited cover some fifteen piers on the Manhattan side of the Hudson River, five on the East River, piers all over the Brooklyn waterfront, and various points in Jersey.

There is no pretense at uniformity of rates, such as theoretically prevails on loading charges. The gangs charge whatever the traffic will bear. The fees vary from pier to pier and from day to day.

The expansion of the racket apparently began gradually, after the loading had been dignified by an agreement between the so-called public loaders and the motor carriers. The agreement calling for an "official" schedule of loading rates, which first went into effect on February 1, 1943, was renegotiated in December 1946, with the rates revised upward.

SPECIFIC PROVISION EXEMPTED UNLOADING

Actually, the agreement has never been worth the paper it was written on, shippers say, but it did contain this paragraph, designed to prevent the loaders from expanding, as they have done, by assuming jurisdiction over unloading as well as loading operations:

"Nothing contained herein shall be construed as giving the International Longshoremen's Association, Public Loaders Division, jurisdiction over the unloading of trucks. The employer at his discretion may hire loaders to unload trucks. The charge for this work shall be agreed upon directly by the employer and the loader."

Shippers complain that the provision has had just the opposite effect intended. The racketeers have assumed jurisdiction of unloading; there is no "discretion" allowed on the part of the shipper, and the "agreement" as to charges is whatever the loading boss says it shall be.

Like the hapless importer who pays for loading, the exporter is compelled to use the loaders whether he wants them or not. Otherwise, his merchandise is left on the trucks. The dealings are all between the truckmen and the loaders, the truckmen passing the charges on to his employer, the exporter, or consignee.

Thus far it appears that the principal victims of the unloading charges are the over-the-road truckmen coming here from distant points.

LEVY ON TRUCKMEN BILLED TO EXPORTERS

"For some reason the purely local truckmen delivering freight to the piers seem to be able to get around these charges," said a spokesman for a trade association. "Maybe they have some special understanding, or maybe the Teamsters Union protects them. I don't know.

"But the over-the-road carrier, who does so much to support this port, gets it in the neck. He pays and he has no choice.

"The driver comes here, say from Pittsburgh. He is hundreds of miles from home. He is told that he'll have to pay such and such a fee to get his truck unloaded. He doesn't know what to do. He finally calls the exporter, who has no way of knowing whether the charge is on the level or not. But he says pay the fee, get the stuff unloaded and on the ship. Then the exporter gets the bill. That's how it goes."

One big company had two truckloads of tires coming here by

truck from Cleveland for export. The drivers were told that they'd have to pay sixty dollars a truck for unloading. There was no choice. The truckmen couldn't unload; they had to pay or the trucks would stand idle on the pier. They paid.

That company is now sending its freight to Philadelphia and Baltimore whenever possible.

"If it's an emergency, a matter of getting urgently needed supplies on a scheduled New York ship, we will use the port here and pay the higher fees," said a representative of the company. "But a substantial amount of all our freight is being sent elsewhere as a result of these higher costs, including such things as unloading fees. It was all a matter of economics with us; the costs are lower elsewhere, so we go elsewhere."

SOME LOADING RECEIPTS INDECIPHERABLE SCRAWLS

The company representative said that his traffic department began paying unloading fees in 1946, and with increasing frequency subsequently. He showed invoices in recent months for varying fees: $9.40, $9.60, $15.69, and so on, for what were apparently small amounts of freight unloaded. Some of the bills were accompanied by "loading" receipts—white slips of paper bearing, in some instances, indecipherable scrawls. Some loading tickets, however, bore the written notation as to where the truckmen should send the checks for the fees.

"Without going into whether such charges are a racket or not, we found them very annoying," said the company representative. "We understand that these loading charges are not imposed at other ports."

But this big, powerful company, in common with other shippers who are paying racket fees, did not want its name mentioned. It wouldn't be good policy, good public relations. It would serve no useful purpose.

"If it were a matter of a company as big as ours coming out and taking a stand and thereby busting a big racket, we'd do just that," said the representative. "But we don't believe it would bust a racket."

LOADERS ON DOCKS BY SQUATTERS' RIGHTS

Other companies are just as reluctant to have their names mentioned. But their anguished complaints indicate the varying sums they are paying for the privilege of having their merchandise unloaded.

One paid $56.20 for twenty-four skids of tinplate weighing 66,123 pounds. Another paid $22.60 for the unloading of ten skids of tinplate weighing 25,650 pounds.

By way of contrast, the unloading charge for 8,000 cartons of foodstuff weighing 160,000 pounds was $30. Typewriters, weighing 89 pounds, cost $3.50. A shipment of rubber coils and copper wire weighing a total of 18,926 pounds cost $45.

"Everybody passes the buck to somebody else," said one official bitterly. "The carriers blame the steamship lines. The steamship lines are scared of reprisals, they say it's none of their business. The loaders are there by squatters' rights on the piers. They have established an iron curtain between the steamship company and the exporter or importer.

"The steamship companies lease the piers and have the right to prohibit the loaders from the piers, but they don't dare do that. The loaders are members of the ILA. If the steamship lines ousted them, they might call out the stevedores, also members of the ILA, in a sympathy strike, tying up the steamship company ships.

"The motor carriers are afraid, too, afraid of violence to their men or property, or both. The carriers have to deal with these loaders. The shipper is caught in the middle. In the end, he's the one who pays."

So the loading-unloading racket continues to flourish, operated by mobsters in control of the piers. They are smart enough to hire

From the turn of the century to the 1940s, New York's loading docks and ships' decks were choked with goods. Moving great quantities of materials exposed the longshoremen to dangerous risks that far exceeded other laborers in America in that period. The involvement of organized crime only increased their mortality and injury rates.

all-union labor, which apparently makes the racket inviolate. The union angle is an invaluable asset in the maintenance of control.

But that official was wrong when he said that in the end it was the shipper who pays. It's the consumer, as usual, who pays. You and every member of your family are affected. For racket costs, like all other costs, inevitably are reflected in higher prices for the things you buy.

NEW YORK, THURSDAY, NOVEMBER 18, 1948

Pickings From Payroll Padding, Kickbacks, Usury, Payoffs, and Contributions Yield Harvest for Dock Mobs

SOMETHING FOR THE BOYS

In addition to the tremendous revenue derived from organized thievery and from the loading racket, the criminal gangs which rule the waterfront find easy pickings from various other rackets: duplicate hiring, or payroll padding at the expense of the stevedoring companies and steamship lines; kickbacks, by which longshoremen are compelled to pay for their jobs; usury or shylocking; simple payoffs, solicited as "voluntary contributions"; gambling, policy, smuggling, and any other illegal enterprise that comes to hand. Since the gang control of the piers is absolute, the gangs take a cut on everything. It all adds up to something for the boys—big money, big business.

Take the matter of duplicate hiring. It is worked with the knowledge and cooperation of the hiring stevedores, handpicked by the mobs, and the pay clerks. It is common practice on the waterfront for longshoremen to have more than one Social Security number, the extra ones obtained under fictitious names.

These "extra" cards for nonexistent employees are easily obtainable, investigators say; anybody can get them. For each Social Security card, the longshoreman then gets a registration card with steamship and stevedoring companies. Then at the shape-up, the antiquated method of hiring on the docks of New York, the hiring boss will pretend to hire ten gangs when he actually needs only nine, the extra gang represented in surplus cards. He collects the cards and gives them to the pay clerk and says: "Put these cards through." The clerk does so, and the gang collects the extra checks. And the irony of it is that the individual longshoreman gets none of this graft.

KICKBACK PROVES COMMON PRACTICE

The kickback is common practice, too. Here, the workman simply pays the hiring boss for the privilege of getting a day's work. Otherwise, he doesn't get hired. The rate often is high as 10 percent, sometimes even higher. The mobsters get this money, too. The kickback has been described as being as regular as the Social Security tax. Here again the method of hiring is blamed—the shape-up, in which the longshoremen gather on the piers daily and wait to be chosen or rejected for work by the hiring boss. The system easily invites graft and favoritism.

The longshoreman in New York has no security; he never knows from day to day whether he has a job. In his eagerness for work, he is easy prey for the racketeers and grafting union officials. He will pay and keep his mouth shut, knowing that if he does not he will not work that day or any other day.

Such exploitation, vicious as it is, goes hand in hand with loansharking or shylocking, another racket controlled by the mobsters. The longshoreman, always hard up, borrows from the shylocks, or sells his paycheck in advance. And the usurers collect from ten to twenty cents on the dollar each week.

"The idea," said an investigator, "is to keep the men poor. Then they can be controlled more easily, controlled through fear—fear of not working and fear of being unable to pay the shylocks."

The shylocks, working closely with the mob, often are able to force the men to take loans because they can help or hinder them in getting jobs.

USURERS GLEAN $200,000 A YEAR

In the case of Frank Savio, convicted of usury in January 1942, the district attorney charged that the waterfront racketeers were making $200,000 a year from the shylocking racket alone. Savio was a boss checker and strong-arm man for the International Longshoremen's Association, the powerful AFL union that controls waterfront labor. He was lending money to the longshoremen and charging them ten cents a week on the dollar. It was shown that Savio was able to have the interest due him deducted from the longshoremen's pay before they received it, thanks to the cooperation of pay clerks. On the occasion of a previous arrest, when Savio was charged with assault, Joseph P. Ryan, president of the ILA, appeared as a character witness on his behalf.

How the key position of the hiring boss leads to graft and racketeering was the subject of this comment in a United States Department of Labor report on waterfront labor: "It is obvious that the hiring foreman occupies a position of the greatest importance on the waterfront. It is largely left to him to decide who shall be employed and who shall be left behind. He is seldom hampered in his choice, especially in regard to the more casual men. He can call them today and ignore them tomorrow. It would indeed be strange if such a concentration of power in the hands of a single person controlling the jobs of so many men did not result in some cases in the abuse of this power. . . ."

This being true, it is obviously important for the gangs in control at the piers to designate all the key men in jobs—the hiring stevedore, the boss checker, and the dock boss. It is accomplished with a vengeance, for these key jobs are held in many instances by members of the mob with long criminal records.

LITTLE PRETENSE ABOUT CONTRIBUTIONS

"Voluntary contributions" are solicited by the mob representatives at many of the piers. There is little pretense about this racket; the rank-

and-file longshoremen recognize it for what it is, a payoff on payday for the benefit of "the boys."

According to one informant, an ex-convict who worked there, this racket is particularly prevalent at the piers above Forty-second Street, now controlled by the Mickey Bowers gang. These piers are under the jurisdiction of Local 824 of the ILA. It is considered one of the richest of the union locals, covering the Cunard, French, and Italian line piers. The fight for control of these piers, now tightly maintained by Bowers and his lieutenants, has resulted in at least eight murders during the last few years.

"Every payday, as regular as clockwork," said the informant, "they'd come around for voluntary contributions. They'd pass a cigar box around, and the collections were made by the shop steward. Every man was expected to kick in a dollar. They gave all kinds of excuses. They were collecting a fund for one of the boys in trouble, to buy flowers for a sick member, or to pay off the cops. They'd tell us anything; it didn't matter what. They got at least $150 from each pier every payday."

"And if a man refused?"

The informant smiled.

"He might refuse once, and maybe nothing would happen to him. But then again something might. He might find he couldn't get work, or he might get kicked around. A man soon got the idea; he didn't refuse more than once."

NEW YORK, FRIDAY, NOVEMBER 19, 1948

History of John Dunn's Surge to Power as Dock Racket Overlord, With Numerous Crimes Attributed to Him

THE DUNN CASE

Along the waterfront they will tell you that John Dunn, the gangster and labor racketeer whose execution for murder has been stayed by his appeal for a new trial, was a suspect in numerous crimes, including murder, before they finally convicted him of killing Anthony Hintz, a hiring stevedore.

Hintz, they say, was murdered because he refused to take orders from Dunn. That's how Dunn ruled the waterfront, controlling all piers between Fourteenth and Cedar streets. Anybody, they added, who got in Dunn's way died, suddenly and violently. It was as simple and as cold-blooded as that.

Dunn is about as tough as they come, and proud of it. He ruled through terror, and his rule in his waterfront territory was absolute for more than ten years. No one dared to cross him.

"I have known John Dunn for years," said an official in the trucking industry. "He is cold-blooded and efficient. He makes a good impression until you notice his eyes. His eyes are a cold steel blue, and when you notice them you know you are dealing with a dangerous man."

DUNN CASE-HARDENED PRODUCT OF NEW YORK

A product of New York, Dunn was a case-hardened criminal long before he rose to power on the waterfront. He was a smooth, convincing talker—shrewd, alert, aggressive. In the school of crime, he was graduated from petty thievery to the big time, with murder alleged to be included in his business.

Dunn was born in Queens, on August 24, 1910. His father, a ship's steward, was lost at sea when Dunn was four. His mother remarried, and her second husband, Thomas Cassidy, was killed in a railway accident. Dunn's mother helped support her family for years by working as a charwoman at Madison Square Garden. Dunn has a younger brother and two sisters. Dunn married in 1938, and he has two children. Despite his long career in crime, the record shows that in his private life Dunn lived circumspectly. He formerly owned a neat, well-furnished home in the Kew Gardens section of Queens, paying nearly $5,000 down in cash for it in August 1938. He appeared a devoted family man.

Dunn's first venture in crime was at the age of fifteen. He stole twenty-nine cents and a box of crackers from a store. That was in 1925. The next year, he robbed a hardware store, and was sent to the Catholic Protectory as a juvenile delinquent. He was paroled in 1927 and promptly returned to his criminal activities. In 1929, he robbed a grocery store of merchandise valued at $625 and was sentenced to the reformatory, from which he was paroled in 1931. On April 15, 1932, Dunn and two accomplices held up a card game and escaped with $9. He pleaded guilty to robbery and was sentenced to two to four years in Sing Sing. He was paroled in November 1933. After his release, the record shows that Dunn teamed up with Ed McGrath, another ex-convict, who later married one of Dunn's sisters. McGrath is pictured as having been the real power behind Dunn on the waterfront and as having assumed open leadership of Dunn's territory since the latter's conviction in the Hintz murder.

DISCHARGED IN KILLING OF FORMER CONVICT

Dunn's next arrest was on May 28, 1935, and the charge was homicide in the killing of one John McCrossen, an ex-convict. Arrested with him was Ed McGrath. Both were discharged for lack of evidence. The record shows that for years Dunn and McGrath were suspected in a series of crimes but were discharged. Dunn's next conviction is on October 17, 1941, for coercion, and he was sentenced to an indeterminate term in prison up to three years.

Both Dunn and McGrath, as graduates of Sing Sing, turned their criminal talents to the waterfront in about 1936, though neither had any previous experience in that field. Nevertheless, their rise to power was rapid, and Dunn soon had complete control of his own union; and both were interested in Varick Enterprises, Inc., organized to conduct the loading racket on the piers. Varick's activities were described in a previous article in this series. On the day that Dunn was sentenced for coercion for beating a boss stevedore, Murray Gurfein, then an assistant district attorney in charge of the Rackets Bureau, told the court that the New York waterfront constituted an "outlaw frontier" and that the bosses of the underworld controlled the entire waterfront. No pier in this city is immune from rackets dominated by the gangsters, he said, and Dunn's mob controlled every pier between Fourteenth and Cedar streets. The underworld bosses, Gurfein said, allocated territory on the waterfront so that the kickback and shylock rackets and thefts of merchandise might "flourish with maximum vigor."

TOUGH COOKIE TELLS OF DUNN'S ASCENSION

Listen to a character named Buster Smith, himself a tough cookie, now doing a hitch in prison, tell how Dunn rose to power and maintained that power on the waterfront.

"In 1936," said Buster, "me and George Keeler and Tom Porter had the loading at Pier 59 at Eighteenth Street. Dunn's mob was trying to get control, so they just moved in on us. Dunn and his boys opened up on us one day with pistols and shotguns. I was wounded. A few weeks later, the gang killed Tom Porter and his girl in Long Island City. A month later, the boys knocked off George Keeler at his home in Brooklyn."

Buster Smith then was sent back to prison for violation of parole. He was released in April 1941. Before he had time to do anything, Smith said that Dunn's gang attacked him again.

"Dunn and Andy Sheridan and one other came into a bar and grill and without a word they shot me again," said Buster. "I heard later that they thought I was getting ready to muscle in at the docks again."

Matty Kane, a gangster also mentioned by Smith, was stabbed to death in Sing Sing prison in December 1938 by a fellow prisoner. The underworld story is that Dunn ordered Kane's death because Kane was getting ready to squeal on Dunn's criminal activities. Andy Sheridan, also mentioned by Smith, was convicted with Dunn and Daniel Gentile for the murder of Hintz. Sheridan, an old-time mobster, was once a trigger man for Dutch Schultz.

According to underworld sources, the gang also ordered the murder of one Johnny Costello, who was in charge of piers at Seventeenth Street until ousted by Dunn's mob. Costello was shot to death on June 15, 1937, as he was wheeling a baby carriage at Seventeenth Street and Ninth Avenue.

By this time, Dunn's organization was really rolling, and Dunn began to look about for new worlds to conquer, to extend his control to inland freight terminals as well as on the piers. Being on the smart side, Dunn already had discovered that the labor racket was made to order for a man of his talents. So Dunn organized a union of his own.

New York, Monday, November 22, 1948

How Dunn Organized Unions Through Which He Dominated Racketeering at Piers and Terminals in His Domain

---

A UNION IS BORN

John Dunn, whose execution at Sing Sing for murder has been stayed by an appeal, has proved an ambitious mobster. His rise to power on the waterfront was rapid and spectacular and was accomplished with ruthless efficiency with guns and strong-arm squads. Dunn quickly turned to labor racketeering as a means of extending his power.

In November 1936, Dunn and his henchmen formed what they laughingly called a "workers' committee" and obtained from the International Longshoremen's Association, the AFL union that controls waterfront labor, a charter for a new union local known as Terminal Checkers and Platform Men, Local 1346-2. With this charter, and without any other union organization behind them, the Dunn mob then approached a number of trucking concerns with the view of "negotiating" a contract. It was Dunn's idea to extend his control from the piers to inland freight terminals, and it will be seen that in this he was eminently successful.

"Dunn had the right technique, all right," said a waterfront investigator. "The modern gangster and labor racketeer doesn't bother to organize the men into a union. He first gets a union charter. Anybody can get one. Then, if his organization is powerful enough, he goes directly to the employers and demands a 'contract.' When he gets the contract, he informs the workmen that they are now in his union—or else."

TRIED TO MUSCLE IN ON TEAMSTERS UNION

The Dunn mob made a bold move to muscle in on the powerful Local 807 of the Teamsters Union, first approaching an official of that local with a proposition to collect shakedowns from employers on the basis of not enforcing contracts, selling out the men, ignoring overtime, and not enforcing the rule on union scale pay. The Teamsters' local refused. That was in February 1937.

At about this time there was some question of jurisdiction between the ILA and the Brotherhood of Railway, Steamship Clerks and Freight Handlers. At the Miami convention of the AFL, the matter was taken up with William Green, the president, who told them to straighten it out with the head of the railway brotherhood. Whereupon the Dunn mob quietly dropped its ILA local and obtained from the AFL charters for three new union locals, under the name of Motor and Bus Terminal Checkers, Platform and Office Workers, the charters being for New York, New Jersey, and Pennsylvania.

Dunn made himself business agent and vice president of the New York local, No. 21510, and Cornelius J. Noonan was named president. Dunn's gunman, Andrew Sheridan, became an organizer for the Jersey local, 21512. Sheridan was convicted with Dunn in the murder of Anthony Hintz, boss stevedore, but an appeal stayed their executions. The Pennsylvania union charter never was used.

DUNN DOMINATED UNION FROM START

It was Dunn's union completely and he dominated it from its inception. It had no connection with the ILA, and it had no international. Nevertheless, through this local Dunn was able to extend his control from piers to numerous inland freight terminals. This got him into the trucking field and opened up numerous other rackets for his organization—hijacking of trucks, the control of checkers at the terminals and, through them, the control of thefts from the terminals. And, of course, there was always the matter of union dues.

Through the Jersey local, Dunn hoped, in time, to control the situation in Jersey as well as in New York. He was balked in this by a criminal as powerful as Dunn himself, Charlie Yanowsky. Yanowsky suddenly seized control of the Jersey piers and in 1946 succeeded Andy Sheridan as organizer for the local. Yanowsky went the way of most big-shot gangsters: He was murdered last July.

But in New York, as business agent of the New York local, Dunn maintained his offices at 265 West Fourteenth Street—the same offices from which he had directed some of the activities of Varick Enterprises, Inc., which was a clearinghouse for the loading racket on the piers.

Dunn's first contract was with a group of trucking concerns organized as the Highway Transport Association, later merged with the Merchant Truckmen's Bureau to form what is now the Motor Carrier Association of New York, representing about five hundred trucking companies. Dunn approached this group for a contract even before his union was born, and the contract was negotiated as soon as he had obtained his charter. It was done through the simple expedient of low pay; in short, selling out the men.

The bait was fifty-five cents an hour. This was in 1937. The truckmen signed. The rate went up by leaps and bounds after that, and today the scale is $1.35 an hour.

TRUCKERS BACKED DUNN IN COERCION CASE

In time, Dunn's union controlled the checkers and platform workers at some 168 inland freight terminals where his union had contracts. Dunn boasted that he had two thousand enrolled members and a thousand "active" members. It was a rich racket, and Dunn's influence was so great that a number of reputable trucking concerns went to bat for him when Dunn was convicted of coercion in 1941.

After Dunn's conviction in the Hintz murder, his union quickly changed its name to Inland Terminal Workers, Local 1730, under charter from the ILA.

Dunn's conviction on a charge of coercion was in connection with his pier rackets. Convicted with him were John Joseph Hughes, Edward Thompson, and George Donovan.

"It is a matter of common knowledge," the prosecutor said, "that for many years the New York waterfront is controlled by gangsters. Below Fourteenth Street, Piers 51 to 11 are controlled by the so-called Village mob, of which these defendants are a part."

Dunn's mob was able to name the defendant Thompson as the hiring stevedore at Pier 45 and the defendant Hughes as the boss checker at Pier 51. Both were key jobs. They attempted also to control the boss stevedore at Pier 51, one Edward J. Kelly, ordering him to hire men favored by Dunn. But Kelly refused to take orders. Dunn then tried to oust him from his job, and, failing in this, resorted to violence, attacking Kelly and beating him up. This was the basis of the state's case.

DUNN MOB–DELAYED SHIP IN WARTIME

The defendant Hughes was an ex-convict and member of the notorious Arsenal mob. He was placed in charge of checkers at Pier 51 after his parole from prison. He hired only criminals friendly to Dunn. The defendant Edward Thompson, placed as hiring stevedore at Pier 45, was a brother of Raymond (Sonny) Thompson, an ILA delegate.

With these handpicked Dunn men in key jobs, it was shown that, among other things, the rate of theft at these piers suddenly began to mount. The thefts at Pier 51 alone during a few months at this time amounted to more than $8,000 in one commodity alone, rice.

Kelly was beaten up in a saloon at West and Tenth streets on September 27, 1941. When this failed to remove Kelly, the Dunn mob had a strike called at Pier 51, ignoring defense problems, delaying the loading of a British freighter, and causing it to miss two convoys to England.

Dunn and his codefendants were convicted on October 17, 1941, and sentenced to up to three years in prison. Then powerful influences began working in Dunn's behalf, that influence extending to Washington.

New York, Tuesday, November 23, 1948

Congressman Tinkham and Army Brass Call for Dunn's Release

"IMPORTANT TO WAR EFFORT"

Despite Strike Ordered by His Mob Making a Freighter Miss Two Convoys

---

WASHINGTON CALLING

John Dunn, labor racketeer and waterfront gangster, now in Sing Sing under stay of execution for murder pending a motion for a new trial, was committed to the city prison at Rikers Island on January 17, 1942, to begin serving an indeterminate sentence, up to three years, on his conviction of coercion in assaulting a hiring stevedore, Edward J. Kelly, who had refused to take orders from the Dunn mob.

Within a few days after he was locked up, a concerted campaign was organized in Dunn's behalf to get him paroled. The Parole Commission literally was bombarded with letters interceding for him, despite his known criminal record. The letters were signed by officials of some of the leading trucking companies in the United States. It is perhaps a mere coincidence that eight of these letters, addressed to Samuel J. Battle, a parole commissioner, bore the same date: January 29, 1942. Others were dated a few days later.

It is, of course, a matter of conjecture as to whether these letters, written by reputable business executives, were voluntary or whether they were "suggested" by influential outside agents friendly to Dunn. The pattern of the letters was the same. They all described Dunn in glowing terms as an upright, honest citizen, a credit to the community. It was a pleasure to do business with him; therefore, wouldn't the parole board return Mr. Dunn to civil life as soon as possible?

EXECUTIVE VOLUNTEERS AS CHARACTER WITNESS

One terminal manager of a large trucking concern wrote that he simply could not conceive Dunn to be capable of the crime "for which he is now charged," and added that he'd be willing to appear as a character witness for Dunn anytime.

Others described Dunn as a gentleman in every respect, and expressed themselves as shocked and horrified to learn that he was in the clink.

"I personally feel," wrote one trucking executive, "that Mr. Dunn's absence from his position may work a hardship on the industry in these trying times and I ask that your Honorable Sir accept this letter in good faith and hope that you will grant a speedy parole for Mr. Dunn."

One wrote of Dunn's "integrity and excellent character." He was an "enlightened labor leader," another wrote, and his loss, especially during the national emergency, would be a severe blow to the trucking industry.

On January 30, 1942, City Councilman A. Clayton Powell, Jr., wrote on Dunn's behalf, stating that he was doing so at the request of some of Dunn's friends. "While I do not know Mr. Dunn personally, I do know the many things he has done for our community in placing Negro men in the Longshoremen's Union, A. F. of L." stated Powell. "I do not know the nature of this case, but will appreciate anything you can do to help him."

CONGRESSMAN MAKES A PLEA FOR DUNN

On February 6, 1942, there was a letter from Representative George Holden Tinkham of the Massachusetts 10th Congressional

HPL Central
Renewals by Phone 832-393-2280

Customer ID: *********1435**

Title: On the waterfront : the Pulitzer Prize-winning articles that inspired the classic movie and transformed the New York Harbor
ID: 33477004526582
Due: 11/4/2013,23:59

Total items: 1
10/14/2013 10:29 AM
Checked out: 3
Overdue: 0

HPL Central

District, written on the stationery of the House of Representatives, Congress of the United States, Washington, D.C., just to make it official. Representative Tinkham wrote that he was interceding for Dunn at the request of a constituent who was a friend of Dunn. The friend informed him that Dunn had a wife and two children, and that he enjoyed an excellent reputation. "I sincerely hope that it will be found possible to exercise clemency in this case," Tinkham concluded.

To these letters, Commissioner Battle of the Parole Board sent a form reply stating that the matter of John Dunn, No. 72910, was still under investigation and no decision had been made.

In the meantime, on February 4, 1942, Dunn and one of his codefendants, John Hughes, were discharged from the city pen on writs of reasonable doubt and the Parole Commission was so notified by the warden.

With Dunn at liberty, the campaign in his behalf, of course, stopped. The Appellate Division unanimously affirmed Dunn's conviction, and on January 25, 1943, Dunn voluntarily surrendered at the prison. His appeal to the Court of Appeals was denied, the court declining to review the case. This was on February 1.

POWERFUL FRIENDS TURN ON THE HEAT

Dunn's powerful friends, whoever they were, then really turned on the heat. On January 29, four days after Dunn was back in prison, Commissioner Battle of the Parole Board received long-distance calls from "officials of the War Department in Washington," according to Battle's statement to the court that had sentenced Dunn. An appointment was made with these officials at the office of the Parole Commission, 100 Centre Street, for 11 A.M., Monday, February 1.

Well, what do you know! The Army "brass" came up here from Washington to lay it on the line for the criminal John Dunn. Present were Lieutenant Colonel Charles E. Martin of the Transportation Corps, chief of the Industrial Relations Division; Major John J.

Lane of the Transportation Corps; and John Bridge, chief of materials, transportation branch, highway division, Transportation Corps.

The brass must have put on quite a show, insisting that Dunn be released forthwith, as he was important to the war effort. That was a laugh, too, for the very case in point, the coercion conviction, showed that Dunn's mob, disregarding defense problems, had called a strike on a pier, delaying a British freighter and causing it to miss two convoys to England with vitally needed war material.

ARMY BRASS STILL CALLED FOR RELEASE

In a subsequent communication to Special Sessions justices Bayes, Oliver, and Burlingame, who had sentenced Dunn, Battle stated:

"The matter of this inmate's case was thoroughly reviewed and we went into it very thoroughly, his criminal record was read to them and also the probation report giving all the facts and ramifications in connection with the activities of Dunn.

"After thorough examination and investigation, all the facts being stated, these officers who represent our Government advised that with all of that they insisted that this man be released for the purpose of facilitating the movement of goods in connection with the successful prosecution of our war. They further stated that because of Dunn's connections with the labor unions and his influence over the men connected therewith, he would be very necessary and that he had already done some excellent work in connection with the movement of supplies for our Government and that they were positive he would be very necessary as a civilian in this connection.

"These gentlemen had come over to New York from Washington, D.C., because of the importance of this case to them and they agreed to appear before the commission at the regular meeting on Thursday, February 4, 1943. They were advised, however, that this would not be necessary, and if this man's presence and services were so necessary to the Government in the war effort, they could write us stating the necessity and making their official request."

COLONEL PRESENTS FORMAL REQUEST

That official request came from Colonel Frederick C. Horner, chief of the highway division, Transportation Corps, in a letter dated February 3, 1943. Horner practically ordered Dunn's release, stating that Dunn had been "extremely co-operative in preventing the spread of what might very well be serious labor disturbances, and also in the adjustment of these disturbances."

"I am mindful of the fact that Mr. Dunn has a record, but in times such as these when there is a goal to attain, such an incident should not be the all-determining factor," Horner wrote. "Nevertheless, consideration of the factors mentioned above and many others which I am not at liberty to divulge compel the decision to ask for his immediate release from your care and custody. It is hoped that the commission can comply with this request immediately."

The commission did. The next day, February 4, 1943, the commission voted unanimously to release Dunn. In the words of Battle, this action was taken "only because of the insistence of officials of the War Department, subject to the approval of the judges of the Court of Special Sessions having jurisdiction on the case."

The matter, however, did not end there, thanks to the intervention of the late Mayor La Guardia, as will be shown in tomorrow's article in the series.

NEW YORK, WEDNESDAY, NOVEMBER 24, 1948

Effort of "Brass" to Free Gangster Dunn Thwarted After La Guardia Carries Case Direct to Secretary of War

WASHINGTON INVESTIGATES

Army brass in Washington came to the rescue of John Dunn, labor racketeer and waterfront gangster, now seeking a new trial after conviction of murder, following Dunn's imprisonment for coercion in February 1943. Dunn had been convicted in the latter part of 1941, released on a writ of reasonable doubt early in 1942, and sent back to prison after the higher courts had affirmed his conviction in February 1943.

As a result of pressure from the War Department in Washington—pressure which included a visit by Army brass to the Parole Commission's office here to intercede for Dunn and an official letter demanding the prisoner's release because of the war effort—the Parole Commission on February 4 voted unanimously to release him.

But the matter did not rest there. The late Mayor La Guardia got wind of the Army brass's high-handed procedure and reacted characteristically. He blew his top. Apparently at the mayor's direction, Parole Commissioner Sam Battle wrote to Secretary of War Henry L. Stimson outlining the whole case and throwing it into Stimson's lap. The letter was dated February 13 and mailed February 20 with the mayor's approval.

Battle told the whole story: how the Army officers had visited him; how, after reviewing Dunn's long criminal record, they had still insisted upon his release; and how this visit was followed up by a letter from Colonel Frederick C. Horner of the Transportation Corps, demanding Dunn's release. Battle enclosed a photostatic copy of Horner's letter.

CONSULTATION URGED WITH OFFICIALS HERE

"The Commission realizes the necessity of co-operating with your department in this great war emergency," Battle wrote. "However, before doing so we thought it might be well to confer with the District Attorney of New York county, Mr. Frank S. Hogan, and also Hon. William R. Bayes, Chief Justice of the Court of Special Sessions. After conferring with District Attorney Hogan and Judge Bayes, it is their belief that in view of Dunn's unsavory past, it might be well to submit the whole matter to your Department. We concur in this suggestion and, therefore, are sending you full details regarding the case."

In a covering letter, dated February 20, La Guardia wrote to Stimson as follows:

"In forwarding the attached letter from the Parole Commission of the City of New York, may I call your attention to the fact that very often junior officers take it upon themselves to make recommendations and to speak most authoritatively for the War Department in personal and small matters. When I doubt very much if they have either the authority or whether the situation requires such ostensible departmental insistence.

"In this case, surely the record of this man is known and the personal appearance and insistence, I believe, is quite inconsistent with your policy."

Stimson wrote La Guardia on March 4: "As you surmise, I was not aware of the request for Mr. Dunn's release and I appreciate your action in bringing the matter to my attention. The situation presented is undoubtedly one which requires further inquiry. In the meantime, you may consider the request for Mr. Dunn's release as definitely withdrawn."

WAR DEPARTMENT CONDUCTS INQUIRY

Presumably on Stimson's orders, the War Department investigated. On March 15, at 11 A.M., Captain William E. Glasscock and Jack Rund, of the Adjutant General's Office, called at the Parole Commission's office and took a deposition from Battle concerning the visit of the Army officers on Dunn's behalf. They stated that they were investigating the matter. On leaving the office, they said that they were going to Rikers Island to interview Dunn.

At the time Battle wrote to Stimson, Dunn had served forty days of his sentence. Dunn stayed in prison until August 29, 1944, when he was released on parole. He went right back to his criminal activities on the waterfront, and to his union racketeering. On September 16, Cornelius J. Noonan, president of Dunn's union, Local 21510, Motor and Bus Terminal Checkers, Platform and Office Workers, advised the Parole Commission that Dunn had been reinstated as vice president and business agent of the local to fill out his "unexpired term" and that his salary was sixty dollars a week, plus expenses of twenty-five dollars a week.

The "reinstatement" didn't stick, however, for on October 2 Noonan, long associated with Dunn in union affairs, notified the commission that he had received and accepted Dunn's resignation as vice president of the local. No mention was made of his capacity as business agent, though the omission was not important, since the union had been Dunn's baby from the beginning. The Parole Commission's jurisdiction over Dunn expired on January 6, 1946.

In the meantime, the full results of the high-pressure intervention in Dunn's case by the Army brass probably will never be known to the public. Top secret stuff, you know, though the war has been over for three years.

However, Colonel Horner, who wrote on Dunn's behalf, was relieved of active duty in September 1944.

NEXT BRUSH WITH LAW INVOLVED A MURDER

With his return to the waterfront and labor racketeering, Dunn's next major brush with the law involved the murder of Anthony Hintz, a hiring boss who, like Ed Kelly, refused to take Dunn's orders. And for this, after a long criminal career, they finally convicted Dunn and two of his gunmen, Andrew Sheridan and Danny Gentile. All three were to have been executed last August, but on August 12 their execution was stayed by Governor Dewey on request of the trial judge of New York County. The request was made to permit determination of a motion for a new trial for Dunn and Gentile after Sheridan, in an affidavit, had declared that his two fellow prisoners had played no part in the slaying.

Of course, the big question before the house is how so much pressure could be brought to bear in Dunn's behalf. Certainly powerful forces were at work, a fact that may or may not fit in with the theory that a super–crime syndicate is back of all waterfront operations and back of all major crime in the United States, making of it a well-organized empire of crime. The mysterious directors in this big syndicate, which has been in existence since Prohibition times, are in a position to exert influence in high places, having strong political alliances. For without such alliances, organized crime cannot succeed.

NEW YORK, FRIDAY, NOVEMBER 26, 1948

How Ed McGrath, Former Choirboy, Made Himself Overlord of Pier Rackets by Application to "Business"

CHOIRBOY TO MOBSTER

Ed McGrath made the grade from choirboy to big-time mobster by diligently applying himself to the business of crime. Today, he is regarded as one of the most powerful behind-the-scenes racketeers on the New York waterfront, the real brains back of the Dunn gang, which rules the piers below Fourteenth Street, and closely associated with certain higher-ups in the big syndicate that reputedly directs all organized crime in the United States.

McGrath's personal history closely parallels that of his brother-in-law and early partner in crime, John Dunn, the waterfront gangster. Both turned to crime early in life, starting with petty thievery and progressing to bigger jobs. Both were graduated from Sing Sing prison, and both started their waterfront operations at about the same time, in 1936.

But there the parallel ends, and though the two were closely associated for years there were sharp contrasts in their personalities. Where Dunn made a career of being tough and trigger-happy, McGrath is more the executive type, a smoother, cooler head, and with a keener eye for the main chance and long-range planning. And so Dunn, the nominal leader of the gang, is in the death house at Sing Sing—where his execution for murder has been stayed by a motion for a new trial—while McGrath still is a free agent.

The New York City docks were among the largest and most expensive crossroads of goods in the world. By 1910, as the above picture shows, the West Side docks by day were larger in population than most American towns, and, by the 1940s, were valued in the hundreds of millions of dollars. Reproduced from the Collections of the Library of Congress.

PLENTY OF EXPERIENCE OUTSIDE OF THE LAW

Not that McGrath hasn't had plenty of experience outside the law. His record shows some twelve arrests on charges ranging from burglary to murder. Today, McGrath, at forty-two, is a tall, well-dressed man, with light gray eyes and brown hair, who lives at a midtown hotel and directs his operations with quiet efficiency and without the open violence that characterized Dunn's movements. McGrath dines at the best restaurants, gets preferred tables at the most popular nightspots, and often hobnobs with politicians and those close to politicians. On the waterfront, especially in his earlier days, McGrath has worked closely with the International Longshoremen's Association, the big AFL union controlling waterfront labor.

The record shows that Ed McGrath came from a decent, hard-working family. He was the only member of the family to go wrong. McGrath was born on January 31, 1906, on the East Side, in the vicinity of Twenty-third Street, the son of Irish immigrants. His father was killed in a trolley accident when Ed was three, and his mother remarried. As a boy, Ed went to church regularly, sang in the choir at the St. Stephen's Roman Catholic Church, and attended St. Stephen's parochial school. One of his first jobs was as a clerk for the New York Telephone Company, at fifteen dollars a week.

McGrath's mother died in 1925, and the boy started living away from his family, in furnished rooms, and working at odd jobs and as a day laborer. It wasn't long before he was associating with young criminals and would-be criminals.

FIRST CRIME NETTED McGRATH FORTY-SEVEN CENTS

McGrath's first crime netted him forty-seven cents in cash. That was on July 27, 1927. At 4 A.M., two cops heard the crash of glass in a neighborhood store in Queens. They saw two men running and pursued them to a vacant house, where the cops found them huddled on the bathroom floor. One was McGrath, the other a youth named Clarence Murray. Murray said he had smashed the glass to get into an ice-cream store, where he robbed the till of $9.47. McGrath got forty-seven cents as his share for acting as lookout. Charged with burglary in the third degree, McGrath pleaded guilty and received a suspended sentence from county judge Adel in Queens.

Thereafter, McGrath began associating with known criminals, most of them older than he. During 1928 and 1929, he was arrested three times for assault and robbery and discharged, and once for violation of the Sullivan law and discharged. These arrests were in connection with a series of holdups. The law finally caught up with him on February 5, 1930, when McGrath was arrested for felonious assault. His original suspended sentence for burglary was revoked after the court got a good look at the intervening record, and McGrath was sent to Sing Sing for a term of five to ten years. He was paroled in September 1933.

In 1935, McGrath and Dunn were arrested for the murder of John McCrossen, who, like themselves, was a parolee. Both were discharged. McGrath went back to Sing Sing for violation of parole, but was paroled again on May 25, 1936.

McGRATH ON DOCKS, HAVEN OF EX-CONVICTS

Two months later, McGrath was on the waterfront, the haven of many ex-convicts. He got his first job on Pier 59, North River, on July 16, 1936, on a call from an ILA delegate. Within less than a year, McGrath was a paid organizer for the ILA, and worked closely with the union—and with John Dunn in the rackets—thereafter.

Meanwhile, both McGrath and Dunn were suspected in a series of crimes not connected with the waterfront. For instance, both were arrested on July 27, 1939, for assault and robbery in connection with the $9,500 holdup of the R. & H. Brewery on Staten Island. They were discharged for lack of evidence.

In October 1940, McGrath was arrested in Boston as a fugitive from Florida, where he was wanted for murder in the first degree. McGrath, together with one Henry Foster Bell, were charged with killing Leon Tocci, alias Macci, whose body was fished out of the waters off Key West on September 23, 1940. Tocci had been shot in the head. According to the police, McGrath and Bell were seen with Tocci the day before the murder. They were indicted in Monroe County, Florida, but the indictment was dismissed.

On the waterfront, opinion has differed as to who bossed whom in the Dunn–McGrath combination. Some underworld sources credit McGrath as being the real leader who directed and planned the mob's operations. But after Dunn's conviction in the murder of Anthony Hintz, a boss stevedore slain for refusing to "co-operate" with the mob, it is generally assumed that McGrath had taken over in name as well as in fact.

NEW YORK, MONDAY, NOVEMBER 29, 1948

How Hintz, Who Told Dunn, Master Mobster of the Docks, to "Go to Hell," Was Shot to Death in Village

THE HINTZ MURDER

At 7:30 on the morning of January 8, 1947, Anthony Hintz, forty-three, a hiring stevedore at Pier 51, foot of Jane Street, Hudson River, was shot and fatally wounded as he stepped into the hallway of his home at 61 Grove Street, Greenwich Village, preparing to go to work. Convicted of the killing were John M. Dunn, leader of the waterfront mob in control of the piers below Fourteenth Street; Andrew Sheridan, one of Dunn's gunmen; and Danny Gentile, formerly a boxer under the name of Danny Brooks.

The three were to have been executed last August, but Sheridan made an affidavit absolving the other two and the executions were stayed by Governor Dewey pending determination of an appeal for a new trial made in behalf of Dunn and Gentile.

(Reargument of the new trial motion, already denied by the trial court, is scheduled for this week before the Court of Appeals in Albany.)

Dunn himself was accused of being the triggerman in this job, pumping six bullets into Hintz. The motive back of the murder was simple: Hintz had refused to "cooperate" with Dunn's gang, so Hintz had to be eliminated.

Hintz died on January 29. On his deathbed, he named the defendants, later convicted of murder in the first degree, as his assailants. At the trial, Hintz's widow, Mrs. Maisie Hintz, testified that immediately after the shooting Hintz had told her: "Johnny Dunn shot me."

KEY JOB ON PIER 51 WAS UNDER DISPUTE

Hintz had been designated as the hiring stevedore at Pier 51 in May 1946, shortly after the Navy had relinquished control of the pier and commercial shipping was resumed. Dunn's gang did not like this. Dunn wanted to designate a member of his own gang in this key job to solidify his control of the pier. He tried to get Hintz ousted and replace him with one of his own men, a notorious ex-convict named James (Ding Dong) Bell, a criminal long associated with Dunn, and one still active on the waterfront.

Failing in this effort, the mob then started to work on Hintz, beginning a campaign of intimidation. There were a series of messages from Dunn: "Play ball with Johnny Dunn and you can keep your job." This was precisely the same approach used a few years back, at the same pier, in the Kelly coercion case, in which a hiring stevedore named Edward J. Kelly was beaten by Dunn's gang for refusing to take orders. Dunn and three codefendants were convicted and sent to prison when Kelly complained and lived to testify against them.

But Anthony Hintz wasn't taking orders from Dunn, or the likes of him, and said so. He was either very brave or very foolish; maybe both. Anyway, Hintz sent back the word: "Tell Dunn he can go to hell!"

With those words Hintz pronounced his own death sentence, though nothing happened immediately. A few days later, three men walked silently on the pier. One was Andrew Sheridan. They said not a word, but walked the length of the pier, as if on a tour of inspection, and then walked away. The men took it as a signal that the mob was taking over, recalling that Andy Sheridan seldom showed up unless somebody was to be knocked off.

HINTZ TRAILED HOME BY MEN IN A CAR

One night later, Hintz was followed home by several men in an automobile. Hintz was with several friends in another car. He saw the car tailing them and asked his friends to let him out at Christopher Street. He stepped out into a brightly lighted area, telling his companions to go on. The trailing car approached, then the driver stepped on the gas and sped away. This was in late November 1946.

Hintz's brother, Willie, was afraid for Anthony's safety and offered to guard him. Hintz laughed and refused. Nevertheless, Willie Hintz made a practice thereafter of calling for his brother in an automobile every morning.

Hintz described the shooting in two deathbed accusations made on January 11 and 13. A transcript of the questioning by Assistant District Attorney William J. Keating was introduced at the trial of Dunn, Sheridan, and Gentile.

"Who shot you on Wednesday morning, January 8, at 61 Grove Street?" Hintz was asked.

"Johnny Dunn," he replied.

"Who was with him?"

"Danny Brooks."

"Who else?"

"Andy Sheridan."

Hintz said he first saw the three men when "they started shooting at me." Sheridan was near a stairway banister, Dunn only a few feet away.

"I went down the stairs," said Hintz. "They popped out—bang, bang. I made a leap at them."

Hintz fell with two bullets in him. As he lay there, four more shots were fired.

"Dunn jumped over me and I tried to grab him," Hintz said. "I pulled one leg down. I was too weak. He hit my mouth."

HINTZ CHARGED DUNN FIRED FATAL SHOTS

"Before these shots were fired, did any of these three men say anything to you?"

"Yes . . . 'Kill the . . . rat! Kill him! And kill that rat brother of his.' "

"Who said that?"

"Dunn."

"Who fired the shots?"

"Dunn; he done well, too."

"How many shots did he fire at you?"

"Six."

Dunn was arrested on the day of the shooting and charged with felonious assault. He was indicted for murder in the first degree after Hintz's death. Sheridan was picked up by FBI agents in Hollywood, Florida, as a fugitive felon and held for the state authorities. Gentile surrendered here.

Brought to trial, the three were convicted of first-degree murder by a jury in general sessions on December 31, 1947. Judge Donnellan, on January 19, 1948, sentenced all three to die in the electric chair during the week of February 23. The defendants appealed, and the execution was stayed pending the outcome of the appeal. On July 16, 1948, the Court of Appeals unanimously affirmed the conviction and set August 26 as the date of execution.

During the investigation of the Hintz murder, before the defendants were brought to trial, Teddy Gleason, a powerful figure in waterfront union affairs, was arrested as a material witness in the case, and released on $50,000 bail. He never testified, however. Gleason was long active as an official of a checkers' union affiliated with the International Longshoremen's Association, is close to Joe Ryan, the president of the ILA, and close to Dunn in union activities.

SHERIDAN CHANGES STORY AT SING SING

From the death house at Sing Sing, Sheridan, on August 5, told a new story about the Hintz murder. In a thirty-six-page affidavit, Sheridan said that he had planned the killing, and absolved his two codefendants, Dunn and Gentile, of any part in it or knowledge of it. On the basis of the affidavit, counsel for Dunn and Gentile appealed for a new trial, and, pending the outcome of the appeal, a stay of execution was granted all three men.

"I planned the killing," Sheridan stated in his affidavit. "I did it to protect myself. Hintz was out to kill me."

Sheridan named two ex-convicts, Little Jeff LePore and John Duff, as the actual killers, saying that he directed them. LePore disappeared shortly after Hintz was slain and is presumably dead. Duff was killed in a train accident on February 10, 1948. Sheridan swore that the car used by the killers was furnished by Charles Yanowsky, big-shot gangster and labor racketeer on the Jersey waterfront who was murdered last July.

The dispute between him and Hintz, Sheridan swore in his affidavit, was over the loading racket and control of a union local. He described in some detail the workings of the pier rackets.

"What was your interest in the docks?" Sheridan was asked.

"Loading—it's a racket," he replied. "I was what was known as a boss loader, and Andy [Anthony Hintz] was a boss loader. The merchants had to pay us for any freight that was loaded on their trucks from the dock. We would hire the loading men. They done the work and we took the money. That is what the fight was over—the profits of loading."

After the murder, Sheridan said LePore and Duff called him on the telephone and said: "The contract has been carried out."

TOUGH TONY QUOTES DUNN WHILE IN TOMBS

During the trial, Anthony (Tough Tony) Tischon, a criminal-turned-informer, testified regarding what Dunn had told him while they were in Tombs prison together after the Hintz killing. Dunn swore and told him, Tough Tony said, that he wouldn't be there if Andy Sheridan had done his part.

"What happened?" Tough Tony asked.

"Sheridan told me his pistol didn't go off," Dunn replied, according to Tony.

"I told Dunn that things like that did happen," Tony continued. "Then Dunn said that pistols McGrath gave them were not toys."

McGrath was not further identified in the testimony.

It was brought out that Sheridan left Florida for New York shortly before the Hintz murder, and returned to Florida, where he was "vacationing" with his family, shortly after the murder. Then Dunn showed up in Hollywood, Florida, and urgently asked to see Sheridan, speaking to Sheridan's young daughter and a girlfriend. Sheridan was not at home. "Tell him I'd like to see him," Dunn said. "Tell him I'll be at the hotel with Meyer Lansky."

During the period that he was in Florida, Dunn stayed at the hotel with Lansky, an underworld figure for many years, once a partner of the late Bugsy Siegel, who was slain in Hollywood, California, and often mentioned as one of the principals in the big crime syndicate that controls major criminal operations in the United States.

New York, Tuesday, November 30, 1948

Killer, Unrepentant as He Faces Electric Chair, Describes His Role in Murder of Anthony Hintz

PORTRAIT OF A KILLER

By his own admission, in sworn testimony, Andrew Sheridan has been a gunman and a killer most of his life. Murder meant nothing to him, he admitted coldly, describing his part in the slaying of Anthony Hintz, boss stevedore. It was "just like ordering a cup of coffee"; no trouble at all. At least, Hintz's murder was like that.

For the record, Sheridan admitted a part in only one specific killing—the Hintz case—but the police and the District Attorney's Office have reason to believe that, all told, he committed at least fifteen murders during his long career as a gangster, racketeer, and gunman.

"But I never killed anybody innocent," Sheridan testified. "I would never hurt an innocent person."

He felt differently about Hintz, who was hiring stevedore on Pier 51, North River. In a flat, unemotional voice, Sheridan said that he was "positively glad" he had planned and directed that murder. He had no regrets whatsoever, and he would do it all over again, he said calmly. "Andy [Anthony] Hintz was no bargain," Sheridan said. "If I hadn't murdered him, he would have murdered me. I'm positively glad he's dead."

MURDERER SKETCHES HIS OWN PORTRAIT

The picture of Sheridan as an unregenerate murderer, though he faced death in the electric chair and felt that nothing on earth could save him, was sketched, in Sheridan's own words, in two days of testimony recently before Judge George L. Donnellan in general sessions. Sheridan was brought from the death house in Sing Sing to testify in support of his affidavit, made last August, stating that his two codefendants, John M. Dunn and Daniel Gentile, who were convicted with him, had no part in the Hintz murder. He swore that he, Sheridan, had planned and directed the slaying, and that two other men, John Duff and Little Jeff LePore, both ex-convicts, were the executioners. Duff is dead, the victim of a railway accident, and LePore is missing and presumably dead.

Sheridan's story was the basis of a motion for a new trial for Dunn and Gentile, and, pending final determination of the motion, a stay of execution was granted them and Sheridan. In opposing the plea, the district attorney contended that Sheridan's story was a lie from beginning to end, told in a last desperate effort to save his codefendants from the chair, sacrificing himself and conveniently pinning the murder on dead men.

Why would Sheridan be willing to do that? Did Dunn, his gangster boss, exert such a terrible power over him that, in blind loyalty or fear, Sheridan would take the death rap to save Dunn? Perhaps. But a more realistic theory is that a deal was made, or that the three defendants drew lots to see which of them would take the rap, agreeing to take care of the loser's family. That is the contention of the District Attorney's Office.

JUST WANTED TO TELL THE TRUTH AT LAST

Sheridan's version of the motive was that he just wanted to tell the truth at last.

"I knew my time was short, only a matter of days," he testified in a low voice. "I knew I was going to the chair and nothing could save me. I figured it was the only decent thing to do. I was just trying to help out two fellows who had nothing to do with this case. That's the God's truth."

Well, true or false, it is the only story Sheridan has ever told in court. None of the defendants took the stand during the trial in which they were convicted, all relying on alibis as a defense. Indeed, Sheridan revealed in the hearing before Donnellan that he had viewed the trial with considerable contempt.

"I never paid much attention to what was said at the trial," he said.

In his two days on the witness stand, Sheridan talked about murder and guns and rackets as calmly as the average citizen would talk about the weather. His manner was cold-blooded, cynical. Occasionally, he favored his questioner with a sour, sneering little smile.

Sheridan is a heavy-set man of medium height. He weighs 220 pounds, is forty-eight years old, and has thick, light brown hair, a pale complexion, and watery blue eyes gleaming behind thick glasses.

"Human life means nothing to you, does it?" Assistant District Attorney George Monaghan demanded.

"Not if it's Anthony Hintz's life," replied Sheridan shortly.

"And even though you are about to go to your Maker there is no repentance or remorse in your soul?"

"Not a bit!"

BARES MURDER PLAN TWO DAYS IN COURT

That was the routine for two days as Sheridan, leaning forward slightly in his chair, described in detail how he planned the murder of Hintz because Hintz was out to get him; how he had told LePore and Duff to "clip" Hintz at the first opportunity; how the killers had "cased" Hintz for days to learn his habits; and how he, Sheridan, had received the report of the mission accomplished while he was at his hotel in Jersey City.

He denied that Dunn was in the rackets with him but freely admitted his own part in waterfront crimes. The enmity between him and Hintz grew out of the rackets, he said. Hintz had the loading racket at Pier 51, was making about nine hundred dollars a week out of it, and was trying to chase him off the piers, Sheridan said. He said that he controlled other piers; that his activity as an organizer for the International Longshoremen Association and as an organizer in Dunn's own checkers' union was just a front for the rackets.

"The police knew I had no legitimate business on some of them piers," Sheridan said, "and I knew that they were trying to involve me in other waterfront murders."

He was asked about other murders—about shooting Joe Moran, a checker in Dunn's union; about murdering a longshoreman named John Whitton, in May 1941, and stuffing his body down a drain.

"If I'd done all that, why didn't youse lock me up before now?" Sheridan countered sourly.

He told how he and Hintz had fought for control of Local 895 of the ILA; how each had tried to elect his own candidates as delegates to the local, and how they had padded the books and conducted phony elections in the battle for control. Sheridan said that his candidate, a fellow named Dutch—he couldn't remember the last name—was elected.

PREPARED TO KILL BEFORE WITNESSES

Sheridan said that sometime before the actual murder he had gone to Pier 51 looking for Hintz, determined to kill him, even if it was in broad daylight and in the presence of witnesses. He didn't find Hintz, and his men, LePore and Duff, got him later, on the morning of January 8, 1947, in the hallway of Hintz's home in Greenwich Village.

No, he didn't force LePore or Duff to do murder for him, Sheridan said. He didn't pay them, either. He didn't have to, for it was to their interest to get rid of Hintz, as both of them were working with him in the rackets and had a "piece" of the loading, Sheridan said.

"To control a pier, you got to control the loading," he explained at one point.

Sheridan said that he himself had supplied the murder guns: a .38 and a .45 caliber. He had lots of guns, kept them all the time. But in this case, Charlie Yanowsky, the Jersey waterfront gangster who was murdered last July, kept the guns for him.

"Charlie knew I was out to get Hintz," Sheridan said. He added that Yanowsky also furnished the stolen car used by the killers.

"You have been a liar and a thief, a gunman and a killer all your life, haven't you Sheridan?" demanded Monaghan.

"Have it that way if you like."

"Well, you are a racketeer, a gangster, and a killer, aren't you?"

"That's right," Sheridan agreed.

FEARS INCRIMINATION AS HE FACES CHAIR

The name of Ed McGrath, Dunn's brother-in-law and reputed partner in the waterfront rackets, was brought into the hearing several times. Wasn't it a fact, the prosecutor wanted to know, that McGrath actually supplied the murder weapons? Sheridan denied it. Hadn't McGrath tried to get Gentile out of town after the murder? Sheridan didn't know anything about that.

Mentioned also were Meyer Lansky, underworld figure, and Vincent Alo, alias Jimmy Blue Eyes, sometimes referred to as a contact man between the waterfront gangs and the big crime syndicate that supposedly controls major rackets throughout the country.

Sheridan said he didn't know Lansky, but that he had seen Jimmy Blue Eyes "around." Didn't know anything about him though.

The spectacle of a man afraid of being "incriminated," though he faces the electric chair, caused laughter in the courtroom when Sheridan was asked about his sources of income and how much he got from the rackets.

"I refuse to answer that. It may incriminate me . . . income tax," said Sheridan.

Before the hearing was over, the court admitted into evidence a statement made by Hintz as he lay mortally wounded. This statement, excluded at the trial of Dunn, Gentile, and Sheridan, shows that Dunn was brought to Hintz's bedside in St. Vincent's Hospital, and that Hintz pointed to Dunn and said: "That's the man who shot me."

Commenting later on Sheridan's testimony and his demeanor on the stand, Monaghan said: "He's as cold-blooded as any man I have ever seen in a courtroom."

DONNELLAN DENIES NEW TRIAL MOTION

On October 18 last, Judge Donnellan, in a nine-page opinion, denied the new trial motion, holding that Sheridan, by his own record and by his admissions on the stand, was a liar and unworthy of belief. Counsel for Dunn and Gentile immediately announced that they would take their appeal to the Court of Appeals.

"He [Sheridan] is now making an abortive attempt to salvage from an inevitable doom his fellow murderers by resorting to a well-known trick of the underworld of substituting for guilty participants dead men whose lips are sealed," Donnellan stated in his opinion. "The creditable evidence produced upon the trial cries out in contradiction of his recital.

"To set aside the conviction of these two defendants, Dunn and Gentile, obtained before a special panel of jurors after a fair trial and whose conviction has since been affirmed unanimously by the Court of Appeals upon the affidavit and the false testimony of an admitted gunman and murderer, to whom the last door of escape has been closed and whose recital is based upon the alleged statements of racketeer gunmen now dead or missing for twenty-one months, would be a mockery of justice and make of the administration of justice a farce. Motion denied."

New York, Wednesday, December 1, 1948

Weak-Eyed Andy Sheridan Reputed to Have Killed Wrong Man and to Have Got Next Victim to Identify Himself

MURDER BY MISTAKE

As a professional gunman, or "knockdown" man, for John Dunn's waterfront mob, Andrew Sheridan was a willing worker, but given to serious blunders. In addition to being a little on the stupid side, Sheridan is almost blind, the result of a cruel incident in his childhood. Consequently, as an executioner for Dunn's gang, Sheridan's aim was poor and he sometimes missed. Once, according to underworld sources, he killed the wrong man by mistake. And, according to Dunn himself, Sheridan blundered again in the murder of Anthony Hintz, hiring stevedore.

It's a problem for the psychiatrists, but it is barely possible that Andy Sheridan might have become a law-abiding citizen had it not been for that incident of his childhood. Dull, but ploddingly honest, and able to stay out of trouble.

Sheridan is a product of New York, born May 8, 1900, one of eight children. His mother died when he was five and the family was broken up. Andrew was placed in the St. Dominican Home, at Blauvelt, New York, where he stayed for about five years. While there, some of his playful little companions threw a chemical into his eyes, permanently impairing his eyesight. That affected his whole life. In later years, his vision grew progressively worse, causing him to lose a succession of jobs. It made him very bitter.

According to his older brother, Frank, Sheridan's criminal tendencies developed while he was in the home, where, Frank says, he came into contact with vicious companions and thereafter showed a distinct preference for disreputable friends over law-abiding ones. Andy was taken out of the home when he was about ten and went to live with his father at the home of a paternal aunt, at Fifty-seventh Street and First Avenue.

SENIOR SHERIDAN STERN DISCIPLINARIAN

The father, Andrew Sheridan, Sr., a native of Ireland, apparently was a decent, hardworking man, but a stern disciplinarian, with little patience or understanding of children. His idea of discipline evidently was to cuff them around. Andrew Jr. hated him and was in continual conflict with him, as well as with other relatives. The boy was always in trouble and frequently stole money from the house. When he was twelve, he stole his father's watch. That was the last straw. The father took him to Children's Court as a delinquent, and Andy was committed to the Catholic Protectory for one year.

After his release, he lived with various relatives, but was unable to adjust himself in any one home. He finally went out to live by himself, and, from that time, little is known about him, except that the records indicate his activities were of a widely criminal character. His father died in 1927, at forty-nine. Sheridan's meager schooling was obtained at the St. Dominican Home and St. John's Parochial School. He never got beyond the sixth grade.

Officially, Sheridan's criminal record dates back to September 24, 1912, when he was sent to the Catholic Protectory. On March 13, 1917, he was convicted of petty larceny and placed on probation. On April 21, 1917, he was sentenced to the House of Refuge for petty larceny. On September 30, 1919, he was convicted of violating the Sullivan law and again sentenced to the House of Refuge, from which he was transferred to the New York City penitentiary. He was paroled on December 14, 1920. Three days later, on December 17, Sheridan and two companions held up a clothing store. He was convicted of robbery in the second degree and sentenced to state prison for a term of seven and a half to fifteen years. He was paroled on July 26, 1926.

CALLED TRIGGERMAN FOR DUTCH SCHULTZ

On December 19, 1927, Sheridan was indicted for criminally carrying a concealed weapon after the commission of a crime, tried in general sessions, and discharged on the recommendation of the district attorney. He was returned to prison, however, for violation of parole, and reparoled on December 19, 1929.

Sheridan was soon in trouble again. On May 21, 1930, he and two others were found seated in a stolen car in front of 18 East 135th Street. When a policeman questioned them, the three were defiant and evasive. The cop drew his gun and ordered them out of the car. As they stepped out, Sheridan drew a .38 caliber revolver and aimed at the cop. The cop fired, wounding Sheridan in the right shoulder.

Two other policemen rushed to the scene. Sheridan and his companions then admitted that they were bootleggers and said that they were waiting in the car to kill a bootlegger who had hijacked a truckload of beer belonging to them. During this period, Sheridan is believed to have acted as a triggerman for Dutch Schultz's beer-running gang.

Indicted for criminally carrying a concealed weapon after the commission of a crime, and for felonious assault in the first and second degrees, Sheridan was permitted to plead guilty to the gun charge to cover both indictments and was sentenced to seven years in state prison. He was received at Sing Sing on July 23, 1930, transferred to Clinton prison on August 4, 1931, thence to Great Meadow prison on April 27, 1934. He escaped from Great Meadow on March 31, 1935, was recaptured, and received a one-year suspended sentence, for escape. At that time, he owed seven years, ten months, and twenty days on his original sentence. He was paroled on October 23, 1936.

PSYCHIATRIC REPORT GIVES PICTURE OF MAN

And this was the kind of man, according to a psychiatric report, who was once more loosed on society: His mental age was 12¾ years. He was of average, dull intelligence; a psychopathic personality, egocentric and unstable. "He leans forward in an aggressive way," says the report, "and has a slight tic of the right eyelid. He has a somewhat sickly smile." He has light brown hair and pale, watery blue eyes.

Immediately after his release, Sheridan first lived with his older brother, Frank, in Brooklyn, and worked at various jobs as a laborer. But Sheridan couldn't get along with his brother, or anybody else, and soon was living elsewhere, though he was careful to keep in touch with the parole board, as required. In February 1937, Sheridan got his first job on the waterfront, working at Pier 14, Hudson River, as a longshoreman. This was, of course, in the territory later under the complete control of Dunn and his partner in crime, Ed McGrath.

Sheridan, known on the waterfront as Squint because of his failing eyesight, boasted that he was able to start work without membership in the International Longshoremen's Association, the AFL union that controls waterfront labor here, because he knew the union delegate. Later, however, he joined the union. During that year, he got married. The next year, he lost his job because of his poor eyesight. Shortly thereafter, Sheridan was hired as an organizer for Local 856 of the ILA at thirty-five dollars a week. His job was to see that all men working on the piers had union books, and to report his findings to the business agent of the local, Charles Piccarelli. Sheridan covered the piers on the East River, and the piers on the North River from the Battery to Pier 27. This was in May 1938.

BOASTED OF BEING HIT-AND-RUN MAN

The record isn't clear as to just when Sheridan joined Dunn's mob, but it was presumably about this time. At any rate, Sheridan began to prosper, and it wasn't long before he was boasting, after he had a few drinks under his belt, that he was a "hit-and-run" man for Johnny Dunn.

That is how he came to commit murder by mistake, according to a commonly accepted underworld story.

At 6 P.M. on November 18, 1938, a young man named John F. O'Hara, a credit investigator for the firm of Dun & Bradstreet, was shot and killed at the entrance of the Celtic Apartments, 43-10 Forty-eighth Avenue, Sunnyside, Queens, where he lived. O'Hara, a twenty-six-year-old college graduate, described by his employers as "an estimable young man," was on his way home from work. He was ambushed by two gunmen who fired seven shots. Two struck O'Hara, killing him instantly. Another bullet struck the eight-year-old son of Patrolman Joseph Monahan, wounding him in the elbow. Monahan, walking through the courtyard as the shots were fired, drew his service revolver and fired two bullets at the fleeing gunmen, who joined a third man, leaped into a car, and sped away.

The police could find no motive for the killing. O'Hara had no enemies, no record, no shady associates. On the contrary, he was a highly respectable young man with a bright future, well thought of by his employers.

Then they learned that a convict, Matthew Kane, had been released on parole from Auburn prison on the day of the shooting, and that, moreover, Kane had promised to go directly to the home of his mother, who lived in the same apartment building in which O'Hara lived. The police were convinced that the murder was a case of mistaken identity, that the intended victim was Matty Kane, an old-time criminal, with a record dating to 1915, and one who had been suspected in a series of jobs with John Dunn.

ANDY SHERIDAN GOT HELL FROM HIS BOSSES

It was O'Hara's misfortune to have been about the same height and build as Kane, though Kane was much older. But it was almost dark—and then there was the matter of Andy Sheridan's bum eyes. True, they were never able to pin this murder on Sheridan, but it is common knowledge in the underworld that Sheridan was one of those two gunmen, and that he was out to get Kane, on assignment from Dunn, because of a grapevine story that Kane was getting ready to squeal on Dunn. Queens detectives assigned to the case strongly suspected Sheridan and so informed the Parole Board. They tailed him for days but could never get anything on him, and he was not picked up.

The mob finally got Kane anyway. Kane was returned to Auburn prison as a parole violator when it turned out that he had not kept his word about visiting his mother that night. Back in Auburn, he was fatally stabbed by a fellow convict, dying on December 13, 1938.

Well, the story is that Andy Sheridan caught hell from his gang bosses for that mistake in murder. They roasted him good, and it made Andy feel mighty low. He felt that his reputation had been impaired, not to mention his integrity. And so on a future professional assignment, Sheridan resolved to make no mistakes.

At 9:30 P.M. on February 7, 1941, Joseph Moran, of 41-20 Fifty-third Street, Woodside, Queens, was working as a checker for the M. Moran Transportation Company (no relation) at 508 West Fortieth Street. As a checker, Moran was a member of Dunn's union, Local 21510 of the Motor and Bus Terminal Checkers, Platform and Office Workers. Moran was standing with several other men in a Mack truck backed up to the loading platform when another man, not then identified, stepped in.

"Who's Moran?" the intruder demanded.

"I am," said Moran.

GUNMAN DISAPPEARS INTO THE DARKNESS

"Okay," said the man, drawing a gun. He fired two or more shots. One bullet struck Moran in the forehead, another in the abdomen. He died instantly. The gunman turned and disappeared in the darkness.

Was the gunman Andrew Sheridan? Dunn himself said he was, though Sheridan was never suspected in that job until after he and Dunn and Danny Gentile had been indicted in the murder of Hintz last year. While in the Tombs, Dunn complained bitterly to a cell mate, Tough Tony Tischon, that he wouldn't have been there "if that . . . Andy Sheridan had done what he was supposed to."

"What's the matter? Sheridan gone yellow?" Tough Tony asked.

"No, he's not yellow," Dunn replied. "He handled Moran like a major."

"What happened, then?"

"Sheridan told me his pistol didn't go off," Dunn said, referring to the Hintz job.

Dunn was believed by the police to have intended to kill Hintz instantly. As it was, six bullets were fired into Hintz's body, but Hintz lived for three weeks, long enough for his dying accusations to convict Dunn, Sheridan, and Gentile of murder in the first degree.

It was another mistake for Andy Sheridan.

Born Francesco Castiglia, Frank Costello was among the longest surviving and most powerful crimelords in law enforcement history. Born in 1891, the "Prime Minister, Irish" was known for his ability to run a business and weave in and out of society. Like Lansky, he avoided jail after his youth, and was known for his incredible business acumen, though he was not above murder. He was known for his close contacts with judges, police, and politicians. He was connected with Meyer Lansky and Bugsy Siegel, among others. In his later years, Costello retired from business, and died at the age of eighty-two in his Long Isalnd home in 1973.
Reproduced from the Collections of the Library of Congress.

New York, Thursday, December 2, 1948

Gang Warfare on City Waterfront Produces Record Murder Crop, With Suspects Often Later Victims of Gunfire

HARVEST OF MURDERS

It has been said that the waterfront here produces more murders to the square foot than does any other one section in the country. That may be an exaggeration, but violence and sudden death on the waterfront are so commonplace that it is difficult to compile a complete and accurate list of the victims whose deaths may be traced directly to the rackets and to the gang warfare during the many years in which the sector has flourished as an "outlaw frontier."

It is estimated, however, that in the last decade at least twenty persons have been slain in the ceaseless battle for control of one of the city's richest racket territories. The figure is admittedly conservative and does not take into account the numerous stabbings and deaths resulting from barroom brawls that may or may not be connected with the gang wars.

One of the most recent of the "planned assassinations," in the words of the District Attorney's Office, is the case of Thomas Collentine, as yet unsolved. The Collentine murder closely parallels that of Anthony Hintz, described in a previous article. Collentine, like Hintz, was a hiring stevedore, a key job. Collentine, like Hintz, was ambushed by his assailants as he was preparing to go to work.

COLLENTINE YOUNG, TOUGH, AND AMBITIOUS

Collentine was young and tough and ambitious. He had been a member of Local 824 of the International Longshoremen's Association since he was sixteen, and he had come up fast. At thirty, he was the hiring boss at Pier 92, one of the busiest on the waterfront, and under lease to the Atlantic, Gulf and West Indies Corporation. Pier 92, at the foot of Fifty-second Street, is in the territory ruled by Mickey Bowers and his gang, and is described by the district attorney's investigators as one of the "hottest piers" on the North River.

Because the territory under its jurisdiction has been the scene of so much violence, including murder, Local 824, of which Collentine was a member, is referred to all along the waterfront as "the Pistol Local."

Collentine was shot and fatally wounded as he left his home at Post Avenue, in the Inwood section of Manhattan, at 7:30 A.M. on April 29, 1948. The assailant leaped out of an automobile and opened fire as Collentine and two companions walked out to Collentine's car, parked in front of the building. It was noted later that the car had two flat tires, a circumstance that probably was part of the murder plot. Collentine's two companions, both longshoremen, were John White, thirty-four, of 121 Vermilyea Avenue, and George Courchesne, twenty-three, of 156 Sherman Avenue.

Stanley Lucksinger, building superintendent at 25 Post Avenue, was emptying an ash can when he saw a black sedan approach from the south on Post Avenue.

"I heard a lot of shots, which sounded like backfire," Lucksinger told the police. "I looked down the street and saw a man with a gun in one hand and a handkerchief in the other, held over his face. A man was lying in the street, and the man with the gun was about two feet from him."

The police said that the gunman jumped from the backseat of the car. Two other men were in the front seat.

Collentine died in Jewish Hospital eleven hours after the shooting. He was tough and uncommunicative to the last. "I don't know who shot me, and if I did I wouldn't tell you," he told the police shortly before he died. His two companions said that they could cast no light on the shooting or the motive for it.

MURDER SUSPECTS OFTEN LATER VICTIMS

A study of other waterfront homicides shows that in many instances the suspects themselves ultimately became victims. There was Jimmy Day, believed by the police to have been slain by Richard (the Bandit) Gregory, delegate for Local 824, who had a record of twelve arrests and three convictions. Gregory was shot to death on November 16, 1940, and one of the suspects in his death, Thomas Cuniff, was knocked off on January 25, 1941.

Dave Beadle, a powerful racketeer who preceded Mickey Bowers in control of the piers above Forty-second Street, was shot and killed on December 9, 1939. Beadle was a suspect in several slayings. Such is the pattern in the racket cases.

Other victims include George Keeler and Thomas Porter, loading racketeers, killed in 1935; Ray Hoffman, found dead in an automobile on Greenwich Street in 1937; Joe Butler, who tried to seize control of the Chelsea piers, slain in 1938; a criminal known as Farmer Sullivan, murdered in 1938; Ralph Clements, 1937; Edward Kenny, a collector for Varick Enterprises, the loading racket outfit, killed in June 1938; Johnny Costello, June 15, 1937; Charles Brady, April 14, 1940; Emil Nizih, February 7, 1941; and Robert Coagnaro, March 6, 1946.

Going much further back, there was William (Wild Bill) Lovett, who ruled a large section of the turbulent Brooklyn waterfront. A would-be rival of Lovett's, Dennis Meehan, was shot to death in his bed on March 1, 1920, and Wild Bill himself was slain in November 1923. Others to die during those earlier years included Peg-Leg Lonergan, Garry Barry, Eddie Hughes, Micky Gilligan, Chris Maroney, John Crowley, Bill Lynch, Bill Quilty, Ricco Brache, Cinders Connolly, Bill Gillen, Dan Healy, Charles (Red) Donnelly, James Monohan, and Linky Mitchell.

WATERFRONT IS HELD HAVEN FOR EX-CONVICTS

In the killing of Emil (Big Moe) Nizih, mentioned above, an ex-convict, Dan St. John, was arrested, indicted, and twice tried for murder in the first degree, but the jury disagreed and the defendant was dismissed. St. John now is working as a hiring boss at Pier 84, in the Bowers domain. His criminal record begins in 1915, and includes some twenty arrests, convictions for larceny and carrying a gun, and two prison escapes. The record of St. John, who is still powerful in his own right, is typical of that of other criminals who infest the waterfront, giving support to official charges that this section of New York is and always has been a haven for ex-convicts.

The notorious Bell brothers are another example. James (Ding Dong) Bell is still active on the North River piers, and his name for years has cropped up in connection with waterfront crimes and the mob activities led by John M. Dunn, the gangster now in the death house at Sing Sing on a stay of execution for the murder of Hintz. Bell's record, beginning in 1922, cites some fourteen arrests on such a variety of charges as petty larceny, burglary, assault, possessing gas bombs, receiving stolen goods, and violation of the Sullivan law. He has done plenty of time.

One brother, Leslie, is also an ex-convict, and another, Henry (Buster) Bell, was arrested with Ed McGrath for murder in Florida but was discharged. Buster was placed on probation in 1944 on a charge of attempted extortion and impersonating an officer. Leslie, put away in 1937 as a mental defective, was a member of a West Side trigger gang and was suspected in assorted murders and pier rackets.

NEW YORK, FRIDAY, DECEMBER 3, 1948

Yanowsky, Sovereign of New Jersey Piers, Died From Twelve Stab Wounds When He Became Too Powerful to Live

---

ALUMNUS OF ALCATRAZ

Until his sudden elimination last summer, the most ruthless, powerful gangster on the Jersey waterfront was Charlie Yanowsky, alias Charlie the Jew, an alumnus of Alcatraz who became an official in a local of the International Longshoremen's Association, the AFL union that controls dock labor.

Charlie was a big-shot racketeer, with interests in several unions, in addition to the ILA, and with close working connections with the dominant Manhattan waterfront mobsters. Like so many other big shots of the underworld, Yanowsky's elimination was swift and permanent. He became too powerful to live.

And so on the night of July 16 last, Yanowsky, the tough guy, was found dead of multiple stab wounds, apparently inflicted with an ice pick, in a lonely field near a public schoolyard in Clifton, New Jersey, about thirty-five feet from the highway.

His killers had made a sure job of it, stabbing him twelve times near the heart. His wallet was missing, but an expensive ring and a diamond-studded belt were left on the body. The police promptly ruled out a robbery motive, despite the missing wallet. It was a gang killing and nothing else, they said.

YANOWSKY CALLED BEEHIVE OF ACTIVITY

There are several theories for Yanowsky's murder and any one of them could be right. He was a man of many rackets, a beehive of activity. In addition to his waterfront operations, he had cut himself in on gambling concessions and was dabbling in the narcotics traffic. He was expanding fast, everywhere he could. He was said to have been enviously eyeing certain lucrative Manhattan piers. Any one of his racket interests could have resulted in his death.

Yanowsky's method of expanding is best illustrated in the story of how he cut himself in on a rich Jersey gambling concession a year or so ago. Preferring the direct approach, Yanowsky went to the gambler and said: "Do I shoot my way in and take it all over, or do I buy my way in for a third interest?"

The gambler looked at Yannowsky, hesitated for a split second, then said slowly: "You can buy a third interest, Charlie."

Despite his power, there were indications that Yanowsky had become highly cautious in the months immediately preceding his death. Two weeks before he was slain, the story went around that Charlie had decided to go underground for a while. No reason was given. He had just decided to step into the background and operate through some of his numerous union stooges.

Maybe Yanowsky thought that the heat was on him at last. In this connection, the words of a private waterfront investigator are prophetic. Two months before Yanowsky was murdered, the investigator said: "Something big is brewing on the Jersey side. There is a feeling that Charlie Yanowsky is getting too big. Something's going to break soon."

EXERCISED FULL CONTROL OF JERSEY WATERFRONT

Yanowsky made his headquarters in Hoboken, and he was in undisputed control of Hoboken and Jersey City piers; undisputed, that is, until he was knocked off. He had strong political alliances in Jersey, and his reputation as a tough, versatile criminal had won him a healthy respect in the underworld. His position had seemed unassailable, and the manner in which he operated indicated that he had the picking of Jersey's most powerful representative in the big crime syndicate that directs most racket enterprises, including waterfront operations, in the big cities of the United States.

Long before turning to the waterfront, Yanowsky, who sometimes used the alias Harry Alberts, was known to the police and to the FBI as one of the most dangerous criminals in the country. He had a record of some twenty arrests, dating back to 1926, and he was suspected in numerous other crimes. He was a hijacker, kidnapper, bank robber, and gunman.

This was the man, then, who was listed in the official directory of the International Longshoremen's Association, of which Joseph P. Ryan is president, with a lifetime job at $20,000 a year. Yanowsky was secretary of the Marine Warehousemen of New Jersey, an ILA local, and he had front men in official positions in various other ILA locals. In addition, Yanowsky had muscled into the Motor and Bus Terminal Checkers, Platform and Office Workers, the union created by John Dunn, the Manhattan waterfront mobster. He was business agent and organizer of the Jersey local of this union, No. 21512. Dunn, whose mob obtained charters for the Jersey and New York locals, as well as one for Pennsylvania that was never used, was business agent of the New York local, No. 21510. Whether Yanowsky got into the Jersey local with or without Dunn's consent is not known. Yanowsky also was connected with a novelty workers' union, a liquor salesmen's union, and an upholsterers' union.

YANOWSKY SUCCEEDED DUNN'S TRIGGERMAN

The minutes of a meeting of the executive board of the Jersey local of the Motor and Bus Terminal Checkers, dated Monday, December 2, 1946, show that on that day Andrew Sheridan, a Dunn triggerman, "resigned" as general organizer, and that "Brother Charles Yanowsky" was appointed as business agent and organizer. Also "resigned" was Anthony Cocasso as secretary-treasurer and organizer. He was succeeded by Steve Wilson, who also happens to be president of the Marine Warehousemen of which Yanowsky was secretary. Andy Sheridan was convicted of murder with Dunn and Danny Gentile, but the execution for all three has been put off pending action on a motion for a new trial for Dunn and Gentile.

"Brother" Yanowsky was a high-minded citizen of Hoboken, judging from the language in the incorporation papers of the Riverfront Democratic Club. Yanowsky was one of the five trustees and incorporators of this club, which announced its intention of participating in this fall's election campaign on behalf of Democratic candidates, state and national.

The announced purpose of the club was social, political, and athletic: "To aid in the administration of government, to advance the cause of democratic government for the people, to campaign for legislation beneficial for the working man and to appose all legislation that seeks to shackle labor." It was also indicated that the club would work for "improvement of pier facilities in Hudson County, and especially in Hoboken, in order to aid in the development of an efficient cargo and marine terminal."

MOWED DOWN IN 1937 BY GUNS OF FBI

Yanowsky was forty-two when he was slain and had been a professional criminal for more than twenty years. In 1937, he attempted to shoot it out with FBI agents, who were trying to arrest him for a bank robbery, and he was mowed down by machine-gun bullets and seriously wounded.

He was born in New York City, the eldest of three children, but was reared in Jersey City. His father was a secondhand furniture dealer. Early in his criminal career, Yanowsky was a member of the Rope Ladder gang specializing in the theft of merchandise from freight cars. Using rope ladders, the thieves would descend from the roof of moving freight cars, break the door seals, and, while the train was in transit, throw merchandise along the right-of-way, to be picked up by trucks by other members of the gang.

Yanowsky's numerous arrests included charges of aiding and abetting a lottery, operating a gambling resort, bookmaking, kidnapping, hijacking, bank robbery, stealing from interstate shipments, and felonious assault. In 1934, he received a suspended federal sentence of three years and a day for stealing from interstate shipments, and, two years later, had to begin serving this sentence when he was arrested for violation of parole. He was sent to the federal prison at Lewisburg, Pennsylvania, but was transferred, as a tough case, to Alcatraz, from which he was paroled on April 21, 1938. In 1935, he was arrested as a suspect in the attempted machine-gun slaying of an ex-convict, James (Ding Dong) Bell, who is a member of the Dunn waterfront gang, and who still is working on the waterfront. On his release from Alcatraz, Yanowsky was promptly picked up as a fugitive from New York, in connection with the Bell case, and sentenced to two to four years in Sing Sing for jumping his bail in that arrest.

NEW YORK, MONDAY, DECEMBER 6, 1948

Underworld Syndicate, With Ties Abroad, Runs Vast Empire of Crime, Reputed to Include Waterfront Rackets Here

---

THE SYNDICATE

There exists in the United States today an underworld syndicate, with national and international connections, which controls organized crime throughout the country. Through powerful political alliances, and with untold millions of dollars to spend, the syndicate can, and does, exert influence in high places. It operates in every major city and it also has big interests abroad. The syndicate rules a vast empire of crime, and it has millions invested in legitimate enterprises as a cover for its shadier operations.

Fantastic? Yes, but existence of the syndicate is accepted without question by federal, state, and city investigating agencies. They say that it has existed for years. Composed of big shots of the underworld, the syndicate has brought efficient big business methods to crime.

The syndicate participates in many rackets, but its principal source of revenue is from gambling. Its total revenue is beyond calculation, but the "take" from gambling alone runs into many millions of dollars annually. It controls the narcotic traffic and all major organized rackets. It controls certain labor unions and certain politicians. The syndicate's power is such that it is not necessary for it to participate directly in every criminal operation or racket. But no racket can flourish anywhere, particularly in New York and other big

Charles (Lucky) Luciano was born Salvatore Lucania, in 1896, in Sicily. Known as a ruthless and cold-blooded archcriminal, Luciano also had an exceptional head for business. During Prohibition and his early years, Luciano worked with Bugsy Siegel, Frank Costello, Vito Genovese, Big Bill Dwyer, Dutch Schultz, and Arnold Rothstein. Luciano and Lansky were largely credited with reinventing the Mafia. Lucky replaced more traditional violent means with more businesslike structures, eventually creating the national syndicate. Thomas E. Dewey sentenced him to jail in 1936 on perjury charges; however, Luciano was released in 1946 for his help in the war effort, then deported to Italy. Though he died in Naples, Italy, in 1962, he was buried in Queens, New York, in his adopted country. Reproduced from the Collections of the Library of Congress.

cities, without the knowledge and consent of the syndicate—and presumably without the syndicate getting its cut.

SYNDICATE MEMBERS HAVE RICH HOLDINGS

In the field of legitimate business, members of the syndicate have investments everywhere. They have huge real estate holdings. They own fashionable restaurants and nightclubs, strings of hotels, expensive resorts, skyscraper office buildings, and stores. Recent reports indicate that the syndicate is planning to extend these holdings on a large scale in Europe, Mexico, and South America. It already has large investments in Mexico.

"No question about it," said Colonel Garland Williams, head of the federal narcotic bureau in New York. "The Syndicate, or Combination, as I call it, has existed for many years. But it is not a dictatorship, not a one-man organization by any means. The personnel shifts. Some of the leaders drop out and others take their places. But the Combination has connections in various cities."

Other officials agree with Williams's estimate, describing the syndicate as a big, loosely knit organization, a sort of trade association in crime.

The syndicate originated during Prohibition, but has long since abandoned the blazing warfare that characterized that lawless era. Today, the organization prefers to operate behind numerous legitimate fronts, with high-priced lawyers, the "cooperation" of practical politicians and crooked policemen, and with an intricate system of interlocking interests in practically every field of business.

REPORTED ROSTER OF THE SYNDICATE

Who are some of the members of this big syndicate?

Well, on the East Coast, names most frequently mentioned by the police, state, and federal agencies include the following: Frank

Costello, Lucky Luciano, Joe Adonis, Meyer Lansky, and Longy Zwillman. There are others, especially in the lower echelons, but these are mentioned as among the top figures.

If there is any head man in the syndicate, Costello is regarded as that man. On that, investigators agree. Certainly he is the top boss in New York, and his name commands underworld respect throughout the country.

For many years, Costello was brilliantly successful in avoiding publicity. During his rise to power, beginning during Prohibition, his name rarely appeared in print, and the police professed to know little about him.

Today, however, newspaper filing envelopes are fat with clippings concerning Costello's activities, or suspected activities, as a judge maker, gambler, slot-machine operator, ex-convict, racket boss, and behind-the-scenes power in local Democratic politics.

LUCIANO IS CALLED BIG MAN IN ITALY

According to Colonel Williams, Charles (Lucky) Luciano, the arch-criminal and vice lord, still is a power in the syndicate, despite the fact that Luciano was deported to Italy.

"Luciano is still very much in the picture," said Williams. "He is handling the movement of narcotics from Italy."

At least three big seizures of narcotics, smuggled here during the last few months, were attributed by federal authorities to Luciano's operations in Italy. From all accounts, Luciano is a big man in Italy today, highly respected and admired. He has his own press relations department, holds "press conferences," and, in general, represents himself as the potential savior of Italy. He has plenty of money, derived from the syndicate, and he boasts that he will enter the motion picture business there and build an industry rivaling that of Hollywood.

Luciano was close to Costello in earlier days. Convicted as a vice lord and sentenced to a long term in prison when Thomas E. Dewey was a racket-busting special prosecutor, Luciano had his sentence later commuted by Dewey as governor during the war under circumstances that have never been explained. Costello personally saw him off when Luciano was deported.

Of the relative power of Costello and Luciano, a former representative of the District Attorney's Office, now in private law practice, said: "If Luciano were back in the United States, it would be a toss-up, in my opinion, as to who would be the big boss—Costello or Luciano. Personally, I'd put my money on Costello. If the Syndicate has a chairman of the board, Mr. C. is that man. In my opinion, Costello is the most powerful, wealthiest underworld figure in the United States today."

HENCHMEN OF ADONIS RULE BROOKLYN DOCKS

Also close to Costello, particularly in the syndicate's multimillion-dollar gambling operations in New York, New Jersey, and Florida, is Joe Adonis, also known as Joe A. Doto and Joe A. Adonis, who is the boss racketeer of Brooklyn, ruling in absentia from New Jersey and points south. His henchmen control the Brooklyn waterfront, where violence and racketeering flourish.

Meyer Lansky, also identified with the syndicate's gambling concessions, is widely known to the police, though he has always managed, somehow, to escape serious difficulty with the law. He has been arrested seven times, but has only one conviction. That was for violating the Volstead Act, in 1931, for which he was fined $100.

Lansky was a partner of the late Bugsy Siegel, the gangster slain in Hollywood, California, in June 1947. They were once the leaders of the so-called Bug and Meyer gang, which started in New York and branched out to Philadelphia, where it became rich and powerful. Lansky and Siegel were closely associated at one time with Louis (Lepke) Buchalter, the industrial racketeer who dominated the garment center, and who finally was executed for murder after the smashing of the organization of hired killers known as Murder, Inc.

Lansky and Siegel, in the old days, were reputed to have supplied gunmen and strong-arm squads for Lepke. In recent years, they extended their operations to the West Coast, with Siegel handling the business there. Siegel is believed to have cut himself in on gambling in Las Vegas, Nevada, and on other rackets, a circumstance that may or may not have provided a motive for his murder.

DIRECT LINK IS SEEN TO WATERFRONT RACKETS

A direct link between the syndicate and the New York waterfront rackets—assuming that Lansky is, as reputed, a member of the syndicate—is seen in the fact that John M. Dunn, the waterfront gangster, sought out Lansky in Hollywood, Florida, shortly before the murder of Anthony Hintz, hiring stevedore, who was shot and fatally wounded in January 1947 in New York.

A record of telephone calls from Lansky's hotel room in Hollywood shows that Dunn made calls from the room to the Colonial Inn, the swanky gambling establishment, of which Lansky ostensibly is one of the owners, and to the Green Acres, a nightclub controlled by syndicate members.

When Dunn showed up in Hollywood in December 1946, he first asked for Andrew Sheridan, one of his gunmen, later convicted with him for the Hintz murder. Sheridan was not home at the time, and Dunn left word that he would be with Lansky at the latter's hotel room.

During the period in which Dunn was there, there were telephone calls from Lansky to Ed McGrath, Dunn's brother-in-law and partner; from Lansky to Dutch Goldberg, another underworld character; from Lansky to Dunn's wife in Queens; from Lansky to Joe Adonis in New Jersey; from Lansky to Hot Springs, Arkansas, identity of the recipient unknown; from Lansky to Bugsy Siegel in Palm Springs, California, and to Siegel in Las Vegas; from Lansky to a member of the old Cotton Club mob, who was then in Havana for the season; from Lansky to Frank Costello and to Dandy Phil Kastel, Costello's lieutenant in New Orleans, who handles Costello's vast slot-machine operations in Louisiana.

ZWILLMAN PASSES WORD THAT HE HAS "RETIRED"

Abner (Longy) Zwillman, another product of Prohibition, was for many years the biggest power in Newark, and maybe he still is, though in recent years he has passed the word that he has "retired." Zwillman, once listed by the late police commissioner Valentine as a "public enemy," is tremendously wealthy, and he still commands a healthy respect in the New Jersey underworld.

Moreover, investigation into the death of Charles Yanowsky, the Jersey waterfront gangster murdered last July, has shown connections between Yanowsky and Zwillman, giving weight to the theory that Yanowsky had strong alliances in Jersey enabling him to rise to power on the waterfront and in other rackets. It also indicates a link between the syndicate and waterfront operations.

Then there is an ex-convict named Vincent Alo, better known as Jimmy Blue Eyes, a very mysterious character. According to underworld informants, he is regarded as a contact man for the syndicate, particularly on the waterfront. He is said to be close to Costello, and, in general, acts as an emissary for the big shots here and in Florida. Questioned by the police in August 1947, Alo said that he was in the restaurant business, and that he owned an interest in the Green Acres nightclub in the Miami area. He was a friend of Bugsy Siegel, the police say, but always has denied that he was ever in business with Bugsy.

Perhaps the most plausible theory connecting the big syndicate with the waterfront rackets concerns the traffic in narcotics. According to this theory, it is vital for the syndicate to control, directly or indirectly, the entire waterfront in order to maintain its grip on dope smuggling, a huge source of revenue.

New York, Tuesday, December 7, 1948

Ryan, President of ILA, Denies Lawlessness on City's Piers

SAYS THERE ARE NO RACKETS

Longshoremen's Leader Declares:
"Let 'Em Prove All This Stuff" About Crime

JOE RYAN AND THE ILA

In his office on the nineteenth floor of the Lawyers Trust Building, 265 West Fourteenth Street, bulky, red-faced Joe Ryan, president of the International Longshoremen's Association, AFL, drummed on his shining glass-topped desk and said that there just wasn't any organized crime on the New York waterfront.

Ryan flatly denied charges of widespread lawlessness on the docks. He denied that gangsters controlled the piers, ruling by terror. He denied that racketeering flourished, denied that any organized rackets existed, and denied vehemently that there was any graft or racketeering in his union, which controls labor on the docks.

"That's ridiculous," said Ryan. "Where is the Police Department? We got a Police Department, haven't we? The police wouldn't stand for a situation like that. Our men wouldn't stand for it. The union wouldn't stand for it. The steamship and stevedoring companies wouldn't stand for it."

ANSWER BY RYAN: UNEQUIVOCAL DENIAL

To any and all criticism of his union, to charges that it is graft-ridden, that it condones racketeering and protects known racketeers, and that, specifically, the kickback in wages is common practice, Ryan's answer was a simple and unequivocal denial. It was all untrue.

"I defy anybody to prove there is any kickback in our organization," he said. "I don't care who says so, and they have been saying it for years. But it's never been proved."

What about the charge that the waterfront is a haven for ex-convicts, that any ex-convict can get a job there, anytime?

"We welcome ex-convicts—well, now, maybe welcome is too broad a statement," replied Ryan. "But we believe every man, regardless of what he has done, has a right to a second chance. If the ex-convicts can't work on the waterfront, where can they work? But we don't ask for them, I can tell you that. They dump them on us all the time—the parole boards. There are some criminals on the waterfront, but they are a minority, and they don't run in packs. Ninety-nine percent of the men in our organization are decent, hardworking, God-fearing men. Men with families, trying to make a living."

What about Mickey Bowers, a known criminal whose gang reputedly controlled the upper Manhattan piers, above Forty-second Street?

"Mickey Bowers? Don't believe I know him," said Ryan. "There is a Bowers who is an ILA delegate or business agent up there, I think."

"That's Harold Bowers, Mickey's cousin," Ryan was told.

"Oh."

RYAN IS QUESTIONED ON OTHER GANGSTERS

The names of other gangsters were mentioned. Gangsters and other criminals who, in many instances, had attained official positions in the ILA, according to the union's own records. Men like Charlie Yanowsky, the powerful Jersey mobster who was murdered last July, who was secretary of an ILA warehouse local and connected with various other locals. Men like John Dunn and Andrew Sheridan, who were convicted and sentenced to death for the murder of Anthony Hintz, an ILA hiring stevedore. And Ed McGrath, Dunn's brother-in-law and reputed partner in the waterfront rackets? What did Ryan have to say about them?

"I'll tell you about Yanowsky," Ryan said slowly. "I didn't put him in that warehouse local. I didn't want him. The first time I saw him, right here in this office, I said he couldn't have the job. He said the men wanted him and had elected him. What could I do? I'll say this for Yanowsky: he's done a good job. The men wanted him and were happy under him. He got things for the men.

"As for John Dunn—he didn't have anything to do with the ILA or the waterfront. He and McGrath and some others organized the motor and bus terminal checkers and platform men. They were underpaid and they needed organizing. They got an AFL charter."

RYAN DENOUNCES PROSECUTOR AS DUMB

"Now, you take a man like Teddy Gleason," Ryan volunteered, referring to one of his right-hand men in the ILA, an official in a checkers' union whose name, next to Ryan's, is mentioned most frequently on the waterfront.

"You probably hear all kinds of things about Gleason," said Ryan. "Well, I have known him all his life. I knew his father, and I worked with his father, and I want to tell you that Teddy Gleason has never been arrested for anything in his life."

As if in afterthought, Ryan did mention that Gleason was taken into custody as a material witness in the Hintz murder case but said that the district attorney obviously didn't have anything on Gleason, for he was released and never was called upon to testify.

Ryan then angrily paid his respect to that "crazy Keating down there," referring to Assistant District Attorney William J. Keating of the Homicide Bureau, whose tireless work was instrumental in helping to break the Hintz case.

"That fellow Keating doesn't know what it's all about," said Ryan. "He's so dumb he doesn't know his own name."

Well, then, what about the loading racket? Wasn't it a racket, and hadn't it existed for more than twenty years, controlled by racketeers who levied a fee on every pound of cargo loaded on trucks at the piers?

Ryan smiled patiently.

"My answer to that is that loading is very hard work," he said. "We do set the rates, and we do insist that three men be used as loaders. That's a matter of union policy. Why, every district attorney for years back has investigated the loading racket—I mean, the so-called loading racket—and has not found anything. If there was anything wrong there don't you think the DAs could find it? They've all had a try at it—Tom Dewey and all the rest. Now the men do the loading, and it's hard work. The men themselves split the fees. It's all divided up. Gangsters do not pocket that money. That's simply not true. Why, the men wouldn't stand for it."

SAYS MEN NEVER ASKED FOR SHAPE-UP CHANGE

What did Ryan have to say about the shape-up, the system of hiring on the waterfront—a system condemned by various investigating agencies, over a period of many years, as antiquated, inhuman, and degrading: as lending itself to abuses, and making it possible for criminals to control the docks?

"The men have never asked for a change," said Ryan. "They could change it if they wanted to. There must be some reason, some benefit from the shape-up, or they'd change it.

"When I went to work on the waterfront, in 1912, we made 30 cents an hour for a 60-hour week, and we had to shape-up from hour to hour, any hour of the day. Today, there are about 65,000 ILA men on the New York waterfront. They make a general rate of $1.75 an hour for a 40-hour week, 8 to 12 noon and 1 to 5 P.M., Monday through Friday. At all other hours, they get $2.62 an hour at time and a half. They now shape-up only twice a day, at 7:55 A.M. and 12:55 P.M. All I can say is that any group of men who can bring their pay and working conditions up that way must have something. The men at no time have asked to change the system. You'd think they'd ask if there was something wrong with it,"

(Since Ryan made the above statement, the ILA workers, as a result of the recent strike, have won wage increases which make their new rate of pay $1.88 an hour for straight time and $2.82 an hour for overtime. They also won better vacation terms, a welfare fund, and other benefits.)

Such was Joe Ryan's defense, delivered calmly and without rancor, of the ILA, and of general conditions on the waterfront. He was unimpressed by any evidence to the contrary, and, as a parting shot, he said: "I'll stand back of everything I've said. Let 'em prove all this stuff you have been hearing about."

HOW RYAN ROSE IN LABOR'S RANKS

Joseph P. Ryan, to give him his full moniker, is a two-fisted, rough-and-tumble labor leader of the old school who came up from the ranks and who has never ducked a fight. He's Irish all the way through, a product of Manhattan's West Side. He grew up on West Nineteenth Street, quit school when he was twelve, and went to work in his early youth on the docks. He received his first union card in Local 791 of the ILA, then a comparatively minor labor union in the Port of New York, on March 23, 1912, and he has been active in the union ever since.

In 1913, Ryan was made financial secretary of his local. Then he was elected an officer of the New York district council, which negotiated wage agreements for the port in 1915. In 1918, he became vice president, and in 1927 he was elected international president. He's held the job continuously, and, today, at sixty-four, he is secure in a lifetime job as president, so voted by his union, at a salary of $20,000 a year. Ryan's thick reddish hair and heavy eyebrows have turned gray, but he has lost none of his vigor and continues to fight his enemies, in and out of the union, with all his customary gusto.

They say that in his younger days Ryan was mighty handy with his fists, never hesitating to wade in and hand out the lumps when he deemed such action necessary.

The charge has been made repeatedly through the years that Ryan condones racketeering in his union, protects the racketeers, and refuses to do anything to eliminate the evils within his organization. Under the Ryan leadership, the union has been denounced as autocratic, a complete dictatorship in which the members are viciously exploited by its leader.

RYAN YEARLY HOBNOBS WITH THE MIGHTY

Ryan also has been publicly accused of associating with known criminals. If he does, it must also be said in fairness to Ryan, that he likewise hobnobs with some of the country's most influential business men, politicians, and high public officials.

Every year, Ryan is the honored guest at the Joseph P. Ryan Association dinner. It's a big affair, and all kinds of people, including criminals, turn out for it. High state and city officials invariably are among those present. In 1931, for example, Franklin D. Roosevelt, then governor of New York; Mayor Jimmy Walker; Frank Hague, the Jersey political tycoon; and William Green, president of the AFL, were listed as honorary chairmen of the Ryan dinner.

Everybody "in the trade," so to speak, attends loyally, and so all kinds of elements on the waterfront are represented. At the dinner last year, held at the Hotel Commodore, the guests included Mickey

Bowers, the ex-convict and gangster, who controls the piers above Forty-second Street; his lieutenant, John Keefe, also an ex-convict; and Harold Bowers, a cousin of Mickey's and delegate of Local 824 of the ILA.

PHOTO SHOWS RYAN POSING WITH CRIMINALS

Similar dinners are held annually in honor of Teddy Gleason for the benefit of the Teddy Gleason Association. At the dinner in 1939, one of the souvenir snapshots taken shows none other than Joe Ryan, posing as big as life, with such known criminals as John M. Dunn, ex-convict, gangster, and labor racketeer, now in the death house at Sing Sing under a stay of execution for murder, and Danny Gentile, also in the Sing Sing death house, having been convicted with Dunn in the Hintz murder.

Also pictured with Ryan in that memorable photograph are such worthies as Robert Baker, alias Barney Baker, an ex-convict who was a collector for Varick Enterprises, which was a strong-arm collection agency for the loading racket at the time; and John Adams, who was vice president of Varick. Adams has a police record, which includes a suspended sentence for felonious assault in 1927.

During the years of Ryan's rule in the ILA, he has been the target of both left-wing and conservative critics. Some of the mildest things they have said about him is that he is an archreactionary, an "enemy of true labor," willing to exploit his men to maintain his power. Ryan either brushes aside such criticism or else replies in kind.

VIOLENTLY ANTI-RED AND WAVES THE FLAG

He is violently, and probably sincerely, anticommunist, and opposes anything or anybody he conceives to be slightly pink, and his standards are ultraconservative. At times, when critics press him too hard, Ryan figuratively waves the flag and yells "Communist." He sometimes waxes fervently patriotic when discussing his union.

"The ILA," Ryan once proclaimed grandly, "stands for 'I Love America.'"

Ryan belongs to the Winged Foot Gold Club in Mamaroneck, Westchester, where the membership also includes prominent business and professional men, judges, politicians, and city officials.. He is a friendly, sociable man, but can be very tough when riled. As a golfer, Ryan is enthusiastic but no par buster.

In his personal habits, Ryan is a "good liver" but prides himself on the fact that he neither smokes nor swears—the result of his devout upbringing, he says. But he likes good food, has a reputation—and the figure—of a trencherman, and he takes a drink when he feels like it. He also has a weakness for expensive, well-tailored clothes.

SUN'S PREPARED SERIES ASSAILED HOTLY BY RYAN

Since the above interview was written, as a part of this prepared series of articles, Ryan has had quite a lot more to say, much of it uncomplimentary, to *The New York Sun*, and to this reporter.

Ryan's blood pressure began to mount when the ILA strike began on November 10, his men having rejected the contract which he had recommended. On the day the strike began, without the sanction of Ryan and his lieutenants, the blustering ILA president charged that the men were striking because of resentment against these articles, which *The Sun* had begun publishing two days earlier, on November 8.

This statement, ridiculous on the face of it, caused only loud and derisive laughter from rank-and-file members of the ILA, who charged that Ryan had sold them out again. Ryan dropped the line of defense quickly enough after the strike spread to the entire East Coast, forcing him to go along with it and make it official.

During the eighteen-day strike, Ryan, referring to the number of ex-convicts in his union, boasted: "*The Sun* has been writing about some of the boys from the old ladies' home up the river who came down to the waterfront and made good. I'm proud to have them as members of this union. I'm proud to have my picture taken with them and proud to be in their company."

NEW YORK, WEDNESDAY, DECEMBER 8, 1948

Ryan, ILA Head, Served With Dunn, Now in Death House, on Committee for 1941 Gala Reception for Gleason

BENEFIT PERFORMANCE

At another "entertainment and reception" for the benefit and glory of the Teddy Gleason Association, held at the Palm Garden Restaurant on December 6, 1941, Joseph P. Ryan, president of the International Longshoremen's Association—with a lifetime job at $20,000 a year—again was prominently identified with some prize characters, including several whose pictures adorn the police rogues' gallery.

At this gala affair for Gleason, long identified with a checkers' union and closely associated with Ryan in the ILA, Ryan was listed in the souvenir book as a member of the arrangements committee. His cocommitteemen were John M. Dunn, ex-convict and labor racketeer, now in the death house at Sing Sing under a stay of execution for murder, and Cornelius J. Noonan, president of Dunn's local, No. 21510, Motor and Bus Terminal Checkers, Platform and Office Workers.

Dunn was also chairman of the "Journal Committee," which got up the souvenir program, a fat, impressive volume filled with congratulatory advertisements—at nice, fat rates, no doubt—from truckmen, union locals, waterfront loading gangs, restaurants, and others who were persuaded that it might be wise to keep the goodwill of Teddy Gleason and his boys.

Mob kingpin Joe Adonis and fellow mobster Salvatore Moretti surrender to charges of racketeering at the Hackensack courthouse, October 31, 1950. Both were later released on $15,000 bail. Photograph copyright © Bettmann/CORBIS.

DUNN WAS ALREADY SING SING ALUMNUS

At the time of this dinner, Dunn, already a graduate of Sing Sing, was under conviction of coercion for beating up Edward J. Kelly, hiring stevedore, at Pier 51, but had not been sentenced. This was the case, described in previous articles in this series, in which powerful influence was exerted in Dunn's behalf, that influence extending to Washington, with Army "brass" interceding in an effort to obtain Dunn's release from prison on the ground that he was important to the war effort.

At a previous Gleason dinner, in 1939, as stated in yesterday's articles, Ryan's picture was snapped in company with Dunn; Danny Gentile, convicted with Dunn of murder, and now, like Dunn, in the death house, pending a motion for a new trial; John Adams, who was vice president of Varick Enterprises, the strong-arm collection agency for the loading racket; and Barney Baker, a collector for Varick and an ex-convict.

In addition to Dunn, some of these same characters were committeemen for the 1941 dinner. Adams was on the reception committee. Serving with him were Baker, who is a stench-bomb thrower, among his other distinctions as a hoodlum; Thomas Burke, whose police record contains some twenty citations; and James Bagley, who was a collector for Varick.

Also on the reception committee were Austin Furey, who has a record of six arrests but has been convicted only of disorderly conduct; Edward Johnson, who has been arrested on such assorted charges as robbery, burglary, assault, and homicide but convicted only of third-degree assault; and, finally, Gene Sampson, a brother of Frank Sampson, former leader of Tammany Hall. Gene Sampson now is Joe Ryan's bitter enemy, and a powerful leader of the anti-Ryan faction in the ILA.

LIST OF ADVERTISERS IN SOUVENIR BOOK

Frank Sheridan, a brother of the notorious Andrew Sheridan, a gunman convicted with Dunn and Gentile in the Hintz murder, was chairman of the box committee. The boxholders included Dunn, Adams, Gentile, and a long list of other notables.

The thick, handsomely printed souvenir book lists only the committee dignitaries and boxholders, and contains, on one full page, a picture of Teddy Gleason, "our honored host." The rest of the book is devoted to advertisements from well-wishers, who were many. There are full-page advertisements from the now defunct Varick Enterprises; various union locals, including Dunn's restaurants and nightclubs; liquor dealers; union loaders of Pier 45—then, as now, a "hot pier" in rackets—and loaders at Piers 84 and 86, in the territory now controlled by the Mickey Bowers gang.

Also, full-page ads from Carmine G. De Sapio, Democratic leader of the First Assembly District; the loaders of Piers 49, 50, and 51, in the territory ruled by Dunn's mob; checkers and clerks of Pier 45; checkers and clerks of Pier 51; the Regular Democratic Club of the First Assembly District of Queens; union loaders of Pier 25 and Pier 46 and local 1261, checkers, ILA.

A number of big trucking firms also paid their compliments in full-page ads, including some of the firms that later bombarded the Parole Commission with glowing letters on behalf of Dunn when he was sentenced to prison on the coercion rap.

BAKER SOMETIMES CALLED OVERGROWN MESSENGER BOY

The record of Committeeman Robert Baker—alias Barney Baker, Big Ben, William Baker, Benny Baker, and Jew Baker—perhaps deserves a little special attention. Baker, an ex-pugilist and all-around thug, is sometimes referred to contemptuously in underworld circles as a sort of overgrown messenger boy for big-time operators.

According to detectives, Baker and Committeeman Jack Adams, the onetime Varick official, worked during the last two winter seasons as escorts or guards at the swanky Colonial Inn, the big gambling house operated in the Miami Beach area by the syndicate which controls gambling and major rackets throughout the country.

When Andy Sheridan was arrested by the FBI in Florida in connection with the murder of Anthony Hintz, a hiring stevedore, in New York in January 1947, Baker is said to have approached Joe Adonis, the racket boss and reputed member of the big underworld syndicate, in an effort to raise money for Sheridan's defense. Adonis, so the story goes, sent Baker packing, and Baker then is said to have taken his quest to Bugsy Siegel, another syndicate member, out on the West Coast. Siegel was murdered in Hollywood in the summer of 1947.

The police "yellow sheet" on Baker shows that he was sentenced on June 1, 1934, to an indefinite term in the penitentiary for setting off stench bombs in a theater. He served a year, and, after his release, he again was arrested for setting off stench bombs and sent back to the pen for an indefinite term.

He was paroled on September 17, 1935, and, while on parole, was shot and wounded on March 15, 1936, in the company of Richard Butler, who was killed; one John O'Rourke, wounded; and one Robert Sullivan, unhurt. The shooting occurred, the police said, on West Thirty-fourth Street, while Baker and his companions were parking their car. The shots were fired from another car. Baker and the others said they were unable to identify the gunmen.

RETURNED TO PRISON FOR PAROLE VIOLATION

Baker's parole was continued until April 1, 1937, when he was arrested and acquitted on a charge of assault in the third degree and then returned to prison for violation of parole. His case history shows that Baker has worked as a foreman of checkers and as a longshoreman and "collector," and that he has been a member of the Terminal Checkers and Platform Men's Local No. 1346-2, ILA, and of Local 895, ILA.

So much for Robert Baker, who served on the reception committee, the journal committee, and the entertainment committee for the Gleason dinner in 1944.

At a testimonial dinner dance for Gleason at the Hotel Commodore on April 19, 1944, the roster of guests was more impressive—in the other direction. On the dais were Alex DiBrizzi, a vice president of the ILA and a power in the union on Staten Island; Captain James J. Braddock, Army Transport Corps, former heavyweight champion of the world—this was in wartime, remember; Lieutenant Colonel Harold G. Hoffman, former governor of New Jersey; Gleason himself; Joe Ryan, James J. Walker, and several colonels from the Transportation Corps.

As noted, all kinds of people turn out for the dinners of the Joseph P. Ryan Association and the Teddy Gleason Association.

NEW YORK, THURSDAY, DECEMBER 9, 1948

Dockers Seeking to Be Honest Are Victims of Vicious Hiring System, Grafting Union Bosses, and Public Apathy

THE LONGSHOREMEN

Though organized crime is rampant on the waterfront, there are thousands of rank-and-file longshoremen who want to be honest, but can succeed only against odds almost overwhelming. These men are victimized on many counts, a condition that has existed for more than thirty years without corrective action.

The longshoremen are the victims of a vicious system of hiring which makes their employment precarious and casual, permits racketeering to flourish unchecked, and makes them the easy prey of criminals who rule the piers.

They are the victims of corrupt, grafting officials in locals of their own union, the International Longshoremen's Association, in which they have little or no voice.

Finally, they are the victims of apathy, and, worse, of public officials and businessmen who steadfastly refuse to clean up their own industry.

ANTIQUATED SHAPE-UP HELD ROOT OF EVIL

Students of the problem, in various critical studies, agree that the root of the evil is the antiquated shape-up, the method of hiring, controlled by the arbitrary whim of the hiring stevedore. In his authoritative book *The Water Front Labor Problem*, published in 1938, Monsignor Edward Swanstrom comments at length on the evils of the system: how it easily lends itself to graft and favoritism; creates and maintains a surplus labor pool, causing as many as five hundred men to appear for work where less than a hundred are to be hired; with the men gathering eagerly in a half circle on the pier, waiting to be chosen or rejected by the hiring boss.

Monsignor Swanstrom also is critical of ILA practices.

"The union has made very little effort to curtail the number of men holding union cards," he writes. "As long as a man is willing to pay the initiation fee and to continue monthly dues regularly, he can obtain admission to the union. Within the last few years occasions have arisen in which it is known that an exorbitant fee has been asked. The business agent of a particular local oftentimes raises or lowers this fee arbitrarily."

The New York Sun's own investigation bears all this out, and more. It shows that longshoremen are at the mercy of loan sharks who work in collusion with grafting ILA bosses; that the kickback, or paying for the privilege of getting a day's work, is common practice; that known criminals have captured control of some union locals, dictate policy, and place racketeers in key jobs on the piers.

DOCKER LEARNS SILENCE CARRIES ITS VALUE

Thus the individual longshoreman gets kicked around plenty. Bitter experience has taught him to be closemouthed, distrustful even of his fellow workers. He knows that if he wants to work on the piers he must bow to the system, do as he is told, and keep his mouth shut. Knowing no security, it is small wonder that he yields to the temptation of turning an easy dollar by working with racketeers. Honest men contend that they have difficulty getting work on some piers; preference is given to criminals.

On the subject of loan-sharking, one ILA informant said:

"At the pier where I work you've got to stay in debt to the loan sharks to keep working. Sometimes the union bosses just take a cut from the sharks, sometimes the bosses do the lending themselves. They charge two hundred percent. As long as you owe them money you find that you keep working. If you are ever lucky enough to pay them off, you suddenly find that you can't work until you borrow from them again."

In a bulletin issued during the recent ILA strike, the directors of Xavier Labor School excoriated the shipping industry for contributing to waterfront evils. Referring to a statement of a stevedoring official, quoted in this series in *The Sun*, to the effect that he was no reformer, that he was "in business to make money and for no other reason," the priests who head this school wrote:

"The Shipping Association fears racketeers and Communists, but does not oppose them. It will make deals with them when forced to, because it is in 'business to make money and for no other reason.'

"It makes no difference if the longshoremen are the ones caught tin the middle, as long as the Shipping Association makes money. It makes no difference if the just rights of longshoremen are violated seriously in their paychecks and work conditions. The Shipping Association is not a 'reform' movement, i.e., it is not bound to observe God's commandments of justice. God's commandments cannot interfere with 'free enterprise.'"

"CONDITIONS SPAWNED BY CRIMINAL NEGLECT"

Enlarging on this theme, the plight of the longshoremen is eloquently presented by the Reverend John M. Corridan, S.J., associate director of the Xavier Labor School, in an article in *America*, a Catholic publication.

"Racketeering and graft are not at the base of troubled conditions on the docks," states Father Corridan. "Racketeering and pilfering are merely manifestations of a condition spawned by the joint criminal neglect of the Shipping Association and the union leadership. . . . The heart of the matter is the system of hiring along the waterfront. Men are hired as if they were beasts of burden, part of the slave market of a pagan era. . . .

"The shape-up cries out against every standard of decency and justice, particularly when you consider the hundreds of millions of dollars spent on docks, shipping and harbor improvements. This degrading system of hiring was condemned as antiquated by Mayor Mitchel's Committee on Employment as far back as 1916. It is a waterlogged relic of the clipper ships when the first anyone knew of a ship's arrival was the cry of the shore watch."

Pointing out that other great ports have long since adopted the hiring hall as a solution to the problem, Father Corridan argues that there must be some regulation of waterfront employment and that present legal difficulties to the hiring hall, as contained in the Taft-Hartley Act, should be removed by the new Congress. There must be a closed shop to solve the problem of casual labor, and hiring must be done through central bodies, he says.

STATISTICS PROVE OCCUPATION HAZARDOUS

In addition to all the other problems inherent in the nature of his work, the longshoreman's occupation is hazardous. According to the Bureau of Labor Statistics, in 1942 more than 138 longshoremen experienced disabling work injuries in the course of every million employee hours of work performed. No other industry for which injury frequency is available had a record even approaching this figure, the report states.

The report shows that a longshoreman has one chance in five hundred of being killed or completely disabled for life, one in forty of suffering permanent physical injury, and one in four of losing thirty-four days because of temporary injury.

The danger and uncertainty of his work has a demoralizing effect on the longshoreman's family and corrodes his character, Father Corridan states.

"If you would blame him," he says, "then you should blast the system that produces him. Living from hand to mouth can do something to a man's idea of fairness. One's ideas of justice fade where injustice is rampant. . . .

"If a longshoreman can't keep straight and yet can't make good at a racket, drink comes easy. He succumbs to the loan sharks and the installment hawks. To get himself out of their clutches he needs to make a 'killing.' He'll despise the chance of a steady income for the big chance to clear himself at once. . . ."

All of these things—often tragic things—are part of the story of crime on the waterfront.

NEW YORK, FRIDAY, DECEMBER 10, 1948

State Action to End Shape-Up; Federal Inquiry or Dewey-Named Prosecutor Urged to Support City Cleanup

It will take more than vigorous police action and successful prosecution to end crime on the waterfront. Such action is necessary, but the problem goes much deeper than that, and it will not be solved until its basic causes are removed. Those causes are the system of hiring and certain other unhealthy practices in which apparently both the union and the employers are at fault.

These are among the inescapable conclusions to be drawn from the facts presented in this series of articles, and from previous investigations, reports, and studies dating over many years.

The Sun's articles have shown that organized crime has invoked a reign of terror on the waterfront. The city's piers are controlled by gangsters who rule with guns and goon squads. Their criminal activity is costing millions of dollars annually and is driving business to other ports.

Some of these gangsters have been named and their methods of operation described in detail. It has been shown that they dominate all the lucrative rackets on the piers and that no pier is immune from these rackets. It has been shown the gangsters are operating through the International Longshoremen's Association, the AFL union that controls dock labor. Known criminals, in some instances, have captured union locals and hold official positions in them.

POLICE ALONE CANNOT EFFECT LASTING CURE

By controlling the hiring and designating their men in key jobs, the racketeers maintain their power and their rackets without serious interference. These conditions exist today, and have existed for more than thirty years. Nothing much has ever been done about it.

Mayor O'Dwyer has ordered an investigation and the police are acting. But the police alone cannot effect a lasting cure. If, with luck and diligence, they could rout all the criminals tomorrow, the remedy would be only temporary. In time, other gangs just as viciously efficient would be ruling the waterfront. For the police cannot dictate the hiring. The ILA, under the stubborn, autocratic leadership of Joe Ryan, does that.

Example: After a notorious waterfront criminal had been released from prison, the police tried in vain to keep him off the docks. They warned steamship operators and contracting stevedores of his record and advised them not to hire him; that he would inevitably resume his terrorism. He was hired. The union forced it, and the employers felt there was nothing they could do about it.

There are other contributing factors to crime on the waterfront. They are political timidity, public apathy, self-interest on the part of both union and employers, reluctance on the part of racket victims to press complaints for fear of reprisal. Moreover, experience has proved conclusively that organized crime cannot exist in any city without a weak police department, a complacent police department, or a conniving police department.

SHAPE-UP HELD KEY TO WATERFRONT EVILS

In the present situation, however, the police can arrest and the district attorney can prosecute, but they cannot eliminate the shape-up, the system of hiring that has been denounced by competent authorities for years.

"The shape-up is the key to the New York waterfront," says the report of the Citizens Water Front Committee, published in 1946. "Every ill and every social waste on the docks sustains itself through the shape-up. No matter with what abuse or social problem one is concerned, invariably the shape-up appears as the crucial factor nourishing the whole system along. It is the bane of the casual employment of the longshoremen."

The Citizens Water Front Committee, a distinguished group headed by William Jay Schiefelin, presented a valuable and comprehensive report of the evils besetting the waterfront, touching on the alliance of crime and politics, condemning practices of the ILA and of the employers, and citing numerous abuses, aside from gangsterism. It described conditions as "shameful and unworthy of the great city of New York" and called for corrective action from the mayor and other city officials; the governor of New York, local and state officials of New Jersey, the ILA, shipowners, business and civic leaders. Nothing was done about it.

Through the shape-up, by which men are hired or rejected at the whim of a hiring boss, it is possible for criminal gangs to place their own men in key jobs on the piers, thus solidifying their rule. Why, then, is the shape-up continued in the face of unanimous condemnation by students of the problem?

TWO REASONS ARE CITED FOR RETAINING SHAPE-UP

Two reasons are cited: From the standpoint of the employers, and the New York Shipping Association, it provides a continuous surplus labor pool, available at any time at no cost to them. From the standpoint of the ILA, it enables the union to control the men through fear of not working. Thus, the men are easy prey for the racketeers and corrupt union bosses.

District Attorney Hogan and others have castigated the shipowners for not assuming more responsibility in cleaning up the situation. There is no doubt that they could do more than they are doing. But they fear to oppose the ILA, because the union can tie up the docks and their ships. And they have shown a reluctance to do anything that does not directly affect them.

All indications are that the steamship lines could eliminate the loading racket, or at least help in that direction, by assuming jurisdiction of the loading operations themselves—setting the rates and hiring the men. That was recommended as far back as 1933. Nothing was done about it.

The late mayor La Guardia didn't do anything about it, either, though he promised to do so. But when complaints came to some of his aides, they wouldn't touch it with a ten-foot pole when they found that a powerful union was involved. Politicians generally have displayed notable reluctance in this respect. As the Little Flower himself might have expressed it in one of his shrill radio broadcasts: Do you get it? Understand? It's politics. P-o-l-i-t-i-c-s!

COST OF RACKETS PAID BY PUBLIC AS USUAL

A trade official put his finger on a sore spot when he quoted Joe Ryan as saying: "It takes two to make a racket; the man who collects a racket fee and the man who pays one."

Added the official: "I don't often agree with anything Joe Ryan says, but he's got something there."

The answer, or course, is that those who pay racket charges are able to pass them on to somebody else. The money doesn't come out of their pockets so they regard it all as a "necessary evil." In the end, the public pays, as usual.

How, then, can waterfront crime be eliminated and the efficiency of the port improved? Several remedial measures have been suggested.

If the ILA and the employers persist in refusing to end the shape-up, District Attorney Hogan urges that the state legislature could do it.

Other obvious steps would be for the ILA to clean its own house of racketeering elements and for the shippers to assume jurisdiction over the property they rent. Judging from the past, no such action is likely.

It is suggested that only federal intervention in some way will provide a lasting solution. In this connection, the Xavier Labor School, which has made a special study of the waterfront, advocates that a federal commission of inquiry be set up to investigate the entire problem.

"There is no better time than the present," say the directors of this school, "while the Marshall Plan shipments keep shipping artificially high. The good of the longshoremen of the Port of New York and national safety demands it.

"In past emergencies, the Federal Government has stepped in, e.g., the Industrial Commission (1898), the Monetary Commission (1912), the Newlands Committee (1912), the Pujo Committee (1913), the Public Utilities Investigation (1928), the National Bituminous Commission (1939). The docks are in need of a long, searching, exhaustive investigation. Here is an industry that is critical in time of peace and absolutely necessary in time of war."

COMBINED ACTION HELD TO BE VITAL NECESSITY

Because the docks present a citywide problem, involving the jurisdiction of the several district attorneys, it also has been suggested that Governor Dewey might step in by appointing a special prosecutor to investigate the entire waterfront.

In the meantime, high hopes are expressed that the current investigation ordered by the mayor will do the job. It enlists the cooperation of the police, the Department of Investigation, and the district attorney.

Certainly, combined action is needed—action aided by citizens affected who are willing to make complaints and to back those complaints with testimony.

The Sun is aware that within the scope of this series it has not begun to tell the entire story of crime on the waterfront. The whole truth would reveal conditions far worse in details than those described. Since publication of the series began, however, this newspaper has been flooded with voluntary information on waterfront evils. This information is being investigated and may produce other stories from time to time.

Rank-and-file longshoremen have volunteered leads and have indicated that they are eager to see the present situation cleaned up. They have attested to the accuracy of the series, but said they wanted to see the whole story told.

NEW YORK FACES PERIL OF BEING "COBWEB PORT"

Crime on the waterfront *can* be eliminated. It can be eliminated by relentless police action, backed by the wholehearted support of the district attorneys, the mayor, and other city and state officials. It can be eliminated with the public-spirited support of trade associations, the New York Shipping Association, honest union labor representatives, merchants and truckmen, and other interested citizens.

If crime on the waterfront is eliminated, it will improve the efficiency of this port and prevent the needless waste of millions of dollars annually and of manpower. It will give rank-and-file longshoremen the opportunity to earn a decent, honorable living, bring increased prosperity to the world's greatest shipping center, and keep this port from becoming "cobweb port," as Mayor O'Dwyer has described other ports where unhealthy conditions have persisted. Unless crime on the waterfront is eliminated, the Port of New York is in grave danger of becoming a cobweb port.

PART TWO

CRIME ON THE WATERFRONT

The Cause and the Remedy

NEW YORK, MONDAY, JANUARY 24, 1949

Shape-Up Enables Gangsters to Rule Piers—Hiring Hall Advanced for Control

---

The New York Sun's recent series of articles, "Crime on the Waterfront," showed that the entire harbor is dominated by racketeers and gangsters and that the key to this gangster rule is the International Longshoremen's Association, the AFL union that controls dock labor. It was shown that control of the piers by criminal elements is made possible through the present system of hiring: the shape-up.

As a sequel to "Crime on the Waterfront," *The Sun* presents, beginning today, a new series suggesting a solution to the problem by eliminating the shape-up and substituting the hiring hall system for it.

As stated in the previous series, successful prosecution alone will not end crime on the waterfront. The present situation poses a grave social and economic problem, and the police, the district attorney, and the other local authorities cannot cope with it. *The Sun*'s principal concern was, and is, to promote a thorough investigation of employment practices on the docks, with remedial legislation as the goal.

SENSIBLE CONTROL SEEN IN USE OF HIRING HALLS

A definite conclusion was reached in the other series: the need for some sensible control of work opportunities on the piers so as (1) to regularize the longshoremen's work; (2) eliminate the possibility of costly criminal activities; (3) permit the shipping industry to operate on a more stable and efficient basis; (4) give needed relief to the shippers of goods; and (5) bring peace and order to an area in which the public has a vital interest.

That sensible control is in the use of hiring halls or some system of registration of longshoremen and rotation of work. The irregular demands of shipping for dockworkers could be coordinated with a controlled supply of longshoremen in such a way as to meet the needs of both. The longshoremen would get work and regular work. Shipping companies would have an adequate, efficient workforce, not the chaotic supply they now have.

In this new series, *The Sun* will explain what the hiring hall is and how it operates, and present the arguments, for and against it, from the standpoint of the employers, the union, and the longshoremen themselves. It will be shown that the entire industry, and the public as well, would benefit from the hiring hall.

ILA HEADED BY RYAN MODEL FOR DICTATORSHIP

Future articles also will prove that the International Longshoremen's Association, as now constituted, is a model for dictatorship, and that the present director, Joseph P. Ryan, is the lifetime president, at $20,000 a year. These charges will be proved by a detailed analysis of the ILA constitution, the history of the union, its conventions and contracts. It will be shown that the Ryan rule does not always promote the welfare of the union members, and that many of the acts of the union leadership are, in reality, antiunion and antilabor.

It will be shown, further, that except through a series of strikes or threats of strikes, directed against the ILA leadership as much as against the New York Shipping Association, the employing group, the longshoremen are unable to help themselves measurably because of their union's laws and the practices of the entrenched leadership concerned only with maintaining its power.

In explaining the hiring hall system in detail, it will be pointed out how rackets now spawned by the shape-up could be eliminated in time by vigorous, honest police action if the shape-up is abolished. The evils of the shape-up will be described.

INVITATION TO COMMUNISTS TO TAKE OVER CONTROL

As matters now stand, the Port of New York, the greatest in the world, is losing valuable business. Shippers are diverting cargo to other ports where they do not run the risk of racketeering costs peculiar to New York. The unstable, high-cost structure of shipping here is a threat to the industry and to all who depend for their livelihood upon the industry.

The public welfare is subjected to the threat of continual strikes that arise out of these chaotic conditions where the law of the jungle prevails. What is even more serious, the present setup, with its discontent, misery, and strife, is an invitation for the communists to assume control of the situation, thereby endangering national defense.

Subsequent articles will indicate by what positive steps the states or the federal government, or both, could substantially correct the dangerous conditions on the docks. It is the intention of *The Sun* to direct this entire series to the attention of the members of the legislatures of New York and New Jersey, and to the representatives and senators from both states, to civic associations, private groups, and prominent citizens in the metropolitan area.

INVESTIGATION BY CITY IS NOW IN PROGRESS

Right now a citywide investigation, prompted by *The Sun*'s recent series, is in progress. It remains to be seen what this investigation will produce, whether any concrete results will be achieved. In all likelihood, however, it can come to only one constructive conclusion; namely, to recommend New York State legislative action.

In addition, the city could require, as a condition for leasing its piers, that the steamship companies assume responsibility for the loading and unloading of trucks, thereby eliminating a costly racket.

New district attorney Frank S. Hogan (*left*) takes the oath of office, while former DA and future governor Thomas E. Dewey (*center*) stands as witness, with Judge George L. Donellan (*right*) administering. Hogan and Dewey would soon team up to investigate the waterfront and longshoremen. Photograph copyright © Bettmann/CORBIS.

To date the city has not done so. But even if the city did, it still could not get at the heart of the problem: the system of hiring.

SIX ESSENTIAL FACTS PRESENTED IN SERIES

In presenting this new series, *The Sun* starts with six facts:

1. Other ports in the world have long since abandoned the shape-up system of hiring and introduced a system of registering longshoremen and rotating their work, operating usually through the joint efforts of the union, employers, and governmental agencies. London did it in 1891, Hamburg in 1906, Liverpool in 1911, Rotterdam in 1916, Antwerp in 1929, Seattle in 1921, Los Angeles in 1922, Portland, Oregon, in 1923, San Francisco in 1934. Thus, New York could benefit from the experience of other ports.

2. A system of registration and a plan for rotation of work as the remedy for New York's waterfront troubles was recommended by:

(a) Mayor's Committee on Unemployment, "Report on Dock Employment in New York City and Recommendations for Its Regularization," New York, October 1946.

(b) New York State, Joint Legislative Committee on Unemployment (Legislative Document No. 69, 1932), "Preliminary Report," February 15, 1932; "Report" (Legislative Document No. 65, 1933), February 20, 1933.

3. The present high hourly rate—$1.99 straight time—the vacation and welfare benefits, together with the increased tempo of criminal activities, do not permit further temporizing or palliative measures.

HOGAN HAS CALLED FOR LEGISLATIVE ACTION

4. After years of investigating crime on the waterfront, District Attorney Frank S. Hogan of New York County has publicly stated

that "the representatives of the people in the State Legislature should take remedial action."

5. Prominent members of both legislatures in New York and New Jersey have endorsed this statement by Hogan: "My feeling about the longshoremen's problem in New York is that it has gotten too big for the local authorities and that the matter should be investigated by the Attorney-General of the State of New York and, after full investigation, recommendations should be made to the State Legislature to pass laws to solve the problem."

6. The steamship interests and the union leadership obviously are unwilling to attack the problem by themselves. Perhaps they could be so persuaded, if the legislatures of New York and New Jersey or the Congress of the United States proposed concrete, constructive measures after a thorough investigation. Competent governmental agencies could get at the problem if so directed by those legislatures through enactment of appropriate laws.

NEW YORK, TUESDAY, JANUARY 25, 1949

Crime and Heartbreak Bred by Shape-Up System on Docks in City

FERTILE FIELD FOR RACKETS

Outmoded Hiring Method Keeps Longshoremen in Grip of Hunger and Fear

---

New York longshoremen know all about the heartbreak and the degradation resulting from the shape-up, the obsolete hiring system still practiced on the docks here and stubbornly defended by the bosses of the International Longshoremen's Association and the shipping interests.

For a picture of the shape-up as it once existed in London, read what Henry Mayhew wrote in 1861 in *London Labor and the London Poor*:

"He who wishes to behold one of the most extraordinary and least-known scenes of this metropolis should wend his way to the London Dock gates at half past seven in the morning. There he will see congregated within the principal entrance masses of men of all grades, looks and kinds. . . . Presently you know, by the stream pouring through the gates and the rush toward particular spots, that the 'calling foremen' have made their appearance. Then begins the scuffling and scrambling forth of countless hands high in the air, to catch the eyes of him whose voice may give them work. As the foreman calls from a book of names, some men jump on the backs of others, so as to lift themselves high above the rest, and attract the notice of him who hires them. All are shouting. Some cry aloud his surname, some his Christian name, others call out their surnames, to remind him that they are there."

"A SIGHT TO SADDEN THE MOST CALLOUS"

"Now the appeal is made in Irish blarney—now in broken English. Indeed, it is a sight to sadden the most callous, to see thousands of men struggling for only one day's hire, the scuffle being made the fiercer by the knowledge that hundreds out of the number there assembled must be left to idle the day out in want. To look in the faces of that hungry crowd is to see a sight that must be ever remembered. Some are smiling to the foreman to coax him into remembrance of them; others, with their protruding eyes, eager to snatch for the hoped-for pass. For weeks many have gone there, and gone through the same struggle, the same cries; and have gone away, after all, without the work they had screamed for."

That was London in 1861. London abolished the shape-up in 1891. But not New York. In the 1930s, in the middle of the Depression here, when good men were going hungry and begging for work, five hundred men lined up in a semicircle in front of a pier, hoping for jobs. A ship was in, the first ship in ten weeks.

A new hiring boss came out, a hundred brass checks in his hand. The men pressed forward eagerly. The new hiring boss took one look at their anxious, desperate faces and lost his nerve. He threw the hundred brass checks into the air.

Five hundred men fought one another like animals for a hundred brass checks and a half day's work. That's your shape-up in New York, the greatest port in the world, and this is the twentieth century.

POWER OF HIRING BOSS IS ALMOST ABSOLUTE

What difference does it make if the hiring boss calls out the names of the lucky ones or tosses the brass checks into the crowd? The hiring boss's power of giving a half day's work is almost absolute. He himself is subject to many pressures. Hiring bosses are usually dictated by delegates of the ILA locals, despite contract provisions to the contrary. Between the two, the kickback racket can be worked, and is, by some. Many a man who is not a longshoreman can get a couple of fat days on the docks for a slight consideration or at the nod of a ward boss. A union book can be had without joining the union. That such men and those who connive with them are depriving longshoremen of their daily bread doesn't bother them.

In some parts of the port, particularly among the Italians, the gang foreman collects the pay of the men and takes his cut out of their envelopes. When men collect their own pay, tribute can easily be exacted on an individual basis. "Voluntary contributions" are solicited by the mob representatives on many of the piers. There is little pretense about this racket. The longshoremen recognize it for what it is. They pay off on payday for the benefit of the "boys."

Why should the public be concerned about such vicious practices? Because "the number of criminals operating on the waterfront is a direct result of the shape-up system." So said District Attorney Frank S. Hogan in this paper on December 6. And what is their take a year? Fifty million in organized thievery. Millions more in the loading racket, $200,000 in loan-sharking of longshoremen, in addition to payroll padding, bookmaking, policy, smuggling, and any other illegal enterprises that come to hand.

How responsible are these criminals, together with the union leadership, for the men rising up with the only weapon that they have, the strike weapon? Are they, together with the leadership, giving the communists their chance to seize control of the world's largest port by winning over the exploited longshoremen?

SHAPE-UP SPAWNS CRIME ALONG WATERFRONT

The shape-up spawns crime. For the police and district attorney to try to stop crime, as long as the shape-up is tolerated, is like trying to block a bursting dam with a pair of hands. The shape-up keeps the men both hungry and begging for work from hands of hundreds of hiring bosses. A combination of fear and avarice grips the industry. No one will speak or testify in a system in which retaliation is often swift and drastic.

The whole system has political overtones. All the men's thinking and actions revolve around protecting whatever work opportunities they have at the moment. In such a jungle setup, it's easy for a gang to move in and take over.

The gangs cannot be touched until they are caught, prosecuted, and convicted of criminal activities. It is rare that they are so unfortunate as to be trapped in this triple set of circumstances. When they are, another gang can move in and take over. District Attorney Hogan said: "The shape-up is the root of the evil. I think it is a system which spawns criminal activities so regularly that the State Legislature might legally abolish it."

GRAPHIC PICTURE DRAWN BY CATHOLIC PRIEST

A graphic picture of the New York waterfront was drawn by a Catholic priest. In his column, "Don Capellano," in the *Labor Leader* for December 27, 1948, he wrote:

"The present West Side dock is a jungle; a matted growth of good trade unionism with graft and sabotage. In the open—families. In the undercover—beasts of prey. Some children of the old Irish dockers are still there, good but poorer than their fathers in spirit and in profession. Every people under heaven mingles in the daily shape-up and some of them look spit up from hell. Every one in the shape-up is coarsened by the all-covering racket which operates by the connivance of management, labor leaders, politicians and policemen. The saloons now are hangouts where the men talk from the side of the mouth about deals, cut-ins and dames. Shifty eyes X-ray the stranger at the bar. In these saloons men drink to watch, to wait or to forget.

"In and out of this jungle slink men, bodily different, face shaped the same. The young wolf-eyed, the old rat-faced. These men don't fight; they hunt in packs and kill in the dark. They kill for the racket, for the slick, softening brains who often eat at Cavanaugh's and sometimes pass the exclusive barriers of the Downtown Athletic Club.

"All this, and much hateful more, shames today's children of the men from Cork and the West of Ireland. The men I knew would have killed with their bare hands those suckers who bleed and feed upon the muscles of the longshoremen today.

"The old-timers from Cork and West of Ireland are not altogether dead. They have sons: priests and judges, district attorneys and policemen in New York. Let these men lift their heads and remember the decency of their fathers.

"The Mayor of New York, better than most, knows the story of the Judases who sold out the workers. He is kin to the old-timers who split their bodies on the docks for greedy Scotch and English shippers, forty years ago. These docks may well be the stumbling block of his political hopes. There was never a secret that involved more than one. There are no political secrets on the docks today."

NEW YORK, WEDNESDAY, JANUARY 26, 1949

Hiring Hall Is Substitute for Reign of Terror Under Shape-Up

WOULD CURB PRESENT BOSSES

Centralized Job Centers Would Be Run by Union, Shippers, and Agents of Public

---

For the shape-up, the present general system of hiring on the docks of New York, with its reign of terror, there is a tried, decent substitute. That substitute is the hiring hall arrangement.

Hiring halls in longshoring would make all hiring bosses walking bosses, with no powers of economic life and death such as they now have. It could cut off the graft and rackets at their source. Centralized places run jointly by representatives of union, employers, and public could distribute work evenly and fairly.

New entries into longshoring could be controlled by a joint board of union and employer representatives. The regular gangs would go to work on radio instructions and without reporting to the hall. Those not in regular gangs would go to one place where all jobs are reported in. There would be no turning out at the entrance of piers in the rain and in the snow. There would be no bitter disappointment to swallow at not finding work at one pier, only to learn later that work could have been had at another if the men had known.

No longshoreman would lose out in the hiring halls. The only ones who would lose out would be the grafting union officials and their crooked satellites. They'd lose their vested interest in keeping the men afraid and hungry and begging for work. Under the hiring hall, they'd have to go to work, or go elsewhere.

HIRING HALL BASED ON SOUND PRINCIPLES

As applied to casual work like longshoring, the hiring hall is based on the following sound principles:

1. The number of men allowed to enter longshoring is limited so that the majority of the men can make substantial earnings in a year's time. If the number of men is too great to begin with, as it is under the present chaotic system of hiring, no more men would be accepted until the surplus disappears. Deaths, accidents, and men quitting longshoring bring about that reduction. When more men are needed, the industry at first issues only permits until the industry is sure it can offer something like regular work. The longshoremen understand this principle and want it. The leadership of the union, the International Longshoremen's Association, understands it but won't want it until the men, and public opinion, as mirrored in legislation, forces them to accept it.

2. All hiring is done through the hiring hall. Employers have to call in their work by afternoon for the following day. The record of all those working on a given day has to be sent into the hiring hall on the same day. These records are necessary for the equal division of work. Special arrangements as to time are made in scheduling extra afternoon or evening work.

The gangs and the men are rotated to the same companies as much as possible. Some longshoremen put in years working on one pier or for one company. Unfortunately, they have no seniority rights. At the time of union elections—where they are held—they can be knocked off the pier by younger men out of work in the interests of a union delegate's reelection.

EQUAL DIVISION OF WORK AND ROTATION ASSURED

3. There is rotation and equal division of work among the registered longshoremen. Regular gangs get work first. Over three

months' time, hours of work come out about the same for all gangs. One hour overtime is counted as one and one-half hours' straight time. Work on munitions is computed on the same basis as far as work time is concerned. All get equal opportunity to get their hours in on this basis. At present East Coast rates, a straight forty-hour week is worth $75.20. With rotation and equal division of work, all the regular gangs in New York could be kept as regular gangs. The average gang, then, would make substantially more in a year's time than the average gang makes now. There wouldn't be roving gangs hogging all the work. Gangs that work at specialties, such as bananas and lumber, would stick to their specialties. All but the greedy longshoremen would go for such an arrangement. The greedy longshoremen are a fraction of 1 percent. You meet that kind in every walk of life.

4. Extra men are the only men to check in for work. The members of the regular gangs would get their work calls over the radio, or by phone, or by coming in and looking at the board for regular gangs. Extra men would check in the type of work they want, including specialties. They would report to the hiring hall, and there the jobs would be called out in the time order in which the men checked in. The advantage of the hiring hall over the shape-up is that all jobs have to come into one place and called out on a first come, first served basis. Extra men would move into regular gangs on a seniority basis when there is an opening, and if a man wants to work in a regular gang.

5. The labor relations committee of each hiring hall—a joint committee of union and employer representatives—sets the weekly port hours based on the amount of shipping expected for the coming week. All the registered longshoremen at a given section, regular and extra, must get work before the special "permit" men or men from other sections are put to work.

AT LEAST FIVE HALLS WOULD BE NEEDED HERE

For the successful operation of a decent hiring hall in a port as large as New York, there probably would have to be at lest five hiring halls in five sections: two in Manhattan, one each for the West Side and the East Side; two in Brooklyn, one each for the Columbia Heights and Bush Terminal sections of Brooklyn; and one for New Jersey.

Under such a setup it would be absolutely essential to have a neutral and competent party to help handle the mechanical details of the hiring halls. There is such a competent, neutral third party in the State Employment Service. It could operate the hiring halls under rules negotiated by the ILA and the New York Shipping Association, in consultation with the State Employment Service.

Such an arrangement would have a decided advantage for all parties. The state could tackle at first hand the unemployment insurance problems presented by casual longshore labor. The longshoremen would be benefited by a system in which they would have confidence, and by a simplified and uniform procedure in applying for unemployment insurance, total or partial.

HUE AND CRY EXPECTED FROM DOCK MOBSTERS

The union and the shipping association would be assured of uniform operation of all the hiring halls and would be rid of an administrative headache. The expenses of operating the halls could be shared by all parties.

Such are the general principles under which hiring halls could be set up here. Details and safeguards for efficient and honest operation could be worked out and negotiated after a thorough investigation and study of the entire problem.

Oh, yes, Joe Ryan, the president of the ILA, and mobsters in control of the waterfront, can be expected to set up a hue and cry to the effect that "an awful lot of people would be hurt by this." The only ones to be hurt will be "the boys" now bleeding the port of millions of dollars through their organized rackets. In one stroke, the longshoremen can be rid of the competition of too many men seeking work on the docks, of having to keep in favor with hundreds of arbitrary hiring bosses, and of the fear of Joe Ryan and his stooges.

The shippers, steamship companies, and contracting stevedores, the police and the public would reap immense benefits from a commonsense system that would bring peace and order and destroy the present jungle setup.

NEW YORK, THURSDAY, JANUARY 27, 1949

Shippers Prefer Shape-Up Because System Provides Labor Pool at No Cost

It is difficult to get from the New York Shipping Association, representing the employers on the waterfront, any real information about work practices and general conditions on the docks here. They are reluctant to talk. Their arrogant attitude seems to be that the public is not entitled to know anything about their waterfront operations; that it is none of the public's business.

In general, however, the Shipping Association is opposed to the hiring hall as a substitute for the shape-up, the present system of hiring, despite all its waste and inefficiency and demonstrable evils. Stripped of a lot of verbiage, the shippers' defense of the shape-up, as stated privately through the years, boils down to this: It enables them to maintain a big surplus labor pool at no cost to them. The shippers are afraid of disturbing the status quo. They say, in effect: "Don't rock the boat," even though the boat is leaking and sinking.

AFRAID OF TROUBLE TYING UP SHIPPING

Actually, the employers here fear change because they know that the archaic union leadership in the International Longshoremen's Association is opposed to any change. The employers are mortally afraid of "causing trouble," and change might cause trouble, might induce the ILA to pull work stoppages on the piers, thus tying up the ships and the investments of the owners,

They feel that, moreover, they can deal with the present leadership of the ILA, as typified in the blustering Joe Ryan, the lifetime president, at $20,000 a year, ruling with the powers of a dictator.

They always have in the past, and Joe, for the most part, has succeeded in keeping the men in line.

Nevertheless, there is a real industrial relations problem on the New York waterfront, and both the union and the shippers know it. That problem is how to coordinate the irregular demands of shipping for dockworkers with the regulated supply of longshoremen in such a way to meet the needs of both shipping and longshoremen.

POOL OF LABOR NEEDED TO HANDLE PEAK PERIODS

The work of loading and unloading ships is subject to frequent fluctuations, to some extent uncontrollable. The causes are natural, economic, and political.

In the first category, the arrival and departure of ships may be held up by tide or weather. However, as far as longshoring goes nowadays, airmail and ship-to-shore radio communications have made possible the exact planning and timing of loading and unloading work.

Economic causes include the foreign trade cycle; the competition of rail and trucks in intercoastal and coastal shipping; harbor facilities, such as pier and loft space; and rail and trucking accommodations.

Political causes include subsidies to the merchant marine, foreign and domestic export and import programs, and the war factor potential.

Thus, each shipping company is faced with the problem of how to draw on a pool of labor to handle its peak periods of loading and unloading. The peak periods of the various companies do not coincide. The shipping companies can follow one of two policies:

1. Each company can build up its own reserve, and you have the shape-up.
2. All the companies can draw on a common reserve, and you have the hiring hall.

New York has the shape-up.

COMPANIES' ARGUMENTS AND ANSWERS THERETO

Here are some of the arguments advanced by company representatives in behalf of the shape-up and the answers to those arguments:

ARGUMENT: "People who attack the shape-up don't know what they are talking about," said one leading shipping representative.

ANSWER: Sociologists, economists, and serious students of labor—all authorities in their fields—have, after thorough investigation, condemned the shape-up here and in other ports. Their reports now are regarded as standard references.

ARGUMENT: Companies say they are satisfied with the present arrangement.

ANSWER: Why should the companies be satisfied with an arrangement in which an estimated 60 percent of their costs are attributable to handling goods from dock to ship to dock, and 10½ percent due to operating and rising insurance costs as a result of grand-scale pilferage? The remaining 29½ percent of the costs go to fuel, wages, and maintenance of the seamen and repairs of ships. If the government granted subsidies on the basis of efficiency, would the companies be as easily satisfied?

NEW YORK COULD CHOOSE BEST OTHER PORTS OFFER

ARGUMENT: "No one has proposed a better system," says H. C. Stevenson, chairman of the board of the National Association of Stevedores, as reported in *The New York Sun* on December 13, 1948.

ANSWER: London, Hamburg, Liverpool, Rotterdam, Antwerp, Seattle, Los Angeles, Portland, Oregon, and San Francisco long ago abandoned the shape-up and turned to a system of registration and rotation of work; that is, the hiring hall. Neither the employers nor the union leadership nor the longshoremen in those ports would go back to the wild, wasteful days of the shape-up. New York could choose from the best that the other ports have to offer. New York would not have to pioneer.

ARGUMENT: "We admit that there are things wrong with the shape-up, but will changing it to something else eliminate the loan-shark and kickback rackets?"

ANSWER: Working a kickback out of hiring halls with thousands of men employed would be a great deal more difficult than where the same men would have to line up before hundreds of hiring bosses and compete for work with those who are not longshoremen and some who have serious criminal records. Under the hiring hall, with the average longshoreman's wages substantially higher and more evenly distributed, with the aid of the present welfare fund and improvements, loan-sharking would be dealt a body blow.

SHAPE-UP GAVE BIRTH TO LOADING RACKETS

ARGUMENT: "I don't see how the shape-up has anything to do with the loading rackets and truck operations."

ANSWER: The shape-up with its swollen surpluses of casual labor gave the loading and unloading rackets their birth. If the shipping companies would assume their former responsibilities, uniform rates for services rendered would end the loading and unloading rackets.

ARGUMENT: "A hiring hall would serve to cut down efficiency and create accidents. Gangs work for years as teams under the shape-up system."

ANSWER: Gangs are more permanent under the hiring hall than under the shape-up. In so far as work is more evenly distributed and more regular under the hiring hall, there are many more regular gangs than in the shape-up. When men know that they will have steady work year in and year out and don't have to eke out an existence under a system of gross favoritism and fear, they are more careful workers. Excessive hours worked at times in the shape-up are not tolerated in the hiring hall. All these factors make for a lower accident rate in the hiring hall arrangement. On the subject of accidents, a government report in 1944 has this to say:

"The New York Code (A Maritime Safety Code for Stevedoring and Freight Handling Operations), 1939, was widely distributed in the East among the employing stevedores. Its application, however, is entirely voluntary, and at the time this survey was made it was found that comparatively few of the officers contacted had a copy on hand or knew what the code provisions were."

NEW YORK, FRIDAY, JANUARY 28, 1949

Shippers and Dockers at Odds Over What Hiring Hall Would Do to Pay Rates

In their opposition to the hiring hall and their defense of the shape-up, the present system of hiring on New York docks, the representatives of the New York Shipping Association, the employer group, argue that, among other things, a hiring hall makes elimination of the unfit difficult.

Well, it's hard to believe that the shape-up, with its hellish mixture of irregular work, favoritism, terror, kickbacks, padded payrolls, and gangsterism, produces fit men. The shape-up cries out against every standard of decency; it is a system under which men are hired like beasts of burden, the men gathering in a half circle at a pier, twice a day, waiting to be accepted or rejected at the whim of a hiring boss.

1909 LIVERPOOL REPORT FITS NEW YORK TODAY

A report written in 1909 on the shape-up on the Liverpool docks fits New York today to a T:

"Everything about the shape-up system of employment seems to foster the formation of bad habits and nothing to encourage the formation of good ones. The alterations of hard work and of idleness disincline the men to steady exertion. The uncertainty of earnings encourage concealment from the wife and by accustoming the family to existence at the standard of bad weeks sets the surplus of good ones free for self-indulgence. The fluctuations of income make the problem of housekeeping impossibly difficult for most of the women, and the consequent discomfort and privations of the home drive the man to the public house, wear out the health, the spirit, and the self-respect of the woman, and injure the health and happiness of the children.

"The consciousness that no certificate of character will be asked and that prolonged absence from the dock on a drinking bout will not perceptibly lessen the chance for employment on reapplication removes all the natural checks and penalties which in other professions do so much to keep the average men straight.

"The haphazard method of selection and the dependence of the men on the good will of the foreman encourages petty corruption and tyranny and lowers the tone of self-respect of the employed." (Report of the Liverpool Joint Research Committee, "How Casual Labor Lives," Liverpool, the Northern Publishing Company, 1909, page 26.)

Liverpool abandoned the shape-up and substituted the hiring hall arrangement in 1911, but New York still has the shape-up, and still defends it.

EMPLOYERS' ARGUMENT REVERSED BY UNION

The employers here also argue that after a period of years the hiring hall system might make the labor supply tight; that the men would take advantage of this, demand raises in wages, and thus increase labor costs.

Answer: This objection has been given all through the years by the employers. It was given when the longshoremen were making 30 cents an hour. It's still given when the straight rate, under the recent contract, is $1.88 an hour, and the premium rate is $2.82 an hour, and attracting still more men to the already crowded labor market on the docks.

Ironically, the union leadership uses an exactly opposite argument in defending continuation of the shape-up. The leadership of the International Longshoremen's Association, AFL, insists that the rate would be cut under the hiring hall. At the same time, the ILA leaders refuse to close the membership books of the union, but continue to pick up all the extra initiation fees and dues that the traffic will bear, without paying any benefits to the members.

WEST COAST PAY HIGHER UNDER THE HIRING HALL

On the West Coast, under the hiring hall arrangement, the men receive six cents an hour less than East Coast men. The last two hours of the eight-hour day, between 8 A.M. and 5 P.M., however, are paid at the premium rate, whereas on the East Coast the men receive straight time for these hours.

The average annual wage of the registered longshoremen on the West Coast is substantially higher than the average annual wage in New York. Yet the West Coast employers prefer the hiring hall system to the shape-up, and so do the West Coast longshoremen who have worked under both: Joe Ryan, the ILA president, and Harry Bridges, the West Coast leader.

All industrial experience indicates that a more regularly employed workforce is more efficient and more valuable to employers than a large and irregularly employed workforce. Under Joe Ryan, the ILA has concentrated on obtaining a high hourly rate of pay, to the exclusion of almost all other benefits. But the worker's take-home pay for fifty-two weeks a year is more important to him than the hourly rate. What good is a high hourly rate of pay if the longshoreman can't get work, or if he gets an insufficient number of hours of work?

On the other hand, the more employers are able to reduce their overall costs through efficient management of an efficient and well-paid workforce, the sounder and more prosperous the industry. On this basis, shipping companies and contracting stevedores undoubtedly would prefer a regularized workforce, if it could be had. They, however, are faced with a double problem.

PIER STOPPAGES STAGED DURING INVESTIGATION

First, experience has taught them that the leadership of the ILA and the lawless mobs in control of the docks are bitterly opposed to any plans for regularizing the industry. That opposition has taken effective form. A little more than a month ago, "spontaneous" work stoppages were staged on Upper Manhattan piers in protest over a man being questioned at the District Attorney's Office concerning illegal activities on the waterfront.

It would be naïve to assume that the men quit of their own volition. They were ordered off the piers under the too obvious threat that if they didn't obey they wouldn't be chosen for work again by the hiring bosses. This was the mob way of defying investigation and the employers, threatened with further such costly stoppages, are keenly aware of the delicacy of their position.

But the mobs have gone even further. Since the city launched its investigation of racketeering on the piers—an inquiry prompted by *The New York Sun*'s recent series, "Crime on the Waterfront"—certain mob representatives have boldly approached steamship lines and stevedoring companies with the demand that the loading racket, one of the juiciest rackets on the waterfront, be given a clean bill of health in case the companies should be questioned by the investigators. The mobsters said in effect: "If you tell them you don't want the loading, we'll see to it that there is no loading or unloading on any pier. You won't get any work done. We'll close down the piers."

WAR VETERANS RISING AGAINST LEADERSHIP

The second problem affecting the employers is an insurgent spirit growing up among the longshoremen against their dictatorial leadership. Ex-servicemen are in part responsible. Young, and with experience of a tough war and many tough places behind them, they say that they are not taking the treatment handed out to longshoremen in the past.

The strikes of 1945 and 1948 are two extreme examples of this new phenomenon. In both strikes, the men defied Joe Ryan and were successful in winning substantial improvements in wages and working conditions against Ryan's opposition. In the fall of 1947, the West Side ILA locals struck against enforcement of a clause in a contract that they contended had not been properly ratified.

Thus, the shipping companies are caught in the middle of a growing internal union struggle. In such circumstances, they should not be averse, privately at least, to a thorough state investigation. Certainly they should not object to the state bringing out facts about the longshoring problem that will help to solve the present costly internal union fight.

FACE LOSS OF BUSINESS TO PORTS ELSEWHERE

In addition, they are faced with a loss of business to other ports, as was reported in *BusinessWeek* for January 8 last—a factor which might make them welcome a solution of the political aspects of the port picture here.

Apart from racketeering costs, the competition from other modernized Atlantic Coast ports may force New York to undertake its own modernization program if New York's leading position is not to be cut down further. A financially embarrassed city administration doesn't seem to be in any position to undertake this program at the moment.

The widespread criminal activities on the waterfront here have sent shipping costs skyrocketing. Competing ports are well aware of New York's troubles, and they are not hesitating to capitalize on them in bidding for more and more business from this port.

NEW YORK, MONDAY, JANUARY 31, 1949

Ryan's Union Opposes Hiring Hall Because Shape-Up Bolsters Leaders' Rule

Under Joe Ryan's leadership, the International Longshoremen's Association is opposed to the hiring hall and favors continuation of the shape-up system of hiring on the docks here. Why? Chiefly because under the shape-up, with its combination of terror, favoritism, and corruption, the union leaders can—and do—control the members completely.

Freedom from fear? The longshoremen of New York never have known that freedom. Everything about the shape-up fosters fear. Fear of not working. Fear of incurring the displeasure of the hiring boss, who can accept or reject men at will. Fear of what will happen to them if the men refuse to go along with the mobsters who rule the waterfront, their rule made possible through the shape-up.

Under the hiring hall, as practiced in other ports, the longshoremen would get a fairer distribution of work through a limited, centralized registration and control exercised by a joint committee of labor, management, and a government agency. It would provide rotation of work, a higher annual wage, and more job security. It would give the men freedom from fear. The ILA doesn't want it, and you can bet your life that the waterfront gangsters don't want it either. It would end the system by which their rich rackets are able to flourish.

OBJECTIONS OF ILA, WITH REPLIES TO THEM

Of course, the ILA leaders don't put it exactly that way. They raise various objections to the hiring hall—all of them strictly phony, according to the opponents of the shape-up. Here are some of those objections and the answers to them:

ARGUMENT: Ryan says that if the men didn't want the shape-up they would get rid of it.

ANSWER: As if the longshoremen had anything to say in an organization in which Gene Sampson, delegate of Local 791 in the Chelsea area, said: "We ended this strike (the last one) with the first nationwide secret ballot in the history of the ILA" (*Labor Leader*, December 27, 1948). The ILA, as now constituted, is a dictatorship, and Joe Ryan is the present dictator, as will be shown later in these articles.

ARGUMENT: Ryan says that the hiring hall is communistic.

ANSWER: There were hiring halls on the West Coast before Harry Bridges came along, and hiring hall was substituted for shape-up in other ports many years ago—in London, for instance, as far back as 1891. In this country, the hiring hall idea is used by such anticommunist unions as Dave Dubinsky's Ladies Garment Workers, the printers, printing pressmen, the seamen, and Marty Lacey's teamsters in Local 816. So why give Bridges or the communists credit for something good in itself and not communistic?

HOW *THE SUN* STANDS ON HARRY BRIDGES

ARGUMENT: ILA officials have suggested that *The New York Sun*, in attacking the shape-up, is really for Bridges.

ANSWER: *The Sun* is for giving a longshoreman a chance to earn a decent living under fair working conditions and with a competent leadership, so as to keep men like Harry Bridges out. True, under the hiring hall as under any other system, proper safeguards must be taken to keep out the communists. But under the present setup, the communists are a far more dangerous threat. They already have made some progress among the exploited Italian longshoremen in

Brooklyn. If the communists should capture control of the union in this, the most important port in the world, Ryan must accept a large share of the blame. He hasn't lifted a finger to clean up the filthy mess on the docks.

ARGUMENT: Ryan says the hiring hall is a squirrel cage. He would have the men think that they have to report to the hiring hall every day for work. He would have them think that there are no regular work gangs.

ANSWER: There are more regular gangs on the West Coast for the number of men working than there are now on the East Coast. The regular gangs can go to work by tuning in on the radio in the morning to find out what pier they are to report to. Once they begin a job, they finish that job. New York could improve on the West Coast setup, perhaps. There is no law that says that if they want the hiring hall they have to take it as the West Coast has it.

RYAN FEARS LONG TREKS; AREA HALLS BAR THEM

ARGUMENT: Ryan says that the men would be sent all over the place. West Side men would be trekking to Staten Island, Coney Island men to Bayonne, and so on.

ANSWER: As stated previously, a port the size of New York probably would have to have at least five hiring halls in as many districts: two in Manhattan, two in Brooklyn, and one for Staten Island and New Jersey. Whatever hiring halls are set up, only men in that section would be hired until all the men in that area had work, and no man would have to go out of his district unless there was work in another and he wanted it.

ARGUMENT: Ryan says the longshoremen would have to be capable of taking any job.

ANSWER: Men in regular gangs would work as they now do in regular gangs. As for the extra men, they would check in for whatever jobs they wanted and could fill. They could check in for only one job at a time. In this connection, Ryan's touching solicitude for the men may come as a surprise. The Watchmen's Union was originally organized to take care of the older or partially disabled longshoremen. Is it? Or are the openings being turned over—after $150 initiation fees are paid—to men getting more in a pension than the average longshoreman gets in a year's work? Ask the longshoremen. They know.

NO SIGN OF UNION TRYING TO END CHAOTIC SITUATION

The ILA conventions are held every four years. You can read through the convention proceedings in vain to find any discussion of the desirability of regularizing the industry. On the contrary, the ILA's policies and practices make it increasingly difficult to set up a scheme of decasualization to end the present lack of job security and chaotic work conditions.

Principal efforts of the ILA leaders have revolved around increasing the hourly pay rate, and getting special rates for handling particular kinds of cargo. At the same time, the union leadership has done nothing to stop the continuous entrance of new men into an already overcrowded field. Ryan's critics, in and out of the union, say that he violates every sound trade union principle by spreading the limited amount of work so thin that the majority of men get no better than a substandard annual wage.

LABOR SCHOOL DIRECTOR STRESSES SUBNORMAL PAY

The Reverend John M. Corridan, S.J., associate director of the Xavier Labor School, stressed this in an article in the Jesuit periodical *America* for November 20, 1948:

> One week's vacation was paid to the longshoremen for the first time in 1946, if they worked 1,350 hours. Seventy per-

> cent of the longshoremen did not earn this vacation pay, because 1,350 hours of work were not available to them. Seventy percent of the men, therefore, could not get thirty-four weeks of work in a year's time.
>
> The majority of the longshoremen worked around 1,000 hours, or one-half year's work at the rate of forty hours a week. Take their present hourly rate of $1.75 an hour, multiply it by 1,000, and you get $1,750, or $34 a week on an annual basis before income tax payments. Say that some of the longshoremen received 500 hours out of 1,000 at the overrate time of $2.62. Their income was $2,187 a year, or $42 per week before income tax payments—hardly a living wage.

Since that was written by Father Corridan, the longshoremen, as a result of the recent strike, have won a higher rate of pay, $1.88 an hour straight time, and a welfare fund—for the first time. They also won a reduction to eight hundred of the number of hours work required for a week's vacation. They won that by striking against "the very fine agreement," without a welfare plan, that Ryan had recommended for their acceptance.

LONGSHOREMAN IS NOW LABOR'S FORGOTTEN MAN

But what of the longshoremen themselves? How do they feel about the hiring hall? They know all about the hell of the shape-up. They know about the padrone system among the Italians hired off the street corners in Brooklyn. The way politics controls hiring in Jersey is common knowledge on the waterfront. Yet they hear Ryan say that he is for the "open" shape; that is, hiring individually and not in gangs, and on a basis of come one, come all, and take your chances. They hear Ryan say that he is for two shapes a day; that it is the best system. Best for whom? For Ryan and his henchmen?

Unfortunately, many of the longshoremen don't know too much about the hiring hall arrangement. Ryan and other officials of the ILA haven't helped them to learn. Some have only a confused idea of what it is all about. Others parrot what their leaders say, that it's communistic, something the Reds want. The men know that their own leaders don't want it, because it works against their interests, which, unhappily, are not always the interests of the members.

What the longshoremen need is some straight facts on the way a decent hiring hall works. *The Sun* is trying to help in that respect. The State Employment Service and the United States Department of Labor could provide additional facts as a service to the longshoremen and to the general public as well. As matters now stand, the longshoreman in New York is the forgotten man of the labor movement.

NEW YORK, TUESDAY, FEBRUARY 1, 1949

How Seattle Led Pacific Ports in Turning From Shape-Up to Hiring Hall

Seattle was the first port in the United States to substitute the hiring hall for the shape-up, the antiquated hiring system still practiced on the docks of New York. That was in 1921.

Since then other West Coast ports, profiting by Seattle's experience, have followed suit: Los Angeles in 1922, Portland in 1923, San Francisco in 1934. Various European ports had blazed the way: London in 1891, Hamburg in 1906, Liverpool in 1911, Rotterdam in 1916. Antwerp joined the parade in 1929.

Seattle's experiment was born of desperation. Seattle then had the same troubles from which New York is suffering today. There were strikes, wildcat work stoppages, grand-scale pilferage and rackets, high accident frequency, and surplus gangs of longshoremen roving from dock to dock seeking work where there was none.

EMPLOYERS REALIZED CLEANUP WAS NEEDED

The employers at last realized that they would have to do something to improve the conditions of the men if there was to be any peace in the port and efficiency and economy in cargo handling. As for the men themselves, like infantrymen they felt that any change was bound to be an improvement.

The results are a matter of record. F. P. Foisie, writing in 1934 for the Water Front Employers Association of Seattle on "Decasualizing Longshoring Labor and the Seattle Experience," summarized Seattle's experience since 1921 as follows:

1. The hiring hall regularized the employment of the men.

2. It gave a more substantial and regular livelihood to a majority of the men.

3. Leisure time was substituted for time formerly wasted in seeking employment or in bars.

4. The central pay service working out of the central hiring hall proved to be an economy and a convenience to the men as well as to the employers.

5. Accident frequency was reduced.

6. Labor relations between the longshoremen and the employers became more cordial, cooperative, and mutually profitable.

SEATTLE PLAN BASED ON BRITISH PATTERN

The hiring hall as it was established in Seattle was based on the pattern submitted to the British Parliament in 1919 by Ernest Bevin, labor leader and now foreign secretary.

Seattle's experience checked with the earlier and much larger experiments in London and Liverpool, ports more comparable to New York in size and importance. In 1931, the ministry of labor in London published "The Port Labor Inquiry Report" on existing registration schemes:

> Among the various measures adopted with the object of overcoming casual conditions, probably none has had such a large effect nor been so generally applied as the system of registration or, as it might be described, the regulation of the supply of labor for port work by granting a general preference in port employment to selected workers, the numbers being determined on the basis of the labor requirements. . . . Of the general good effect which registration has had on the industry as a whole there can be no doubt. (Pages 16–17.)
>
> In our opinion no port can hope to make any real progress

toward regularization of port employment without a registration scheme. It is clearly impossible for the most satisfactory workers' organization alone, as it is for the individual port employers among a number operating in a port to create an organization by themselves for the engagement, distribution and general control of the pool of labor so as to meet the just needs of both the employers and the work people. Experience has clearly shown that this can only be done by an organization operated by all the parties concerned. We have no hesitation, therefore, in reaffirming that a jointly administered registration scheme is the only satisfactory foundation upon which to build hopes of eventual decasualization. (Page 43.)

NEW YORK'S TASK EASIER THAN LONDON'S OR SEATTLE'S

Students of the problem say that the introduction of hiring halls in the Port of New York would not prove as difficult as in the ports of London and Liverpool or Seattle. For one thing, New York could draw from the experience of these ports. Then, too, whereas the other ports had no accurate knowledge of the number of men working on the docks prior to registration, New York has. From the records kept on vacation pay since the 1945 contract, and the recent welfare clause, won as a result of the last strike, some reasonably accurate estimate should be available. To date, no one has published those statistics.

Under the new contract between the International Longshoremen's Association and the shipping companies, eight hundred hours worked in a year's time is the minimum qualification for one week's paid vacation and welfare benefits, but records have to be kept for all men working. The only men for whom records might not be had are the shenangoes.

Shenangoing is the term used for work at such odd jobs as bringing the lighters and barges into position for cargo handling. The shenangoes—the most casual group in the port's waterfront labor market—are hired at any moment of the day and are paid for the time worked on the day itself. You will find plenty of ILA men among the shenangoes, from whom the ILA accepts dues, but for whom the ILA does nothing, absolutely nothing.

FOUR GOALS SET FORTH IN GOVERNMENT BULLETIN

To sum up, hiring hall requirements are set forth as follows in "Cargo Handling and Longshore Labor," Bulletin No. 550, United States Department of Labor, Bureau of Labor Statistics, February 1932:

> First, there must be complete registration of all longshoremen in the port, these to constitute the total supply of labor which is to be reduced or enlarged in accordance with the demands of the port. Only those on the register should be permitted to work on the waterfront.
>
> Second, all employers on the waterfronts must give up their right to hire longshore labor individually at their piers or elsewhere and must secure their labor from the central office where the registry of longshoremen is kept. Without these two important points, namely, the workers giving up the right to seek work individually along the waterfront, the employers giving up their right to hire labor individually, no scheme of decasualization can succeed. In fact, what decasualization really implies is a coordinated organization of each port as a single employing unit, under a single administration, with the power to direct the supply of labor and to swing it from point to point as needed.
>
> Decasualization does, or should, accomplish the following:
>
> 1. It guarantees to all the employers an equal chance to obtain workers as needed.
>
> 2. It guarantees to all the longshoremen an equal chance of getting a job when work is available.

3. It tends to eliminate the power of the hiring foremen and the abuses and favoritism that go with it.

4. It gradually reduces the total number of longshoremen in port to that approximating the actual needs of the port and thus raises the average earnings of the men on the register.

CONTRASTING CONDITIONS IN NEW YORK LISTED

By contrast, New York under the shape-up has the characteristics of a port not decasualized. These are summarized as follows:

1. A large, highly immobile body of workers scattered over the entire waterfront and ignorant of the actual time and place where work is to be had.

2. A large number of individual employers, each aiming to create as large a reservoir of labor as he may need to satisfy his maximum demands, thus increasing the total supply of workers to a number far in excess of the demands of the entire port.

3. Complete dependence of the longshoreman's job on the goodwill of the foreman and on chance.

4. Conditions of hiring longshore labor which, because of the autocratic power concentrated in the hands of the foreman, pave the way for unfair practices.

5. Periods of enforced idleness alternate with long stretches of hard labor. It may be added that on payday these workers are still under the necessity of tramping from pier to pier standing in line at each, in order to collect the small amounts of money earned in their scraps of employment.

("Longshore Labor Conditions in the United States," *Monthly Labor Review*, United States Department of Labor, Bureau of Labor Statistics, Part I, October 1930, page 6.)

NEW YORK, WEDNESDAY, FEBRUARY 2, 1949

Ryan, Dictator With a Life Job, Rules Union as Securely as Stalin Does Russia

As now constituted, the International Longshoremen's Association, AFL, is a model dictatorship, the like of which might be found in Russia. In the Soviet dictatorship, Stalin at least submits to the mockery of an election, though no rival slate is permitted. In the ILA dictatorship, Joseph P. Ryan, the international president, has dispensed with elections, at least in his own case. In 1943, Ryan got himself elected for life.

There are elections—of a sort—for the other international officers at the ILA conventions held every four years. In reporting Ryan's announcement of the opening of the last ILA convention, in 1947, the press stated: "The convention will elect seventeen vice presidents, thirteen of whom are expected to be reelected. Four vacancies left open by the death of members will be filled."

That's about par for the course. The convention elections in 1931, 1935, and 1939 were all cut and dried, without one rival candidate for any post.

BILL OF PARTICULARS AGAINST THE ILA

Critics in and out of the labor movement charge that the ILA violates virtually every principle of good trade unionism. Here's the bill of particulars:

1. No good union subscribes to the principle of cutthroat competition between men for jobs. The ILA does. There are more than

twice as many men seeking longshore work as there are jobs on the docks here. Last year, twenty-two thousand men out of forty-five thousand or more longshoremen in the Port of New York got more than twenty weeks of work—sixteen thousand in New York and six thousand in New Jersey, according to the central records bureau kept by the New York Shipping Association. Despite this condition, the New York District Council of the ILA has not recommended closing the membership books of the union. Initiation fees and dues are the gimmick.

2. No good union tolerates a condition of job insecurity. The ILA promotes it with a two shape-ups a day system of hiring. On the record, the best it's been able to do for the men is guarantee them a minimum of four hours of work—if and when they are lucky enough to be hired in shape-up. The ILA's official policy was well stated in the 1935 convention by its first vice president, Walter B. Holt: "We do not believe in the gang system. The men have to shape individually and be hired." In practice, though, the ILA does nothing to stop certain stevedores from hiring gangs from so-called clubs. A longshoreman pays weekly "dues"—the kickback—to keep his membership in the club as some assurance of getting hired.

3. No good union gives preference to nonunion men over union men where work opportunities are limited. The ILA does every day. Longshoremen see nonunion men go to work and union men left in the street. "The foreman stevedore shall give preference in hiring to men who have regularly worked on the pier for which they are being hired." So reads the contract negotiated by the ILA.

ILA NOT CONCERNED WITH ACCIDENT PREVENTION

4. All good trade unions are concerned with accident prevention. Not the ILA. "The unions of longshoremen have done little to

increase the safety of longshore operations. Safety is rarely mentioned in the union agreements, and such references as do appear are usually vague generalities, such as 'The employers shall provide safe equipment and safe working conditions'" (page 14). An auditor for a stevedoring company gives the compensation rate on white-collar workers as 5 cents for every $100, for longshoremen $10 for every $100.

5. Every good union pays some benefits to its members. Not the ILA. In the 1931 convention, Ryan forbade—and his prohibition still holds—locals to pay death benefits out of their treasuries unless they charge a higher rate of dues than that dictated by the international. "My reason for this recommendation," Ryan decreed, "is that I know our organization is rendering service to the membership in full measure for what they receive by seeing to it that their wages and conditions are maintained; and if they are properly protected during life, they should be able to provide for themselves, or their dependents, in time of sickness or death."

Earlier in the convention, Ryan praised the ILA for its organizational job despite the prolonged shipping depression. No doubt his own job improved as the depression continued, for Ryan's salary was raised to $8,000 in 1931 to $15,000 in 1935, and to $20,000 in 1939.

ANY MAN FILING GRIEVANCE IS ASKING NOT TO BE HIRED

6. Good trade unions prize and work for contractual grievance machinery so that small beefs can be quickly settled and not allowed to fester. Not the ILA. Any man not in a regular gang who goes to the shop steward on a pier and asks him to take up his grievance is asking not to be hired again. As a result, men don't go to the shop steward but form separate cliques nursing their particular "wrongs" until they explode in a work stoppage.

7. Reading through the ILA directories and the ILA convention

proceedings, one finds a striking similarity of names. Often, one man is president of one local and organizer for another, a business agent for a third, a secretary-treasurer for a fourth, delegate or officer of the District Council, and a delegate to convention after convention, representing a local's full voting power.

For example, John (Ike) Gannon is president of the New York District Council of the ILA; president of Local 824, ILA; and secretary of Local 1693, General, Special Cargo, Mail and Baggage on Airborne Freight Carriers, ILA. By a coincidence, Gannon also is an organizer of Local 1496 of the Port Watchmen's Union, formerly affiliated with the ILA, but technically not so affiliated as of the moment because of the Taft-Hartley law. Officially, it is now an "independent" union.

MEN WITH CRIMINAL RECORDS AMONG UNION OFFICERS

Another example was Charlie Yanowsky, the ex-convict and gangster on the Jersey waterfront who was murdered last July. Yanowsky was secretary of the Marine Warehousemen of New Jersey, an ILA local, and was also business agent and organizer of Local 21512, Motor and Bus Terminal Checkers, Platform and Office Workers, the union created by John Dunn, Manhattan labor racketeer now in the death house at Sing Sing for murder. In addition, Yanowsky held official positions in various other unions, and had front men, or stooges, in several ILA locals.

ILA history shows that other men with serious criminal records held union office or were paid organizers. They include, to mention only a few, Ed McGrath, Dunn's partner and brother-in-law; Andy Sheridan, onetime triggerman for Dutch Schultz, and now in the death house with Dunn at Sing Sing; and several who were murdered: Joe Butler, Farmer Sullivan, Dave Beadle, and Richard (the Bandit) Gregory.

The longshoremen had a history of striking in the 1930s and 1940s. Sometimes the strikes were for more pay or better work conditions; other strikes were caused by hardships placed on them by the oppressive climate of corruption, betrayal by their own union, and by organized crime. Reproduced from the Collections of the Library of Congress.

Is such a record consistent with good trade union policy and practice?

LOCAL'S ELECTION MEETING PACKED WITH OUTSIDERS

8. Local 895, the Greenwich Village local, has no bylaws and rules of order. No monthly meetings were held in this local between March 1, 1942, and October 1, 1945. Raymond (Sonny) Thompson, business agent, and Peter Hussey, secretary-treasurer, called a sudden meeting for the purpose of getting themselves reelected to office for a five-year term. Without authorization, the elections were moved up from their regular date, March 1946, to December 1945.

When the members came to the meeting, they found the hall packed with nonunion members. The men, including five recently returned GIs, protested. For seeking to protect the rights of the membership, Ryan and Thompson barred them from work. If it were not for Edward Scully of the Catholic Labor Defense League taking their case into the courts, these men would have been kept off the waterfront, as so many men have been before and after them.

Their case had been called for trial before Supreme Court Justice Henry C. Greenberg when the ILA officials capitulated. They agreed (1) to the resignation of the officers illegally elected in December; (2) to set up a five-man elections committee, two to represent the rebels and two for the local machine. A fifth person, Professor Milton Handler of Columbia University, was selected by Judge Greenberg as chairman. Despite a new administration slate, and Ryan's continued opposition, the rebels won three out of the seven offices. It was the first secret election ever recorded in that local. Regular monthly meetings have been held ever since.

NEW YORK, THURSDAY, FEBRUARY 3, 1949

Dockers Have Constitution Called a Blueprint for Dictatorship

ENSURES RULE BY JOE RYAN

Most of Longshoremen Never Have Seen Document That Sets Forth His Powers

---

The constitution of the International Longshoremen's Association is a blueprint for dictatorship. It contains twenty-seven articles, a neat appendix on rules of order, and a convenient index, all bound in a blue-and-gray cover, pocket-sized, streamlined for the one-man rule of Joe Ryan, the union's lifetime president, at $20,000 a year plus expenses.

The majority of longshoremen are not familiar with the ILA constitution. They know vaguely that there is such a document, but many of them have never even seen a copy of it, much less read one. They should read it and weep, for Ryan's dictatorial powers are stated in black and white.

The first six articles of the constitution are conventional enough, setting forth the name, duration, jurisdiction, objects, organization, and powers of the ILA and its convention. Longshoremen may be interested to learn that among the objects listed in Article IV are "to increase the job security and to better the work and living conditions of its members . . . to promote welfare programs; to instill the spirit of patriotism. . . ."

REAL FLAVOR OF RYAN'S MOLOTOV COCKTAIL VERSION

Strictly hearts and flowers. The longshoremen know that the only job security Ryan has ever negotiated for them is a guarantee of four hours of work, if and when they are lucky enough to be hired in the shape-up. They won a welfare fund late last year by striking against the Ryan leadership as much as against their employers, the shipping interests.

But to get the real flavor of Ryan's version of a Molotov cocktail, read section 4 of Article V on "Organization and Powers":

> All executive, legislative, and judicial powers of the ILA shall be vested in its convention. When the convention is not in session, they shall be vested in the Executive Council; when the Executive Council is not in session, they shall be vested in the international officers as herein provided.

Now read Article VI, which states: "The regular convention of the ILA shall be held every four years." Then read Article XIX, section 5, on "Appeals," and remember that the convention is the last source of appeal:

> No member or local union shall institute any civil action, suit, or proceeding in any court against the ILA, any of its local unions, or District Council, or District Organization, or any officer or member of the ILA or any of its local unions or District Council or District Organization on account of any controversy for which a remedy by trial or appeal is provided for in this constitution, unless and until he has first exhausted all such remedies of trial and appeal.

That means, of course, that an aggrieved longshoreman may, if he is brave and patient enough, take his case through union channels, get turned down all along the line; wait four years and appeal to the convention, and then, and only then, go to court. Did anybody say something about infringement of civil rights? Yet some people hereabouts are saying that the trouble along the waterfront is just a management–labor problem.

POWERS GRANTED TO RYAN BOTH TO HIRE AND FIRE

Now take a look at some of the powers granted the international president, Ryan. Article IX provides that he shall be the principal executive officer of the ILA, preside at conventions and meetings of the Executive Council, which he may convene, and that he shall have the power to attend meetings of local unions, district councils, and districts. It then states, in part:

> The International President may employ and discharge such representatives, organizers (who shall be members in good standing of the ILA), administrative, technical, or other employees as may be required.
>
> He shall fix the salaries of all persons employed by him; he shall appoint all committees not otherwise designated by this Constitution; he shall designate the duties and direct the performances of District officers, organizers, and vice president. All bills covering expenses incurred must be approved by him before payment. . . . He shall have such other and further powers in addition to those herein enumerated and shall perform such other and further duties as are usual to his office, and as are performed by the President in accordance with the usages of the ILA. The compensation for the services of the International President shall be $20,000 annually and he shall receive in addition thereto, traveling, hotel and incidental expenses.

EXTRAORDINARY DISCIPLINARY POWERS POSSESSED BY RYAN

Ryan's omnipotence is further protected by extraordinary disciplinary, financial, and patronage powers.

Disciplinary Powers: Article XII, Local Unions, Section 4:

> The International President, with the consent of the District Council, and where no District Council exists, with the consent of the governing body of the district, may consolidate two or more local unions, or may reorganize or dissolve any Local Union, or amend the charter or jurisdiction of any Local Union.

In other words, stay in line or Joe may abolish you.

Article XVIII provides that a copy of any charges preferred against a district council or district organization officer, delegate, or paid representative must be transmitted by the recording secretary of the local union to the international secretary-treasurer. It then states:

> The District Council or District Organization, its Executive Board, or the Executive Council, as the case may be, shall have the right by notice in writing to such Recording Secretary to assume jurisdiction of any such charges and, in that event, no action upon such charges shall thereafter be taken by the Local Union with which they were filed, but all further proceedings shall be taken by such District Council or District Organization, its Executive Board or the Executive Council, as the case may be, in the same manner as though such charges had originally been filed with it.

CLAUSE GRANTS "THE BOYS" A DOUBLE PROTECTION

That clause affords a double protection. It conceivably could protect some of "the boys" against an unsympathetic court; it also could protect the leadership against rebellious officers.

For example, in their fight for an honest election, the rebels of Local 895 petitioned the District Council to oust Raymond (Sonny) Thompson as their delegate on the ground that he owned a saloon, in violation of Article XXIV of the constitution, prohibiting such ownership, direct or indirect, by any officer in the ILA. The District Council ignored the petition.

Further disciplinary power is granted under Article XVIII, section 7:

> Whenever charges have been filed with the Executive Council, or whenever it has assumed jurisdiction over the charges against an officer or officers of a Local Union, or District Council or District organization, the Executive Council shall have the following powers which it may exercise prior to a hearing or decision on such charges:
>
> (A) Summarily to suspend the accused officer or officers.
>
> (B) To appoint a temporary officer or temporary officers who shall have all the powers of the officer or officers so suspended, and who shall serve pending the decision of the Executive Council upon the charges against the accused. . . .

Any stooge, of course, can file any charge whatsoever against a "rebellious" officer, and he and his supporters can be taken care of, but good.

AUTHORITY TO RAISE DUES IS ALSO DULY PROVIDED

Under financial powers, the constitution provides that dues and initiation fees of local unions shall not be "inconsistent" with any rules promulgated by the District Council, and that such dues shall not be less than $2 a month.

The dues now are being raised to a minimum of $2.50 a month, and the per capita tax from each local, payable to the international treasury, is being raised from 30 cents to 50 cents a month.

The constitution further provides that assessments on the membership may be levied by the Executive Council "whenever it deems such assessments necessary to the welfare of the ILA."

In addition to the disciplinary and financial powers, the ILA dictatorship is further solidified by patronage as provided for in Article XXII, section 1, on "Organizers":

> The International President may appoint regular and special organizers as he deems necessary or proper for the welfare of the ILA. Such organizers shall hold their positions at the will of the International President.

NEW YORK, FRIDAY, FEBRUARY 4, 1949

Practically All of Longshore Union Funds Go for Officers' Pay and Expenses

In return for their contributions in dues, initiation fees, and assessments, the longshoremen never receive a financial report from the International Longshoremen's Association. They probably will be glad to know, in case they have any doubts, that practically all of the union's funds are spent on officers' salaries and expenses.

The secretary-treasurer's report at the 1939 convention gave some breakdown of expenses. Those at the 1931 and 1935 conventions did not. The conventions are held every four years.

The report in 1939 showed that for the six-month period ending December 31, 1935, the per capita tax collected by the ILA was $73,107.30, and the total income $75,361.51. Officers' salaries and expenses came to $77,931. The balance in the treasury was $39,246.64. (Pages 108–109.)

OFFICERS' SALARIES GROW AS TAX RECEIPTS RISE

As the per capita tax collected rose, so did officers' salaries and expenses. For the six-month period ending December 31, 1937, for example, the per capita tax collected was $105,481.32. Officers' salaries and expenses were $116,698.60.

For the four-year period 1935 to 1939, the total per capita tax collected was $727,821.48, 88 percent of all income. In that same period, $621,488.46 was paid out in officers' salaries and expenses, 85 percent of all per capita tax collected.

Of those salaries, Joe Ryan, the lifetime president of the ILA, gets $20,000 a year, plus "traveling, hotel and incidental expenses," as guaranteed under the ILA constitution, the blueprint for Ryan's dictatorship.

The constitution also empowers Joe to "employ and discharge such representatives, organizers . . . administrative, technical or other employees as may be required." Still another provision (Article XXII, section 1) authorizes him to appoint "regular and special organizers as he deems necessary or proper for the welfare of the ILA. . . ." Ryan fixes their salaries, and the organizers hold their jobs "at the will of the international president," says the constitution. Ryan evidently uses his power to appoint rather freely. That's why there is so little left in the treasury. The balance as of May 1, 1939, was $36,566.39.

Other salaries, as listed in the constitution, are $7,500 a year for the first vice president and $10,000 a year for the secretary-treasurer, plus "all necessary expenses."

LIMITATIONS ARE IMPOSED ON LOCAL DEATH BENEFITS

By way of contrast, the longshoremen get no benefits from the international. And just to make sure that the union locals don't spend money foolishly on their deceased union brothers and their families, this safeguard was put in the constitution:

Article XXVI, Miscellaneous Regulations for Locals, Section 24:

Donations from local treasuries in case of sickness or death shall not be made, excepting where special arrangement is entered into by the local itself, providing a fund for this purpose. Such donations not to be made out of monthly dues, excepting where monthly dues are higher than two dollars ($2.00) per month prescribed by the international constitution.

With dues now raised to $2.50, the local would have to charge more than that amount to make any donations. No benefits are paid. Strike benefits could be paid if Ryan declared a strike official and sanctioned the payments of benefits. The first "official" strike in Ryan's regime—since 1927—was called last November after the membership rebelled against the "very fine agreement" negotiated and accepted by Ryan.

SOME OF RYAN FAITHFULS GOT GRAVY FROM STRIKE

Ryan, blustering and fuming, first said that the men had quit because they were "insulted" by the series of articles, "Crime on the Waterfront," which had just started running in *The New York Sun*. But finally, as the strike spread, he had to go along, making it "official." No strike benefits were paid.

There was some gravy in it, however, for some of the Ryan faithful. The constitution provides that the president of the union local "shall appoint and be an ex-officio member of all committees not otherwise provided for. . . ." Thus, as president, he can appoint the members of the negotiation committee. They receive $25 a day per member for each day of negotiations. A Ryan man can put other Ryan boys at the trough as a reward for faithful service.

The last negotiations were rich. An eighty-day injunction prolonged the negotiations and paid the negotiators handsomely. Except for three rebel West Side locals, Nos. 791, 895, and 1258, it was this wage scale committee, 125 men in all, at twenty-five dollars a day each, that went along with Joe in accepting that "very fine agreement" that resulted in the strike on the Atlantic Coast down to Virginia.

HOW RYAN MAINTAINS HIS ROLE AS DICTATOR

Well, that is the Ryan dictatorship in the ILA, and here, in part, is how he maintains it:

Through two shape-ups a day, but not enough work to go around, in a union that refuses to close its membership books and continues to accept dues and initiation fees in a field already overcrowded.

Through protecting a vicious system of hiring—the shape-up—which enables gangsters and other criminals to control key jobs on the piers and exploit all manner of rackets, at the same time keeping the longshoremen deaf, dumb, and blind.

Through the disciplinary power of the ILA constitution.

Through the financial control of many locals, in so far as they need not pay their full per capita tax, with the knowledge and acquiescence of Ryan, as long as they "stay in line."

Through Ryan's power of appointments.

Through the reluctance of steamship companies and contracting stevedores to disturb present operations.

Through the ignorance and apathy of the public.

Through the paralysis of politicians.

A vigorous, overall state investigation, with remedial legislation as the goal, is the only sensible answer to this waterfront problem—a problem in which the union, workers, employers, and the public all have a vital interest.

SIDELIGHT ON RYAN, FEARFUL OF CRITICISM

Now for a sidelight on Joe Ryan.

Like all dictators, Ryan is particularly sensitive to and fearful of criticism, no matter how objective or how mildly phrased, or how sympathetic with the longshoremen.

In 1938, the Reverend Edward E. Swanstrom, a priest for many years in a Brooklyn waterfront parish before assuming the post of associate director of Catholic Charities, received his doctorate from Fordham University. The Fordham University Press published his thesis, *The Water Front Labor Problem*. It was of Father Swanstrom that Ryan spoke at the 1939 ILA convention, and this is exactly what Ryan said, according to the official minutes of the ILA:

> If he had permitted it here the other day you would have circulated around here asking you to read by a Catholic priest whose name I won't mention because I won't give him any free advertising; he is looking for a dispute with myself and our officials; he is from the same faith as myself and he is not the type of priest who believes in minding your own business. I am not going to refer to him by name, but we had to tell the messenger, Charley Spencer, and the sergeant-at-arms to take the circulars from him and ask the management of the hotel (Commodore) to put him out of the lobby.
>
> They asked you to read this certain book. Of course, we don't care if you read it or not, because we know you know more about your conditions than this priest from the Brooklyn waterfront." (Page 240.)

Father Swanstrom has since become Monsignor Swanstrom, and, at present, is director of the War Relief Services of the National Catholic Welfare Conference. His excellent thesis is now published by Declan X. McMullen, 23 Beekman Street, New York, N.Y. It tells the truth about waterfront labor conditions. Read it and find out what Ryan fears.

APPENDIX

ADDITIONAL WATERFRONT REPORTING

by Budd Schulberg

The New York Times Magazine,
December 28, 1952

Joe Docks, Forgotten Man of the Waterfront

Behind the Current Investigation into Longshore Racketeering Is a Plain Guy Whose Hands Perform One of the City's Toughest Jobs

---

We all know the big names of the current investigation into crime and corruption on New York's waterfront. The headlines are hogged by Anastasia, Joe Ryan, Mike Clemente, "Big" Bill McCormack, the polished executives of the great shipping lines, and influential stevedores. But there is a forgotten man on the waterfront. His voice is lost among the gravel-throated alibis of high-bracket hoodlums, the oily explanations of labor politicians, and the suavely martyred inflections of the shippers.

You whiz by him on the West Side Highway but you don't see him. You hurry past him as you board ship for Europe or a winter cruise through the Caribbean, and never notice his face. But his muscles move your groceries and your steel; he carries your baggage on his back. From his pocket comes the notorious kickback you've been reading about. He's the one who has to show up every morning for the "shape-up" you've been hearing about. He is the human material with which racketeers, masquerading as union officials, pull flash strikes to shake down shipping companies and force the employment of such key personnel as boss loader and hiring boss. He is the man who performs the most dangerous work in America, according to the statistics on labor injury and death.

He's the longshoreman, the dock walloper, the little man who isn't there at investigations: the forgotten man in the great city of New York, the forgotten man of American labor. Miners, railroad men, even sailors were fighting fifty years ago against the kind of medievalism that passes for working conditions on the docks this very morning. In a day when Social Security and old-age pensions are accepted as economic facts of life by both major parties, the longshoreman hasn't got job security from one day to the next.

If he's the forgotten man of the current investigation, here's the forgotten fact: It is this basic insecurity—breeding fear, dependence, shiftlessness, demoralization—that feeds the power of the mob. The weaker, more frightened, and divided are the dock workers, the stronger and more brazen are the Anastasias, Bowers, Florios, and Clementes who manipulate them.

Who are these longshoremen? What kind of lives do they lead? What do they think of these investigations? What are they after?

I went down to the waterfront two years ago for what I thought would be a few days' research for a film about the docks. Long after I had enough material for a dozen waterfront pictures I kept going back, drawn by these forgotten men performing a rugged, thankless job in a jungle of vice and violence where law and constitutional safeguards have never existed.

In the past few weeks, I returned to watch the shape-up. I talked with dock wallopers in the bars from the Village to the mob hangouts along the midtown docks. I went to the homes of longshoremen who talked to me frankly (over cases of beer) about their lives, their fears, and their hopes for a decent setup on the piers. I talked to the defeated who shrug off every investigation as just one more political maneuver and who are resigned to grabbing a few crumbs from the gorillas who rule them. I talked to "insoigents," as they call themselves, who think the time finally is at hand when honest unionism can remove the killers, grafters, and seller-outers, and institute regular and honest employment on the docks.

About thirty-five thousand men are paid longshoremen's wages in the course of a year. Of these, about half are regular longshoremen, men who depend on this work for their livelihood. The rest are what you might call casuals, now-and-theners who drift in to pick up an occasional extra check. Many of these are city employees, policemen, and firemen who like to grab off the overtime money on nights and weekends. Some 50 percent, for instance, earn less than $1,000 a year. Another 10 percent earn less than $2,000. About a third of all the longshoremen, fifteen thousand at most, earn from $2,000 to $4,000 a year. These are the regulars, the ones who have to hustle every day to keep meat and potatoes on the table for the wife and kids. An upper crust of favored workers averages more than $75 a week on a yearly basis. The base pay of $2.27 per hour sounds all right. It's the irregularity, and mob intimidation, that make longshoremen the most harassed workmen in America.

Nine out of ten are Catholic—if not Irish Catholic, then Italian or Austrian. This accounts for the influence of certain waterfront priests who have championed the dockworkers, in a few dramatic cases going so far as to challenge known hoodlums face-to-face on the piers. You'll find the Irish on the West Side and in Brooklyn, some six thousand of them, but they are now outnumbered by the Italians, which explains the growing influence of the Italian underworld that controls the Brooklyn waterfront, as well as the Jersey, Staten Island, and East River docks. Irish longshoremen are devout. Before the 7:55 A.M. shape-up, you will see them going to mass at St. Bernard's, St. Veronica's, or St. Joseph's. Italians follow the Latin tradition of letting the wife handle the church responsibilities.

The Irish longshoremen, while kept in line by strong-arm boys and plagued by an inhuman hiring system, have a better deal than their fellow Italians, who, in turn, are a niche above the Negroes, who work in traveling gangs picking up the extra work when they can get it and are often relegated to the hold, the job nobody wants. The Irish are hardly ever asked to kick back anymore. In other words, when the hiring boss picks his four or five gangs of twenty men each from the two hundred to two hundred and fifty men who shape themselves into an informal horseshoe around him, the Irish no longer return part of their day's pay to him in order to assure themselves of a job. But the Italians and Negroes systematically kick back as much as five dollars per man per day. With seven or eight thousand men kicking back, this quickly becomes big business, some $30,000 or $40,000 a day in illegal fees being passed up from the hiring boss to his superiors as part of the $350 million illegal take from the New York harbor each year.

"It's a stinkin' feelin' standin' there in the shape every mornin' while some thievin' hirin' boss looks you over like you were so much meat," one of the Irish dockers was telling me the other day. "But once in a while, an Italian gang is brought into work with us, and that really looks like something you've heard about in Europe, not America. They work in a short gang—sixteen instead of twenty—so the cowboys c'n pick up the extra checks for themselves. But they've got to do the work of twenty—or else. If they squawk, the boys work 'em over—or they don't get no more work. I've actually seen 'em beaten like cattle for askin' a question.

"So the rules take a beatin'," my Irish friend went on. "In the first place, ninety percent never read the contract. In the second place, it's just a piece of paper if the shop steward and the delegate are part of the mob. Jerry Anastasia, for instance, he's a delegate. A lotta help you get from a stiff like that. Half them I-talians are ship jumpers, which leaves 'em at the mercy of the trigger boys. They ain't citizens, and they can't even apply for unemployment insurance. The way I see it, we got it lousy, and they got it double lousy."

Today, most of the Irish workers are picked up by gangs—in this case, a legitimate work group, not the Mickey Bowers type. Each gang has its own leader, and when the hiring boss points to him it means his whole crew works that day. But the Italians, Austrians, and Negroes are still hired on an individual basis by gang carriers, exactly as Henry Mayhew described it in his book *London Labor and London's Poor* a century ago:

> He who wishes to behold one of the most extraordinary and least-known scenes of this metropolis should wend his way to the docks at half past seven in the morning. . . . [When] the "calling foremen" have made their appearance there begins the scuffling and scrambling forth, countless hands high in the air, to catch the eye of him whose voice may give them work. . . . It is a sight to sadden the most callous to see thousands of men struggling for only one day's work, the scuffle made fiercer by the knowledge that hundreds out of their number must be left to idle the day out in want. . . . For weeks many have gone there, and gone through the same struggle, the same cries; and have gone away after all, without the work they had screamed for.

Not a word need be changed in this description to apply it to hiring methods in New York harbor a hundred years later. Now, as then, two or three times as many men as will be needed loiter near the dock entrance waiting for the hiring boss to blow his whistle when a ship is ready to be loaded or unloaded. Now, as then, he will pick them out according to his own whim and preference. But on too many docks in the great harbor of New York, the nod is given to the man who plays ball, kicks back, buys a ticket for the benefit he will not be expected to attend, signs up for haircuts in a barbershop where all the seats are filled by labor racketeers. Too often the numbered tag which a dockworker gets from the hiring boss, his admission card to a four- or eight-hour shift on the pier is a badge of compliance, an acceptance of inferior status on the waterfront.

Thousands of longshoremen are wondering why a modern metropolis insists on maintaining a practice so barbarous that it was outlawed in England sixty years ago and is now abandoned in nearly all American coastal cities but not in the great Port of New York.

Work is slow right now, and even the longshoreman who stands in with his hiring boss is lucky to pick up three split days a week. How does he make ends meet? "Ya live for t'day—ya never put nuttin' away—if ya need money, ya borry it," I was told. Borrowing comes easy on the docks and is deeply imbedded in the system. The men passed over in the shape must have eating money, and they get it from the loan sharks who are part of the mob.

If you "borry" four dollars, you pay back five, and the interest keeps mounting each week. A rap of 30 percent isn't unusual. Nor is it unusual for a longshoreman getting the nod in a shape to turn over his work tab to the loan shark who collects the debtor's check directly from the pay office. So our longshoreman winds up a day's work by borrowing again.

"I was born in hock and I'll die in hock," a longshoreman told me in a Chelsea saloon. In some locals, a longshoreman who wants to be hired has to go the route—come up with a bill for spurious "relief" drives and play the numbers and the horses with books belonging to the syndicate. In Brooklyn, Albert Anastasia had everything for six blocks in from the river. Longshoremen have to buy their gin from the mob liquor store, and the groceries and their meat.

Unquestionably, their incomes are supplemented by regular filching of meat and liquor from the supplies flowing through the piers. Even the insurgents who are doing their best to buck the graft and large-scale pilferage are no different in this respect. Their ethics may be questionable, but they stem from a deeply ingrained cynicism that is easy to understand. For years, they have watched the fantastic loading racket make off with whole shipments of valuables. The pilferage of ten tons of steel, reported to the Crime Commission by a shipping executive, may have been front-page headlines to the general public, but it was hardly news to the dockworkers. "If five percent of everything moving in and out is systematically siphoned off by the mob, why shouldn't I take a few steaks home for the wife and kids," a longshoreman figures.

"Takin' what you need for your own table is never considered pilferage," it was explained to me rather solemnly. Shortly before Thanksgiving, a longshoreman who could double for Jackie Gleason noticed barrels of turkeys being unloaded from a truck. He was not working that day, but he simply got in line and waited for a barrel to be lowered onto his back. Everybody in his tenement got a free turkey.

Another longshoreman, known for his moxie in standing up to the goons of a pistol local ("one of them locals where you vote every four years with a gun in your back"), told me he was starved out on the docks for sixty straight days. "I stand there lookin' the crummy hirin' boss right in the eye but he never see me." In a whole year, he made less than $1,500, and he had kids to feed. "We couldn't've made out if I hadn't scrounged the groceries on the dock," he said.

What are their politics? Traditionally Democratic, as befits good New York Irish and Italians, but you might say their universal party is cynicism. Because so many mobsters were aligned with the Democratic city machine, some longshoremen took to wearing Ike buttons on the docks as a sign of defiance, and undoubtedly the president-elect was well supported. Like the majority of voters nationally, they hope our political change will break the ties between racketeers and the officeholders who have been protecting them.

But longshoremen have a feeling of being political orphans inevitably betrayed by the people for whom they vote. They'll tell you their cause has been ignored by the politicians, the police, and even the press. Still, they aren't fooled by communism. Despite periodic outcries against subversive influences on the docks—unfortunately used as a cover-up for various forms of racketeering—communism is as unpopular among longshoremen as among stockbrokers, farmers, or railroad workers. The insurgents who led the harborwide wildcat strike a year ago have a hatred for Joe Stalin and his slave labor system that burns just as fiercely as their feeling for Mickey Bowers, Mike Clemente, and the whole waterfront system that keeps union racketeering in power.

Men in the Chelsea area are still bitter at the editorials calling their strike communist-inspired. The local involved, 791, is made up of staunch Irish Catholics, many of them under the influence of the waterfront priest Father John Corridan, and are so rabidly anticommunist that they have been refusing for years to load war materials headed for Russia or China. It is safer to call these men communists in print than to deliver that opinion face-to-face.

"I belt guys for less 'n that," said an embattled member of 791, identified with opposition to Joe Ryan, to strong-arm methods, and to chronic insecurity on the docks. "Anastasia—that great patriot—he calls us commies. Florio and DiBrizzi—to those bums, we're communists. Strange breed o' commies who never miss mass in the morning, and who'll give up a day's pay before they'll work a Russian ship. But I'll tell you one thing, if we don't clean this mess up ourselves the commies'll have a nice fat issue all ready to take over."

Father Corridan, of the Xavier Labor School, on the Lower West Side, who has become a kind of one-man brain trust of the rank and file, sums up the communist angle this way:

"In '45, the communists did move in and try to take credit for the leaderless, rank-and-file strike. But right now their influence is nil, no matter what the ILA brass says. The men down here—almost without exception—are loyal, God-fearing Americans. The way to fight communism in the labor movement is to accentuate the positive—in other words, find out what the men really need in order to live healthy, happy, dignified lives, and then fight for it."

What longshoremen want has nothing to do with ideologies and millenniums. Their aims are so modest as to be taken for granted by some sixty million American wage earners. What they want most is an assurance that the job they're lucky enough to have today is the same one they'll have tomorrow—and next week—and next month. They don't want to go on shaping up twice a day hoping for work.

An old man with forty years on the docks compared his status—or lack of it—with a railroad engineer's. "Look at him, he goes to work every morning knowing he's got a place in the world. The more time he's got behind him, the more secure he feels. That's seniority. He knows if he does his job well his pay'll increase, his position improves, and he'll finally retire with a good pension. He's got dignity, that's what he's got. Now, take me. All my life on the dock. And I know my job. I know how to handle copper in the rain, and how to get my fingers into a bag of flour. I c'n work fast. I like to take pride in my work. But what kind of pride c'n I feel when some punk comes out of the can and starts makin' five times as much as I am for doin' nothin' except pushin' us around?"

The old man insisted on buying me another drink. It may have been loan-shark money, but longshoremen are proud and open-handed, and fine drinking companions when they feel they can trust you.

"After forty years, I get up t'morra mornin' and stan' over there on the dock like an orphan. I'll be lucky if I bring home twenty-five bucks this week. Is the hearings gonna change it? Well, lad, I'll tell ya one thing, it can't make it any worse. I just hope it goes all the way."

This hope is echoed all up and down the waterfront. Joe Docks, bottled up in his cramped cold-water flat or his waterfront bar, doesn't get much chance to tell us about his life. But he doesn't like it. Hard-drinking, two-fisted, high-strung, a rabid sports fan, an all-out friend, a dangerous enemy, he's also a loyal, religious, hardworking, responsible family man concerned with getting his kids through school and seeing them get a better break than their old man. He lives for the day when his job will be systematized through some plan of work rotation based on an equitable, democratically accepted schedule as to where and when he's going to work. Today, there is not even a central information service on shipping traffic, and the men pick up their information as to job chances in the same haphazard, chaotic way they did a hundred years ago.

Joe Docks thinks he deserves something better than the hopelessly outmoded hiring system that delivers him into the hands of hardened criminals. He's hoping, but not counting on, the hearings, which are the most thorough ever held on the problem, to rescue him from the underworld bondage and raise him to a level of dignity and security enjoyed by other American workers in legitimate unions.

He's too solid and useful a citizen to be left to stew in his own bitterness and bewilderment in the waterfront bars. Antihoodlum, anticorruption, anticommunist, antiuncertainty, and antihunger, he is the real forgotten man of American labor.

The other morning, a little fellow who sounded enough like Barry Fitzgerald to make the *Ed Sullivan* TV show was left standing on the dock by an ex–Sing Sing hiring boss for the fourth consecutive jobless day. "In Liverpool, back in 1912, they knocked out this kinda hiring," he was saying. "I could tell them judges on the Crime Com-

Louis Waldman (*left*), general counsel for the International Longshoremen's Association, and Joseph P. Ryan (*right*), president of the ILA, are shown conferring right before Governor Dewey opened up hearings on plans to end racketeering on the New York waterfront, the Bar Association Building, June 8, 1953.

mission a thing or two about this stinkin' setup." Even now, early in the morning with another jobless day ahead and the Good Lord only knew what tomorrow, there was a twinkle in his eye. These are indestructible men (until a strong-arm man, a [Danny] St. John or an [Albert] Ackalitis, has the last word), and laughter comes easy to them for all their grief and frustration. "When those high muckymucks get all through and there's a zillion words of testimony all nicely bound, they'll know what we knew in the first place—down here it's really time for a change."

He gave his cap a jaunty poke, stuck his hands into his battered windbreaker, pushed his chest out in a gesture of general defiance, and crossed Forty-fourth Street to McGinty's Bar and Grill.

As you read this over Sunday breakfast or in the paper-littered parlor, Joe Docks may be in church, or playing with his kids, or lying in bed reading about the basketball games. He'll be back on the docks tomorrow morning around half past seven. If he's passed over, he'll be over at McGinty's, or some other place, looking for the loan shark, drinking a little beer, worrying about the wife and kids, playing a number, wondering if the Crime Commission can really get these gorillas off his neck, and waiting for the general public to respond to a golden challenge: "If you do it to the least of mine, you do it to me."

THE NEW YORK TIMES MAGAZINE,
SEPTEMBER 27, 1953

How One Pier Got Rid of the Mob

The Story of Pier 45 Offers a Guide to the New Port Commission: The Rank and File Wants To—and Can—End Corruption on the Docks

---

For the Port of New York, these autumn months have a strange and unreal quality that may be likened to the hour before dawn. The long night of mob domination is nearly over. At least on paper.

After years of lethargy, the state governments of New York and New Jersey have acted. Congress and the president have backed them up. On December 1, it will not only be a crime to employ longshoremen through the shape-up, it will no longer be lawful for homicidal criminals to serve as hiring bosses and union officials, as they still do this very Sunday. Labor racketeers, entrenched for over a quarter of a century, have been brought to the bar of public opinion. It took a long time, but, to the credit of Spruille Braden's New York City anticrime committee, the New York State Crime Commission, governors Dewey and Driscoll, and the president, it has been done.

On paper. Joe Docks, our average longshoreman, shrugs and says, "Let's wait 'n' see." On mob-dominated docks, he hesitates to express enthusiasm for the new New York–New Jersey waterfront commission because he fears his overlords will make good their threats to defy the government and the AFL and hang on somehow. When some local gauleiter tells him to march, he is all too likely to.

But if Joe Ryan & Co. is finally on the skids, who is to fill the vacuum? Dave Beck and his teamsters? Or one of the insurgent groups within the International Longshoremen's Association? Or some new labor setup not yet in existence, and perhaps, as yet, not even in the planning stage? Are there any natural leaders among the longshoremen? And is there a rank and file with guts enough to think for themselves?

In the course of asking these questions, I heard about an "honest" pier, Pier 45, the Grace Line dock on the Lower West Side. Here an interesting experiment in dock reform has been going on, unknown to the general public, for the past seven years. This was one-pier reform, spontaneous, improvised from below, rather than the harborwide, bistate, high-brass reform from above, but, in a general way, it may be studied as a preview of the working conditions and type of leadership that may prevail after the new law takes hold.

Eight years ago, Piers 45 and 46 were the private preserve of the Thompson brothers, Sonny and Eddie, lieutenants of the Dunn-McGrath mob that terrorized the Village waterfront until Dunn went to the chair in 1949 for murdering a hiring boss. In 1945, Sonny Thompson was doubling as union delegate and saloon-keeper, Eddie as hiring boss. Sonny's West Shore Bar and Grill, on West Street, facing the Hudson, was both an unofficial union headquarters and hangout for the pistols, loan sharks, and bookies who preyed on and intimidated longshoremen. The shakedown, organized pilferage, and most of the other waterfront vices flourished.

The men grumbled but the Thompsons, through their grip on Local 895, had absolute power. "Take it—or else," was their motto. There was always a human surplus willing to take it. A favorite trick was to recruit unemployed garment workers. Of course, there is a skill to handling cargo, and inexperienced men can endanger fellow members of a hatch or dock gang, but this was no skin off the Thompsons' noses. Demoralized longshoremen showed their resentment by hurling rocks into Thompson's bar. "It got so nobody would sit near the window," a customer recalls.

An ebb tide in the fortunes of Pier 45 was the departure of the Navy, which had kept the pier alive during the war. The Thompson piers, with their wholesale grafting, low efficiency, and disaffected dockworkers, offered slight inducement to shipping companies. Pier 45 lay idle and men went hungry.

In this moment of despair, a new, youthful "rebel" group began their search for a solution to the problem of unemployment and underworld rule. Their leader was stocky, thirty-year-old, dead-square and dead-game John Dwyer, who had come home from two years in the Pacific with the Navy in no mood to tolerate the shabby situation on West Street. Dwyer is not a verbal man; he's a hard, honest, practical man. His strength is in his physical courage, his dockside savvy, and his incorruptibility. Said one of his associates: "He drew you to him just by standing there and looking at you. You know he won't turn his back on a fight and you want him on your side." To his side came other longshoremen of 895, Pete Laughran, Jackie Mullins, John (Bibbles) Barrieo, Vincent (Bangles) Kuscinski, Eddie Barry . . .

The rebels of West Street challenged the mob by demanding regular meetings of 895 and a new election of officers. This was fantastic. Like most other longshore locals, 895 had had no membership meeting in some twenty years. But by fearless badgering and persistence, Dwyer and his men finally got their way.

The hierarchy of 895 consented to an election in November 1945. But this show of democracy was hardly an indication that the Thompson boys had reformed. To the polls established in the basement of St. Veronica's Church on the waterfront came hundreds of unexpected "voters." Said an ex–Thompson man who switched over: "Sonny brought some of those voters in from Greenpoint by taxicab. Their union buttons were so shiny new that all of us could tell they had never seen a union before." There were fistfights as the regular union men tried to save their election, but the "three hundred strangers" won the vote. "Officers were elected for five years that none of us had ever seen before," Bibbles Barrieo still recalls with bitterness.

That Christmas of '45 was Valley Forge for the rebels. Home relief and unemployment insurance provided the only means of subsistence, and the holiday pickings for their wives and children were unforgettably lean. It must have seemed, in the early months of 1946, as if they had committed themselves to a hopelessly one-sided battle. The Village mob was their sworn enemy now, and behind Thompson and Dunn was the power and constitutionality of the top ILA officialdom.

Although Alcoa was now ready to lease Pier 45, the embattled insurgents were unwilling to be victimized by the Thompsons, who, they claimed, had no right to negotiate a contract since they held their union offices by ballot stuffing and violence.

The rebels turned to the Association of Catholic Trade Unions, which provided them with free legal counsel in the person of Ed Scully. He advised them to bring official charges against the Thompsons, and a hundred men put their lives and their waterfront careers on the block by signing a court order requesting a new, free election. Hiring bosses were forbidden to employ them anywhere from Brooklyn to Hoboken. Dwyer had gone to work with an ammunition gang on the Jersey shore, but when Sonny Thompson passed the word along Joe Ryan had him fired. Dwyer's crusade against Ryan and the Ryan type of unionism (Sulka shirts and vacation luxuries on union funds) stems from this bitter period.

The Thompson–Dwyer deadlock continued into the summer of 1946, when, finally, Justice Henry Clay Greenberg appointed Professor Milton Handler of Columbia University to supervise a new, free election. Alcoa and the McGrath Stevedore Company were still anxious to open their pier, but they knew if they let Eddie Thompson blow the whistle to summon the men to the shape-up a majority of them would walk away. On the other hand, if they asked a "rebel" to do the hiring they were inviting trouble from the Thompson mob. Cockeye Dunn's boys had a habit of knocking off hiring bosses who refused to play ball with them.

One morning in August 1946, a stevedore superintendent said to Dwyer, "Do you think you could blow the whistle?" What he meant was, if Dwyer took charge would the regular longshoremen back him up? Although Dwyer has a strong back and a strong heart, he admits, "To tell the truth, I was scared to death. They threw me the whistle, and there I was, the new hiring boss. I was so scared I couldn't blow it. It's a tough job under the best conditions. You have work for maybe a couple of hundred men, and there are five or six hundred staring at you, begging for a day's work, and ready to call you every name in the book if you turn 'em down. When a hungry man looks at you, his eyes go right through you. It's a terrible responsibility."

The decision to let Dwyer handle the whistle was justified that December when the first legitimate election took place. Without his taxicab brigade to tip the voting scales, Sonny Thompson suddenly lost interest in running for union office and beat a strategic retreat to Miami, where he took up life as a bookie. The men of Pier 45 had won the right to govern their own affairs.

When John Dwyer blew that whistle seven years ago, he was heralding an unprecedented square deal for Pier 45. There was no way to eliminate the shape-up as long as it remained an official ILA policy approved by the shipping interests. What Dwyer did was to bring to it a fresh sense of fair play and judgment. Regular gangs were formed from men who were known as reliable workers and had families to support. The work was rotated. On many a gang run, dock veterans of twenty and thirty years are often pushed aside for hoodlums who can be of service. Here, on Pier 45, Dwyer tried to reward old-timers with the relatively easy work in the pier loft. As somebody said in Max's saloon, opposite the pier, "There's a heart on West Street."

But in the summer of 1948, Alcoa moved out to a smaller pier in Brooklyn, and 45 was dark again. The hint came from Joe Ryan's headquarters that shipping companies would be wise to let it remain dark. For months, 45 stood idle while the new leaders of Local 895 vainly petitioned the mayor and the port commissioner to bring it to life again.

Finally, they called a mass meeting at St. Veronica's to pressure the ILA and city officials and publicize their cause. Teddy Gleason, the West Side union boss allied today with die-hard waterfront criminals like Mickey Bowers and Eddie McGrath, was trying to hamstring the meeting when John Dwyer rose and accused him of fronting for Bill McCormack, the powerful waterfront multimillionaire, and Joe Ryan. "I'm walkin' out, and anybody with me can follow me out," he said. Every longshoreman in the hall, some six hundred, rose and followed Dwyer out, leaving Teddy Gleason talking to himself.

When the McGrath Stevedore Company left Pier 45 with Alcoa, they had taken Dwyer with them as an assistant superintendent. Immediately after Dwyer had led the walkout on Gleason, he was fired out of hand. "You shouldn't have sounded off at that meeting," he was told. But Dwyer had won something important: the overwhelming support of the membership of 895. "The night John got up and blasted Gleason, he lost his job, but he won the neighborhood," Pete Laughran recalls.

Again, there were lean months for Dwyer and his mates, but they persevered, and early in 1949 the Grace Line decided to take its chances with them. The gamble has paid off. For the last five years, Dwyer has been the hiring boss of 45. To suggest the ethical revolution that has come to West Street, one longshoreman put it this way: "Before John Dwyer, if you refused to play ball you never got a job there no more. A.D.—'After Dwyer'—it was the same thing in reverse. Anybody offering John anything was washed up."

* * *

The new slate that came in with Dwyer was a refreshing change. On too many piers, a safety man is more interested in selling his numbers and collecting his graft than in saving lives. On Pier 45, Jackie Mullins, the first reform president of Local 895, keeps an eagle eye on the equipment that has a life-and-death relationship to the men who use it or work under it. Pete Laughran is a unique shop steward. A steward is supposed to look out for the welfare of his men and channel their complaints to the hiring boss, the walking foremen, and the union and stevedore officials. On a mob pier, to put it mildly, he seldom does. On a Sonny Thompson pier, there were no shop stewards at all.

Today, Laughran keeps a solicitous eye on the men in the dangerous work on the dock. He can sense their moods, get them to air their grievances before they "blow their corks," causing work stoppage losses to the company and to their own take-home pay. A good shop steward makes the difference between a "happy ship" and a surly bunch laboring under a slave psychology and filching anything they can carry away.

Pilferage is a traditional vice among longshoremen, and on a mob-ridden pier it is easy to rationalize dishonesty. If you don't lift it, the "boys" will, by the truckload. On Pier 45, pilferage has been reduced to an almost invisible minimum. "Men who used to be consistent offenders can now make an honest living of four or five thousand a year. When you give them good conditions, men don't need to steal," Dwyer says.

In their desperation, the labor racketeers have tried to pin a Red label on Local 895. This makes the boys on West Street fighting mad. The fact is, they are predominantly Irish Catholics, who first turned for help to the ACTU, and who have been backed by Father Thomas G. Conboy, of St. Veronica's, and Father John M. Corridan, "the waterfront priest," whose recommendations to the New York State Crime Commission were closely followed in framing the new bistate law. Says Pete Laughran, "I think a real turning point was the time Father Corridan came down to bless the men during our tough strike for fairer conditions in 1951. We were being sold out by Joe Ryan and his council of stooges. Musclemen were roaming the waterfront. City Hall looked the other way, and most newspapers thought we were radicals. The mob called us Reds, and the Reds called us Fascists. Then Father John came down to the docks. It was like a sword cutting a path for us, separating us from the commies on one side and the mob on the other—a road for longshoremen to move ahead on."

Curiously enough, the men on 45 have not welcomed the new bistate law, as might have been expected. Having stabilized their own working conditions, they would rather keep the bird in hand than go after the two birds said to be nesting in the bush of harborwide reform. And the new law is a poser for John Dwyer himself. Under this law, he is faced with the alternative of remaining a hiring boss and dropping out of the union or continuing his union membership as a regular longshoreman. This makes sense in the abstract, although Dwyer managed to double in brass as a good union man and a fair hiring boss. He is ready to sacrifice his status in the interests of his union work.

This is only one of a number of differences between the longshoremen's own reform through Local 895 on Pier 45 and the new commission plan that will be supervised by Lieutenant General George P. Hayes of New York and Major General Edward C. Rose of New Jersey. Nevertheless, Pier 45 may be considered as a one-pier forecast of what could happen when the gangsters are driven off the docks. It is certainly to be hoped that the men of Pier 45, or men like them, will come forward to help restore the health of the Port of New York, and to bring to its thirty thousand regular longshoremen the dignity enjoyed by organized workers in responsible unions and responsible industries.

FROM BUDD SCHULBERG'S COLLECTION OF *SATURDAY EVENING POST* ARTICLES

Father John Knows the Score

PART I

Last winter, when crime on the New York waterfront hogged the headlines as a result of a thorough State Crime Commission investigation, a tall, ruddy-faced Irish priest with a salty West Side twang to his speech was making front-page news. PRIEST PUSHING PLAN FOR BETTER PIER CONDITIONS, said *The Herald-Tribune*. DOCK PURGE MAPPED BY WATERFRONT PRIEST, cried *The Daily News*.

Father John Corridan, a man who looks as if he could hold his own with a loading gang if ever he wanted to swing a cargo hook, was using moral and mental force instead as he came in swinging at the encrusted evils that have continually plagued the giant harbor of New York. He spoke on the Garroway show, and with Tex and Jinx; he debated waterfront problems on the air with City Council president Rudolph Halley, and punched home to an audience of many millions his eight-point plan for ridding the port of labor racketeers, criminal violence, inhuman working conditions, and wholesale pilferage.

Astonished TV viewers, accustomed to the more pious and conventional type of clergymen, could hardly believe their eyes and ears as they heard Father Corridan talk to them straight from the shoulder in crisp, waterfront language. "Y'know what the mob is sayin' about this latest investigation?" said this rapid-talking, slangy descendant of Saint Francis, Saint Vincent de Paul, and other inspired champions of the underdog. "They're warnin' longshoremen, 'We'll still be around when this thing blows over. We'll take care of the guys who talked. They'll be bodies floatin' in the river.' "

No wonder his TV audience asked itself if this was a clip from a forthcoming movie. A dynamic, good-looking Catholic priest standing up to the Sing Sing alumni who have corrupted stevedoring into an organized racket worth $350 million a year. What was this if not a Hollywood writer's hokey dream?

One skeptical viewer actually went so far as to ask me whether this rangy, fast-talking gent in the turned-around collar, full of bristling facts and figures on waterfront crime, was in truth a priest at all. I assured my doubting friend that he was—though I was similarly surprised three years before when I had first gone down to St. Xavier's on the Lower West Side to see Father John Corridan for myself. I had asked some reporters to fill me in on the waterfront story, and their advice had startled me: "Go down and see Corridan, Father John Corridan, that Father John, he really knows the score."

Next day, I was having lunch at Billy the Oysterman's with a chain-smoking, g-dropping, quick-witted West Side Irishman in his early forties. He was so full of his subject that he hardly looked at his food. It was the damnedest talk I had ever heard, a highly flavored verbal stew combining the gritty language of longshoremen with mob talk, the statistical trends of a trained economist, and the teachings of Christ.

"A frien' o' mine, a real holler-guy for the men, who's been talkin' up to the pistol boys in his local, died last month—fell off a cliff at a church picnic. *Fell?* That's a hot one. I'm tryin' to find out who did it. But I've got to play it very cute or they'll take it out on his widow. Geez, things're really hot down here!"

". . . sometimes these muscle boys get the idea—only it's a little late. Like that beer barrel across the river, Florio, the great trade unionist who owns a piece of everything on the Jersey side. Outside the Jefferson Democratic Club—which the mob owns—the brothers of a murdered hiring boss work him over with a lead pipe, and what does he holler? 'Saint Anthony, save me!'" An infectious grin spread across Father John's face. "Funny thing about those tough guys. They're not so tough when the heat is turned the other way."

Listening to Father Corridan with unconcealed amazement, I found myself in a new world—a world which I would have refused to believe could exist in America—just as I would have been skeptical if I had seen a movie about a Catholic priest who becomes a leader among rough-and-tumble dockers and stevedores, as tough in his own way as the killers who rule too many New York docks. In waterfront bars, I heard big-shouldered men with telltale cargo hooks in their belts swear on the heads of their beloved mothers that Father John was one of the very few men the waterfront racketeers really feared. They may sneer at him, curse him, ridicule him, and threaten him, but, when the smoke clears away, there he is, picking his way quietly and surely through the battleground described by the present district attorney as "the city's most depressed slum area—a spawning place of crime."

As Father Corridan's influence grew, one young hood was heard to remark, "Turned-around collar or no turned-around collar, if he keeps bucking the boys he's gonna get it." The youthful, tenement-hardened priest laughs off that kind of threat. "Tough kids don't frighten me. I feel sorry for them. The smart guys go to their funerals. In some of these West Side parishes, half the kids raised in parochial school grow up to be mobsters. The other half become priests. It's so tough that it seems like you have to go to one extreme or the other. There's no middle ground."

Mention any pier on the West Side and Father Corridan can name the mob that controls it, with the names of the hiring boss, the delegate, and the boss loader, together with an accurate account of their crimes, past and present, convicted and unconvicted, their political contacts in City Hall, their ties with multimillionaire waterfront tycoon "Big" Bill McCormack. He can make an educated guess at the incredible take, estimated at well over three hundred million a year, that has made New York harbor the happy hunting ground of the Anastasia, Mike Clemente, and the Mickey Bowers "pistol local" boys.

"Father John is a human encyclopedia of waterfront crime," a ship's reporter told me, "a one-man Kefauver committee, who carries on a round-the-clock investigation every day in the year." All he has to do is enter the DA's building and the whole waterfront is buzzing. Maybe he's got the dope on the murder of that hiring boss by the young mob trying to muscle in. Maybe he's going to needle the DA into taking some action. The boys watch him like a hawk.

When I asked Corridan about his growing reputation as "the conscience of the waterfront," he grinned at me, a little slyly, I thought, and made a humorous confession. "Once in a while, if I don't have anything to do for half an hour, I take my hat and coat and stroll over to the DA's office. I just walk in and out of the building. Then I wait to see what the boys in the back room think I went over there for. Sometimes I even pick up a little piece of news that way, because the boys think I'm on to something I haven't even heard of yet."

But most of the time Father Corridan's missions are no hoax. Whether he's called to Washington or interviewed by the press, it's a sure thing that he's been able to light up still another murky corner of that dark frontier along the Hudson.

A year ago, there was a good deal of talk about a young mob moving in on the Lower West Side. When I asked Father John about this, his answer was prompt and characteristically direct. "Scanlon. He's starting to throw his weight around. We're watching him."

[Johnny] Scanlon left a couple of Corridan's followers in a side street with concussions, after laying in wait for them with baseball bats. Today, he is in Sing Sing for assault, a rare example of law enforcement on the waterfront. For as Father John points out, of the hundreds of murders on the waterfront there have been only two convictions since 1928. Crime may not pay, but you could never prove it by New York harbor.

Up through the years, the piers have been divided among different gangs, Father Corridan explains, much as Chicago and New York were carved into mob empires in Prohibition days. The piers above Forty-second Street on the West Side are the domain of the Bowers gang, headed by the notorious Mickey Bowers and his cousin Harold, former bank robbers who muscled in and took over the local that controls all the jobs on the midtown piers. The great luxury lines, like the French, the Cunard, and the United States, submissively pay tribute to these racketeers, who grow fat on pilferage, shakedowns, public loading, numbers, loan-sharking, and half a dozen other angles blatantly pursued, although for years not blatantly enough to arouse the wrath of the law-enforcement agencies and the ILA officialdom who looked the other way. Below Thirtieth is the Chelsea area, once the province of Tanner Smith and that celebrated professor emeritus Owney Madden, but now the home of a "reform movement." While it would be stretching a point to say that labor racketeering is unknown to the Chelsea piers, there is an honest, insurgent group that draws its inspiration from Father John. Uncompromisingly antimob and anticommunist, they have been scrapping to establish a democratic beachhead on the docks.

The mob's grip on the Chelsea docks was loosened when a sinister figure called "Cockeye" Dunn went to the chair some ten years ago. Dunn, who ran these piers in partnership with his brother-in-law, dapper Eddie McGrath, admitted to more then a dozen murders when he was convicted for killing a hiring boss who had refused to pass on to him and McGrath the loot he was expected to exact from his strategic position on the pier. Dunn, an associate of the select circle that included such operators as Meyer Lansky, Frank Costello, Joe Adonis, and Phil Kastel, clammed up throughout his trial and while awaiting execution.

"They were just about ready to throw the switch on Cockeye when the tough guy started coming apart," Father John says, with a knowing grin. "He was ready to sing if the state would spare his life. The bait he held out was his willingness to turn in the real Mr. Bigs of the waterfront. The assistant DA hurried up to Sing Sing. But, suddenly, Dunn changed his tune. Or someone changed it for him.

Anyway, he sold himself on taking his chances with the chair instead of buying his life with the information that might have led to the conviction of the real movers behind this stinking mess on the waterfront." Dunn's widow has been drawing a payoff pension from the mob ever since. And Eddie McGrath merrily went his way, an ILA organizer for ten more years, with a yacht in the Bahamas and plushy suites in Miami Beach hotels. Called before the Crime Commission last winter, the smooth-talking, slick-haired, smartly tailored McGrath wouldn't even give his mother's name, on the ground that this—like every other answer—"might tend to incriminate and degrade him."

The Lower Manhattan piers, Father John will tell you, are the prize of the old Socks Lanza mob. There Mike Clemente has been operating so brazenly that you could go into the Twelfth Avenue saloon where he counted off the thousands of dollars in kickback money on the bar every Friday. Another old Sing Sing boy, Alex DiBrizzi, has the Staten Island territory, while the Brooklyn and East River docks are Anastasia country, controlled by America's most proficient and illustrious murderer, Albert Anastasia. It was against slippery Albert A. that clay-footed ex-mayor O'Dwyer once boasted of having "the perfect case," a case that literally went out the window when Murder, Inc., employee Abe Reles, held in a hotel room month after month by O'Dwyer's stalling boys in blue, found that flying was easier than singing and wound up as silenced meat on the pavement five floors below. Anastasia, Father John points out, despite his position as chairman of the board of Murder, Inc., has been singularly free of legal embarrassment these past thirty years. There was a time when mystery writers used to make quite a production of "the perfect crime." Shucks, Albert A. has committed dozens and dozens and dozens of them.

Not that there's anything so special about that on the waterfront, says Father John. And to prove it, he will cite chapter and verse on any number of interesting assassinations that have gone unpunished, and, indeed, unheeded. "Take Collentine, the hiring boss up at Pier 92 a few years ago. He was working with the Bowers boys—the Pistol Local, it's called for pretty obvious reasons—but I guess he got a little too big for himself, decided to go into business for himself, you might say. So he was knocked off in broad daylight right in front of his home, with three or four witnesses. No arrests, just a little routine questioning, and after a few months it's forgotten."

Father John went on describing, rapidly if somewhat matter-of-factly, the atmosphere of violence and sudden death in which he lives and teaches desperate and suspicious men the teachings of Christ. "There's an old-timer in the Red Hook section of Brooklyn, worked the docks before the First World War, one of his sons was killed by the mob several years ago. Recently, another son was bumped off by one of the young hoods as he came out of a saloon. The old man couldn't take any more. He got himself good and loaded and went to the meeting of his local and blew his stack. The place was full of trigger boys, but the old man got up and told 'em off. I was afraid they'd give it to him sure but he got away with it, maybe because of his age. Now, here's the end of the story . . ."

Some of the intensity of this fierce, almost unbelievably melodramatic but authentic experience seized the earthy, realistic priest as he talked.

". . . There's a third son, and he knows who rubbed his brother out. I'm worried about him. One of these days he's liable to get a few too many belts in him and blow his cork." Father Corridan patted the side of his cassock as if to draw an imaginary gun. If this seems an incongruous gesture for a man of the cloth—as if Chesterton's Father Brown were to be brought up to date and rewritten for Humphrey Bogart—it must be remembered that everything about Father Corridan is incongruous if you think of a priest in any of the established stereotypes.

Full of the nervous energy of the waterfront he serves, Father Corridan understands and hopes by this understanding to help correct the brutal and desperate measures used by hunters and hunted alike in the industrial jungle of New York harbor. Corridan is not the first, but he is by far the most active and involved of the waterfront priests who have made a unique effort to apply the teachings of Christ to the primitive struggle for survival on the docks.

Father Corridan's parents came from County Kerry, and although the older Corridan died when John was only nine years old the young priest remembers him as an incorruptible policeman whose sense of honor cramped the style of his superiors to such an extent that he spent most of his career in Rockaway and the hinterlands of Brooklyn. From his father, John Corridan inherited his keen sense of right and wrong; from his hardworking, warmhearted mother, he learned compassion and a never-failing belief in social justice. To these qualities, and his own determination to serve men by following as closely as possible the example of Christ, Corridan adds a master's degree in economics, and a realistic grasp of the waterfront labor–management picture that impresses everyone who comes in contact with him.

"Violence begets violence, and the dockers fight back because for too many years it was the only law they knew," Father Corridan explains. "They learned it in the streets when they were kids. The big man on the block, the one all the kids looked up to, was the neighborhood pistol. What I try to do—what all the waterfront priests try to do—is to help 'em learn how to defend themselves, how to hold their own in a meeting, how to cope with double-talking parliamentarians, and how to bargain for themselves in a lawful, intelligent way. You can pass all the reform laws you want; what we'd still need down here if we really want to clean up this mess, once and for all, is for the legitimate longshoremen to build their own, strong, honest organization, democratically, from the ground up. That way, they won't get pushed around by any kind of vested interests, neither by corrupt labor leaders, nor the shipping companies, nor the commies or the mob."

Democracy and more democracy, Christianity and more Christianity—but of the practical, down-to-earth variety that Christ Himself preached and practiced, and that the Xavier Labor School represents—that's the key to the unique class for longshoremen that Father John has been conducting for the past seven years. Today, this group spearheads a significant revolt against the Anastasias, the Camardas, Bowers, Clementes, and DiBrizzis, and the labor officialdom that was either too lazy or too contaminated to clean its own house, despite its repeated promises to do so. Today, Father Corridan is front-page copy, and his plan for harbor reform has been endorsed by the big metropolitan newspapers and vindicated by the unprecedented action of the AFL convention in publicly blasting its waterfront international. But when Father John first came to St. Xavier's in 1946, it was a different story.

The school had enjoyed notable success among the teamsters, printers, and municipal employees, but the waterfront was tough to crack. To understand why, you have to know something of the nature of longshoremen. Like all men who live in constant danger—either from industrial or extracurricular causes—they are clannish, secretive, and traditionally sullen with outsiders. Having spent the whole of their lives in an atmosphere of violent death, with privation, insecurity, greed, and corruption as a way of life, they have developed a hard, almost impenetrable core of cynicism. They drink hard and talk hard, and the majority of them will tell you—if they ever reach the point of confiding in you—that they live for today, drink and spend and take everything they can get today, for tomorrow who knows, a winch may slip, a truck may back up, a hook might swing in their direction, a gun go off, or they may find themselves passed up in the shape-up day after degrading day.

Father Corridan has seen for himself the shocking spectacle of men offering themselves on a human auction block. And he has become even more deeply convinced that the shape-up method of hiring is the foul root from which crime and political corruption inevitably spreads through the waterfront. His conclusions, interestingly enough, are identical with that of the New York Anti-Crime Commission, headed by the Honorable Spruille Braden. Its wire to Governor Dewey warned him that the graft and criminal violence on the waterfront could be traced to "the unfair and even brutal shape-up system." The New York Port Authority and AFL leaders have also formed the campaign to outlaw the "shape."

This system, Father Corridan maintains, is not only un-Christian and un-American but a positive menace to our national efficiency and security. For him, Christianity is not an abstract dogma but a living force; the most cynical agnostic could not help feel the presence and the power of Christ when he describes the inhuman conditions he has witnessed and studied on the waterfront. "I figured out, on the basis of yearly income and man-hours, that there is about enough work to support seventeen thousand longshoremen and their families," he told me. "There are more than twice that many shaping up. The uncertainty, the humiliation of having to stand there and beg with your eyes for work while brutal ex-cons look you over like you were so much meat in a butcher-shop—no wonder the men who get passed over drift off to the bars and fall deeper into the clutches of the loan sharks."

The average longshoreman doesn't tell his wife what pier he's going to be working at for fear she will worry, or that some crime or act of violence might lead to her being questioned. Even though it's honest work at an unsteady wage earned with muscle and sweat, a longshoreman goes off to his job with some of the stealth a thief would exercise if he were meeting his cronies to rob a bank. It may be a somewhat perverted tradition, but it is well known that longshoremen will clam up even about the murders of their own pals and coworkers.

Collentine, for instance, the murdered hiring boss whose case is one of hundreds Father Corridan has studied, went to his death refusing to divulge the name of his assailant. To some extent, the code of the mob has infected even the honest and law-abiding dockers. In addition, there's the constant fear of getting involved, of risking your own neck for a futile gesture, for the longshoremen have come to take it for granted that suspected murderers are either overlooked completely or receive a routine questioning and allowed to return to their easy pickings and their murderous ways.

It was this "little iron curtain," as Father John calls it, this wall of cynicism and fear, distrust, and moody resignation that Corridan prayed for the strength and the savvy to break through in 1946. Now and then, a lone workman would wander in off the docks out of curiosity or some terrible personal need. But the potential leaders, the catalysts that Father John had hoped to find, kept their distance. In fact, he had almost despaired of "cracking the waterfront" when, near the end of 1947, a delegation of about twenty men, a number of them from the militant and relatively democratic Local 791, finally showed up at Xavier. They were only a few, compared to the tens of thousands who depend on the waterfront for their living, and in their work clothes and with their hard-jawed, weatherbeaten faces they looked no different from the working stiffs on the docks who seemed, in Father Monaghan's vivid language, to have been "spit up from hell."

But these men had come to Father Corridan out of a deep-rooted instinct for fair play and human welfare, for their fellow workers as well as for themselves. They were rank-and-file leaders, not professional union organizers with soft berths and fat expense accounts. They were the real, rock-bottom holler-guys not afraid to stand up and be counted, even when the counting was done by hired goons at the business end of a .45. They came to Xavier one by one at night because they knew their enemies; they knew that even entering Church property in a body would be considered a hostile move by the wolf pack who preyed on the labor and the shipping of the port.

They had their doubts, they admitted later, as to whether or not this young priest with the print hardly dry on his diploma in economics could do them any good. They had come only as a last resort because they felt stymied, frustrated, bewildered, and all other avenues of counsel seemed closed off to them. Although they were Catholics, as are most longshoremen, overwhelmingly Irish and Italian—they had no illusions about the wisdom or infallibility or even the integrity of priests per se. On the waterfront, along with "good priests" who understood their dilemma, like Father Monaghan, and Father Head at St. Veronica's, there was another who was, to put it mildly, less than a spiritual example to the men. This priest, longshoremen believed, had the backing of stuffed-shirt labor leaders and waterfront hoodlums. When he had wanted to build a new church, these rather soiled Christians had chipped in from their blood money, or had pressured the men on the docks to pay tribute, just as the men are systematically "encouraged" to kick in for other "causes" that too often turn out to be the welfare of the boys in the double-breasted suits. The rank-and-file dockers who had seen this other priest play politics with their welfare happened to be not only good Catholics but men who went to church every day, perhaps because death is not just an eventuality for them but a daily threat. But life on the docks had made pragmatists of all of them, even if they would probably gag on the word. A little ill at ease, self-consciously trying to comb the rough spots out of their earthy waterfront vocabulary, and half convinced that all this technical waterfront stuff would just be wasted on a man of God, the longshoremen told their story.

Father John listened. Occasionally he made notes in a rapid, half-shorthand scrawl. At times, he leaned back and put the tips of his fingers together, to form something that looked a little like a bishop's hat—his only parochial gesture. Most of the time, he studied the faces of the men just as intently and frankly as they were studying his.

"We didn't expect him to pull no rabbits out of a hat," a member of this original delegation told me recently. "Fact is, I don't know what the hell we did expect. We just figured we'd lay our story on the line and see what kind of a fella he was."

What Father Corridan learned was this: The work longshoremen do is vital to the nation, and as arduous as mining—and even more dangerous. But where the miners have a powerful union responsive to their needs, the longshoremen were held in check by too many mob-controlled locals so accustomed to bribes from employers that they had developed into company unions. As AFL president George Meany has wisely observed, these were no longer unions at all but simply fronts for every kind of waterfront racket, from extortion and systematic pilferage to smuggling of aliens and traffic in narcotics. In these hijacked locals, the key figures were the business agent, the hiring bosses, and boss loaders, and since these jobs had become the hand-me-downs of the underworld the ordinary longshoremen had to depend on the whim and malicious approval of the mobsters for his employment. His daily bread was measured by his willingness to play ball with the mob, which means kicking back as much as five dollars a day to the hiring boss for every day he was chosen. This made him a vassal and an unwilling ally of the mobs in power on all but a few of the docks.

Meanwhile, the benefits to longshoremen lagged behind that of nearly any other worker in America. While autoworkers, steelworkers, miners, and garment workers were forging ahead, longshoremen had no pension plan, no welfare plan, no equitable vacation plan, no safety rules, and, worst of all, no security from week to week, or even day to day. In 1945, Corridan learned from this historic visit, Joe Ryan had signed a new contract for the longshoremen without their knowledge, much less their consent.

With returning servicemen wanting a better deal than they had had in prewar days, with prices climbing, with Joe Ryan asking the men, or, rather (Corridan's group asserts), telling them, to be satisfied with a dime-an-hour raise that was not even compensated for by regulated employment, restlessness and discontent began to seethe on the waterfront. The first of a series of costly wildcat strikes was a spontaneous rebellion against the callous officialdom. In the absence of responsible leadership, the communists, usually an isolated minority, were able to move in, exploit, and take credit for the uprising.

Now, in 1947, another contract had just been signed without the democratic participation of the forty thousand longshoremen. Again, the men on the docks were muttering "sellout." Whether the city authorities, whether even the ILA bureaucrats were aware of it, another flare-up, another costly wildcat strike was imminent. Once more, the communists would be ready to make political capital of the leaderless demonstration. What was the answer? The little group who had crept in out of the darkness to lay their cards on Father Corridan's desk felt hopelessly hemmed in by rival totalitarians: the union racketeers, who watched and controlled their every move on the docks, and who operated with the support or the connivance or, at best, the disregard of the shipping companies and the city authorities; and the communists, who agitated for longshoremen's interests but were always ready to change their tune the moment this policy no longer suited the aims and ambitions of Soviet Russia.

The problem with which Father Corridan had been presented that night was a technical and pressing one: How could the locals, including the relatively unfettered 791, reestablish their right to vote on the contract agreement? Father Corridan's answer was simple. He said he didn't know. He would have to study their constitution and bylaws. He would need a more detailed knowledge of the relationship of the men to their leaders, or overlords, in each local. He wasn't there to make snap judgments or hasty decisions. Then he played the card he had been holding up the sleeve of his cassock for almost two years. Whether or not they could solve their immediate problem in time to do something about the pending crisis, he frankly doubted. There was a long-range problem of decent leadership on the waterfront. There was no use going from panic to panic and defiance to defiance. The way to defy mob rule and undemocratic action on the waterfront would be to train a body of potential leaders who could go among the longshoremen armed with facts and fortified by a program. He and Xavier were willing to tackle the job if they were ready to go back to school—to spend a number of evenings a month thrashing out their common problems and hammering out a strategy that would appeal to and serve the best interests of the men.

Father Corridan admits he held his breath while the men looked at each other in questioning silence. He waited for their answer. Finally, a short, wiry, broken-nosed man of sixty spoke up for the group. "Well, I never got further 'n grammar school, and I ain't too sure about this class stuff, but I guess I'll give it a try."

These few tentative words muttered by a little old man who had gone to work on the docks as a child-laborer before the First World War were to have some of the effect of the first shot fired at the battle of Lexington. If they were not to be heard around the world, they were certainly, before another year had passed, to be heard around the New York waterfront, whose traffic and whose health, or disorganization, acutely affects the world.

PART II

After several years of watchful waiting, of futile efforts to break through the wall of suspicion behind which longshoremen labored and were treated like beasts of burden, Father Corridan finally had managed to draw in off the docks a handful of disciples. After that first, historic meeting, they slipped out into the night—careful not to be followed, for this was as much an underground as any in Europe. But one man remained behind. He was the gnarled, flat-faced, dock-hardened old man who had been the spokesman for the group. His name was Tim McGlynn—at least, we'll call him that, for the waterfront situation is still too explosive at this writing to identify him more definitely. (Last winter, one of Corridan's most outspoken supporters was shot at by goons while watching a TV program with his young son in his own parlor.) Tim and Father John were sizing up each other. In many ways, they represented the two extremes of Irish Catholicism.

Although from origins as humble as McGlynn's, Corridan was a master of arts from St. Louis University. He had studied for the Jesuit Order, at the same time continuing his studies in economics, statistics, and labor law. He was well read in half a dozen fields; he was urbane, well rounded, at ease with the most sophisticated as well as the most humble group. McGlynn, on the other hand, was a true product of the Irish West Side and the docks. He was, he admitted, not adverse to a drink now and then; in fact, his wife was apt to describe him as "taken with drink." As a man of four-, five-, six-, and seven-letter words, he could hold his own with the loudest, coarsest mouths on the docks. He had spent his entire sixty years on the waterfront; midtown Manhattan was almost as strange to him as it would be to an immigrant. But, like Corridan, his parents had battled the British Black and Tans in the cause of Irish Republicanism. And, like Corridan, he was a natural scrapper who had stood up to the union goons and the triggermen of the mob for decades. His face looked like an old ex-pug's, for he had lost count of the times he had been beaten into unconsciousness. He knew how it felt to take a bullet. And twice he had been left for dead, with cargo hooks in his neck and in his ribs.

"I'm on borried time," Tim confided to Father Corridan, "I shoulda been dead twenny years ago." A marked man because he refused to knuckle under to the boys who pocketed union dues, he seemed to bear a charmed life, as if his very defiance had clothed him in armor plate and lent him a legendary indestructibility.

Corridan was pretty sure he had found his man at last, a worker short on education and grammar but long on native intelligence and guts, who could absorb the teachings of Francis Xavier and put them to practical use on the waterfront. McGlynn, he realized, was a natural labor leader; for years, he had been fighting a heroic, futile, lone-wolf, undisciplined battle against union sellouts, gunmen, greedy shipping interests, and Stalinist opportunists. He had stood up and shot off his mouth and gotten his head bashed in for it, and then stood up again.

He admitted a lot of things to Father John that night. Some of the corruption of the waterfront had poisoned his own soul, he confessed, though he didn't say it that fancy. On his record was a stretch in reform school, and another for petty larceny. The line at which larceny begins is a delicate and often invisible one on the waterfront. In the code of the longshoremen, for instance, it is not considered pilferage for a man to lift articles for his personal use. Larceny doesn't begin until you steal enough to sell off the surplus.

Father John told McGlynn to forget about the bad raps. After all, he was a West Sider himself, from a family as poor as any in the neighborhood—poorer, perhaps, because his father had died when he was nine, and his mother had had to work as a cleaning woman, and deprive herself and struggle every waking hour to raise four sons. Petty larceny was something for which he had a special understanding.

McGlynn grinned. In the course of the evening, he had begun to trust this priest who talked a language seldom heard on the docks—that of honest trade unionism. He had been a faithful churchgoer all his life, but he had never thought of a priest as an adviser and an ally in the bitter struggle for survival on the docks. "But you, you're okay, Father." He winked at Corridan. "You seem to know the score."

So began an alliance, and the first steps toward a profound friendship that may yet affect the balance of power on the waterfront. McGlynn was afraid he was too old to submit to the discipline of a classroom and the supervisory eye of a teacher-priest. But to his own amazement, and Father John's prayerful satisfaction, he soon developed into a prize pupil. "The Father didn't hand us any crap," he explains. And Father Corridan says, "It was a fifty-fifty proposition. I learned as much from them as they did from me. It was from them that I got a firsthand picture of how the system works, the gang pressure, and the terrible inadequacies of the hiring system. In return, I gave them a clearer idea of their rights, and how to go about asserting them in a parliamentary way. We worked together, and we strengthened each other, and we hammered out a plan."

It was Corridan who enlightened the men as to their rightful claim to some $15 million in unpaid overtime under Article 731 of the Wage-Hour law. He wrote a letter to every senator and to all the key representatives explaining in detail the legal and moral justification for the longshoremen's case, at the same time urging a senate investigation of the chronic infection that has paralyzed—and will continue to, until effective reforms are instituted—the greatest harbor in the world.

Corridan's efforts are double-edged. Through the widening circles of dockworkers who have come under his influence, his principles and economic tactics are carried to the larger body of longshoremen by such disciples as McGlynn. At the same time, with the information he gleans from his waterfront contacts he operates as a one-man, but surprisingly effective, lobby, bringing unreported murders and assaults to the attention of key reporters who have the honesty and conscientiousness to buck the waterfront curtain of lead, encouraging meetings under the protection of the Church so they will be reasonably safe from underworld marauders, alerting city authorities to the trouble spots in the hope that action will be taken, feeding telling facts and inescapable conclusions to civic groups who can help dispel the confusion and ignorance that has long beclouded public opinion of the waterfront blight. It was an open secret that during both the Kefauver and New York Crime Commission investigations of waterfront crime, some telling evidence came from Father John's unofficial but deadly effective fact-gathering system. A waterfront figure who had once been close to the mob gave a detailed picture to the Crime Commission of specific illegal operations on the docks he had worked. The newspapers had been playing up the death threats that had been hanging over him the week he was to testify, and there was a good deal of speculation in the press room as to why this man was taking such a chance. A short time after he testified to murders, kickbacks, and shakedowns of which he had firsthand knowledge, I had an opportunity to ask him the question that was in everybody's mind, What made you want to do it? How did you get the nerve? This man whose life was said to be in imminent danger shrugged casually and said, "Corridan."

Sometimes a dockworker who has stumbled on some particularly incriminating fact will sneak into Father John's chambers at night, and then hurry off again, never to return. For as Father Corridan's influence grew, it had become more and more dangerous to be identified with him. Fortunately, the men had found a man who could be as closemouthed as they were. He has never been known to reveal a source or betray a confidence. He is a natural intelligence officer, with his sure instinct for which men to trust and which to avoid.

One young longshoreman in his class, for instance, was a real fire-eater, a young militant ready to push the mobsters right into the river. Father Corridan was wary of this excess of spirit. He had McGlynn and some of the other "Corridan men" keep an eye on the kid in the waterfront saloons. Sure enough, the kid was talking too much. He was shooting off his mouth about plans and tactics that were still in the discussion stage at Xavier's. The kid, for all his good intentions, had to be eased out of the Xavier group.

By 1948, when the emotions of the men on the docks were gathering toward another eruptive strike, Father John Corridan was ready to play a decisive, if discreetly off-stage, role in the tumultuous events of the waterfront. By this time, "Father John knows the score" was a popular saying among the reform element, and "Father John is a no-good son of a bitch" was an equally popular saying in the mob-ridden beer joints that look out on the docking and sailing of such luxury liners as the *Queen Elizabeth*, the *United States* and the *Île de France*. Whenever some prickly issue arose, men had begun to ask, "What's Father John got to say about this?" His realism, his ability to foresee some workable pattern for the chaotic working conditions, plus plenty of good old-fashioned moxie that never loses its appeal to the boys of Hell's Kitchen, was finally beginning to pay off.

During one of his talks, for instance, a heckler kept interrupting. As a Corridan admirer described it to me, "Father John had his number. Right in the middle of his talk he stops and goes up to this sharp-looking character. He says, 'I know who sent you so go back to your bosses and deliver this message: Tell 'em if anything happens to the men I'm trying to help here, I'll know who's responsible, and I'll see to it that they're broken throughout this port. They'll pay, and I'll see that they pay.'" The Bowers boys, the Clementes, and Scanlons tried to dismiss Father Corridan with sneers and muttered threats. Men suspected of "Corridanism" were brutally worked over in the dark side streets near the river.

But the class in self-help and up-from-under leadership continued. Men came in off the docks in their work clothes, their faces still grimy from the hold or sweating from the heavy work. The only way that Father Corridan ever touched upon religion in this waterfront class was to ask his students what they considered the basis of economics. Invariably, they would name "money," "break," "profit," or "labor supply." And, invariably, Corridan's answer was "Man." "Only man is capable of knowing and loving," he would tell them. "In other words," he said to me, "I teach 'em the dignity of man."

The inhumanity of the shape-up haunts Father Corridan. The things he has seen with his own eyes are intensified by what he has heard from Tim McGlynn and the other veterans. There is unforgettable suffering, as frenzied as anything in Dante's *Inferno*, in McGlynn's description of a particularly chaotic "shape" that took place in the hungry thirties. A new hiring boss didn't know how to cope with the hundreds of job-hungry, wild-eyed men pressing in around him. Instead of going among the men with torturous poise and coolly passing out brass checks, representing work, to his favorites, the new boss got panicky and flung the brass checks in the air. Like a medieval rabble scrambling for crusts of bread, the men threw themselves on the ground and punched, gouged, wrestled, and kicked each other for the little brass checks and the few dollars for which they could be redeemed when their four-hour job was through—the all-important four hours' work that would mean food in the bellies of their wives and children that day. Men were knocked unconscious. Vicious gashes were opened and bones were broken. It sounds more like a throwback to the days of Roman tyranny than an event that took place, and went unnoticed, in the modern city of New York some fifteen years ago.

Father Corridan regarded the incident as marking a new low in waterfront inhumanity, but McGlynn didn't agree. This was a squarer shape than the usual ones "rigged by the boys." At least, this was every man for himself, and may the best man win. "I got my nose busted," McGlynn remembers, "but I got a chance to work without no kickback."

Sometimes Father Corridan walks the streets of the waterfront and ponders the horror of this scene. Where does one man—and that man usually a thug and convicted criminal—get the right to control the livelihood, the very life's breath, of other men merely by pointing or not pointing a finger at them? What would Christ say if He were standing here on the waterfront among these desperate men? This question inspired a memorable sermon on the docks, one of the few times when Father Corridan revealed the spiritual passion behind his interest in human welfare on the waterfront.

Said Father Corridan:

> I suppose some people would smirk at the thought of Christ in the shape-up. It is about as absurd as the fact that He carried carpenter's tools in His hands and earned His bread by the sweat of His brow. As absurd as the fact that Christ redeemed all men irrespective of their race, color, or station in life. It can be absurd only to those of whom Christ said, "Hav-

ing eyes, they see not; and having ears, they hear not." Because they don't want to see or hear. Christ also said, "If you do it to the least of mine, you do it to me." So Christ is in the shape-up. . . .

He stands in the shape-up knowing that all won't get work and maybe He won't. What does Christ think of the efficiency argument of the shape-up. . . . Some people think that the Crucifixion took place only on Calvary. Christ works on a pier and His back aches because there are a fair number of the "boys" on the pier. They don't work, but have their rackets at which so many wink. What does Christ think of the man who picks up a longshoreman's brass check and takes twenty percent interest at the end of the week?

Christ goes to a union meeting. Sees how a meeting is run. Sees how few go. Sees how many men don't speak. Sees a certain restraint. At some meetings, he sees a few with $150 suits and diamond rings on their fingers . . . drawing a couple of salaries and expense accounts. . . . Christ walks into a tenement and talks with the wife of a longshoreman. Her heart is heavy.

As an audience, there's nothing tougher than longshoremen. They're edgy, suspicious, and quick to smell a phony. They gag easily on verbal syrup. They've *had* the silver-tongued orators, from the president of their international up and down, trying to sweet-talk them out of their rights. Their name for former mayor O'Dwyer, even in the days when his prestige was at its height, was "Weeping Willie." "So maybe we don' have too much education," a docker told me in a Chelsea saloon, "but you don' hafta go t'collich t'know who's with ya and who ain't. Father John is with us. He ain't tryin' t'sell us out like these itchy-finger boys posin' as organizers. And he ain't signin' us up for some phony peace pledge like the commies either. He's one of us. We believe in God up there and a fair shake down here."

Father Corridan studied economics and labor problems at two universities, but he didn't learn about poverty and the cause of humanity out of any book. When his father died, his mother, Hannah, was left with five boys, of whom one died in childhood. The oldest was John, and although he was only nine he now had to pitch in and help care for his four brothers. "The old man didn't leave any money—he was an honest cop," Father John explains. The pension was not enough to feed and clothe them properly, so his mother went to work as a cleaning woman at the neighborhood police station. John and his brothers still call her "the Little General" for her ability to run her household and raise her sons so successfully on her meager income.

The boys learned how to handle themselves in the free-for-all of tenement life. The only way the Corridan boys could get enough money to see a ball game was by pooling their few pennies and hoping to run them up into dimes and quarters in a crap game. Once, when John was about eleven, he hit a lucky streak. With pass after pass, the money was beginning to bulge in his pocket, and he had practically cleaned out the game when he looked around at the hard faces of the fifteen- and sixteen-year-old boys with whom he had been playing. He saw he was never going to be able to take his winnings out of the game. With apparent recklessness, he began to lose back the money faster than he had won it. When he convinced the bullying crapshooters that he was "cleaned," by showing them his empty pockets, he was allowed to go on his way.

His younger brothers followed him listlessly; they had set their hearts on the ball game. John kept walking until they were around the next corner; then he reached down into his knickers—way down—and produced four dollars. He had pushed them through a hole in his pocket before ostensibly playing his winnings back into the game. Today, when Father Corridan prepares for a showdown by holding some special information in reserve, his phrase for the proverbial "ace in the hole" is "the hole in my pocket."

One Christmas season, when John was about eleven, there wasn't enough money in the house to buy any real presents for the

Corridan boys. An uncle had given each boy fifty cents, but the four sons had pooled their money to buy stockings as a Christmas gift for their mother. John and his brothers braved the hostile East Side to attend a Curb Exchange party for underprivileged children, in the hope that they would get the sort of presents they were realistic enough not to expect in their own home on Christmas morning. The gifts turned out to be ten-cent store items of a practical nature. The intention might have been there, Father Corridan now thinks, but the true Christmas spirit was lacking, as was any understanding of the real desires of poor children deprived of playthings.

Guiding his brothers through the enemy streets to the West Side, young John couldn't fight down a growing sense of bitterness about this season of goodwill toward men. He wasn't so concerned for himself; the one he was brooding about was Bobby, his three-year-old brother. He knew the youngest of the Corridan boys had asked Santa Claus for a fire engine. Now, as the day approached, Bobby's confidence that Santa would answer his prayers was reaching such proportions that John was overwhelmed with temptation.

The day before Christmas, he went to a toy store and priced a red fire engine. Two dollars. He hid out until the store was closed, then sneaked up to the cash register and jimmied it in a way he had learned from the hoodlum element on his block. The drawer shot open. "I looked at all that money," Father John remembers. "I could've taken it all. But all I wanted was that two dollars." When the fire engine turned up under the Corridans' skimpy tree on Christmas morning, John's mother said nothing, but she looked at him. The boy tried to avoid her eyes. He was troubled, for now he faced the problem of how the priest would react to his crime at confession.

"That was a turning point in my relations with the Church," Father Corridan says now. "Seeing how much that fire engine meant to my little brother, and knowing what an empty Christmas it would have seemed if Santa had let him down, I made up my mind that if the priest gave me too much hell I was through with the Church. That would have broken my mother's heart, of course, so I went to confession that day with my knees trembling." Fortunately for Father John and the Church he later was to serve with such devotion, the priest was understanding and helped put John's mind at ease. "I did penance," Father Corridan recalls, "but I didn't have to make my kid brother give up his fire engine."

When he grew up to become a priest himself, he never forgot this incident. It was the story that was in his mind, for instance, when Tim McGlynn confessed his petty larcenies. Father Corridan isn't condoning dishonesty and disrespect for law. But he feels his own brief adventure in bad means to a good end helps him to understand the desperate measures his parishioners can sometimes be driven to when poverty pins them to the wall, especially when their children are made to suffer for reasons of greed and indifference.

He still remembers entering his railroad flat as a child and seeing, when she greeted him at the door, a set, embarrassed expression on his mother's face that meant only one thing: a social worker was in the apartment checking up. Yes, Father John doesn't have to draw on any books or secondhand knowledge when he describes the life of a longshoreman's wife in her cold-water flat, pinching pennies to feed her kids. For a short period of his life, he was a runner for a Wall Street brokerage firm, and he even had dreams of becoming a millionaire. But gradually, he says, as he watched men in the boom days accumulate fortunes without any sense of social responsibility, he came to the decision that he should follow in His steps. But, with his memories of hunger and humiliation, he would serve God among the poorest of His children; he would devote his life to social justice. "If you do it to the least of mine, you do it to me," became the core of his faith.

Three years ago, another contract with the shipping companies was up for consideration, and Father Corridan learned from his Xavier group what the majority wanted: not merely a raise, but a welfare fund and a vacation clause. Once more, there was a general suspicion on the waterfront that the ILA leadership was preparing to sell them out. The men sat up late that night analyzing the situation with Father John. Tim spoke for them all when he said, "If this deal goes through, Father, it means a strike, sure, no matter what Joe Ryan says. The men need that welfare plan and a better vacation setup. If we don't try to get it for 'em, the commies will grab the issue and try to make themselves the heroes."

Father Corridan proceeded in a characteristic way that drew this summation of him from Pulitzer Prize–winning reporter Malcolm Johnson: ". . . cool as a cucumber, as patient as Job, and as tough as the situation demands." Instead of flying off the handle in an emotional way, he sat down night after night with an experienced insurance man and worked out a practical plan on the Blue Cross model that could be operated for less than four cents an hour. Then, early one morning, he went down to Washington and managed to see both John Steelman, the president's labor adviser, and Cyrus Ching, then head of the National Mediation Board. Father Corridan wasn't relying on a spiritual, humanitarian appeal. He had carefully marshaled the facts and figures to prove his case. He was still talking to Ching as the shadows lengthened on the government buildings. The needs of the dockworkers had never had such specific presentation. Ching listened, patiently poker-faced, as befits a veteran mediator. What were Corridan's qualifications as a spokesman for the longshoremen? he wondered. Was he really speaking for the majority? He wasn't speaking for them at all, Father Corridan protested. He was merely describing the situation as he knew it to exist, from his day-to-day experience as a waterfront priest. Nor was he advocating a strike. He was merely assuring Ching, from his knowledge of the mood of the men, that the dockers would rebel against Ryan and tie up the port if the proposed inadequate contract went through.

When the strike did break out, exactly as Father Corridan had predicted, and Joe Ryan refused to take it seriously, Corridan wrote an article for the Jesuit magazine *America* detailing the case for the longshoremen and had twelve thousand reprints of it distributed on the waterfront by Tim McGlynn and the Xavier group. The program Father Corridan laid out responded exactly to the long-frustrated de-

Longshoremen on the Chelsea docks sit it out after refusing to obey the shape-up whistle on November 10, 1948. The wildcat strike on the waterfront was a rejection of a ten-cent hourly wage increase that had been accepted by union leaders. Joseph P. Ryan, president of the International Longshoremen's Association, initially blamed the walkout on Johnson's articles. Photograph copyright © Bettmann/CORBIS.

sires of the majority. The name of Father John became a byword on the waterfront. When the Conciliation Board met to settle the strike, the men saw to it that a copy of his article was placed before every negotiator. When the shipping association accepted both the welfare fund and equitable vacations with pay, Father John was widely credited with having won something for the men that they had been after for twenty-five years.

He just grins when you mention this. "All I did was tip the conciliation boys off to the pitch." And he maintains that he is not a waterfront leader, just a friend and adviser of the rank-and-filers. "It's simply that I have the confidence of quite a few of the men," he says. "They come to me for advice and I give it. They want information and I dig for it."

Holding services for striking longshoremen three years ago, Father John offered this prayer: "For those longshoremen who are straight and are good family men, God be praised; / For those who slip every once in a while and lose hope, God have mercy; / To *those responsible*, God grant the grace to see things as Christ sees them on the waterfront, for the time is growing short when God will have no mercy."

Last November, the pattern of the 1948 rebellion was repeated again. Once more, President Joe Ryan and his ILA committee of 125 approved a new contract with the companies and once more the longshoremen rose up against it. The Chelsea local 791 that Xavier men had taken over from the remnants of the old Cockeye Dunn mob called a strike because they had rejected the contract and believed the vote to be fraudulent. A spirit of protest and a demonstration of independence spread up and down a waterfront that union racketeers could no longer control. And Father John Corridan was back in the news again. At daybreak, he was on the waterfront leading the aroused dockworkers in prayer:

"God grant that our government will order you back to work only with honor. May God protect and preserve you this day."

It was difficult for the average citizen and newspaper reader to make any sense out of the heated charges and countercharges as the great Port of New York stood paralyzed day after day. One of the more reputable papers in the city, for instance, charged that the strike inspired by Local 791 was a communist plot. Father Corridan is an implacable and effective foe of communism. But he believes that to cry "Communism!" every time American workers make a move for self-protection and social betterment is to play into the hands of the communists.

"You think these fellers are communists." Father John grins at you. "Strange breed of communists who never miss mass and who come to me and our Catholic labor school for help and advice. Better not call 'em that, unless you want to get belted. Joe Ryan wishes they were communists. Then he could wrap himself in the old flag and have it easy. Actually, he does more for the C.P. than he'll ever realize. Since '48, Bridges on the West Coast has had twenty-four strikes with a man-day loss of seventy-five thousand. Ryan has had forty-five strikes with a man-day loss of five hundred thousand. In other words, as a labor columnist put it recently, Ryan has given Stalin five times as much pleasure as Harry Bridges. And Ryan's do-nothing, know-nothing policy serves up on a platter a lot of big fat issues the communists can exploit. The men who walked off the docks in protest against a contract that had been voted for them but not by them are loyal and decent, God-fearing Americans who don't want mobsters to capture their locals, and who don't need or want the communists to win their battles for them. The way to stop communism—graduates of Xavier have done it in the Teamsters Union, on the telephone, and lots of others ways—the way to stop 'em from dominating these unions is to accentuate the positive—in other words, to find out what the men really want, what their real beefs are, what they need in order to live healthy, happy, dignified lives, and then to fight for it fairly and squarely, and even harder than the commies do. Social progress, American style, will do more to cut the ground from under the communists than all the noisy Red-baiting of the unholy alliance of shipping owners, mobsters, and union opportunists."

Without any mock heroics, Tim McGlynn told me that he was ready to do anything Father John asked of him—even if it meant laying down his life in the cause of honest unionism and the cleanup of waterfront crime. "What've I got to worry about?" this embattled old man assured me. "I'm on borried time anyway. Like I told the old lady. Any day I don't come home, just call Father John. The boys will always chip in to see my family's taken care of, and Father John'll look after everything. Long as I'm sure he's gonna be with me at the end to give me the last rites, I figger I'm on velvet." This was no speech. The way he said it, it was the simplest thing in the world. Then his wizened, scuffed-up, weather-beaten face split in a funny grin. What he said next had something spiritual about it, but it was 1953, waterfront style. "Sure the mob's tough, but Father John's tougher. One of these days he's gonna run 'em right into the river. That Father John—he really knows the score."

An up-to-the-minute economist, an astute politician, a down-the-liner for human rights, a man who lives his Christianity and shepherds the hard-talking, hard-drinking, pugnacious men of the waterfront jungle—that's Father John Corridan. His work on the docks may be just beginning. His plan for long-range dock reform, officially submitted to the New York State Crime Commission, calls for the elimination of the shape-up, systematized employment for the regular gangs, hiring centers run by the Port Authority for honest employment of extra men, registration (but not licensing) of dockworkers so that old-timers can enjoy seniority and other union benefits and casuals and drifters can be weeded out, removal of hardened criminals as hiring bosses, elimination of the public loading racket, and, of course, the institution of democratic procedure from top to bottom in the ILA.

With most New York newspapers, the AFL, the Port Authority,

and the state Crime Commission demanding a thorough cleanup and genuine reform of the waterfront, Father John is no longer a voice crying in the wilderness. "All honest longshoremen, which means most of them, look on Father Corridan as a friend and the ILA certainly cannot call him a Communist," the *Newark Evening News* observed the other day.

"If something constructive doesn't come out of all this—something that'll give security to the men and build the port, I'll throw in the sponge," Father John told me recently.

"Him throw in the sponge?" old Tim was saying a little while later over boilermakers in an Eleventh Avenue bar. "About as much chance as I have of stayin' sober on St. Paddy's Day. This business of cleaning up the harbor is an all-or-nothing proposition. A feller like Father John figgers to be in it all the way."

Cosmopolitan,
March 1954

Docker's Wife

In an Atmosphere Charged with Insecurity, She Puts Up a Rugged Battle to Build a Stable Home Life for Her Family

---

For years Joe Docks, the ordinary longshoreman of New York harbor, worked at his vital but unpublicized job of loading and unloading the thirty million tons of general cargo that pass each year through the greatest port in the world.

Then came the Kefauver and New York State Crime Commission investigations, leading to a head-on collision between the crime-infected International Longshoremen's Association union and a new antiracketeering AFL union. We, the public, were staggered to learn that New York's 650 miles of coastline was virtually an outlaw frontier harboring a $350-million-a-year racket.

Now Joe Docks is no longer a cipher buried in the shipping news section. Today, his activities make front-page stories across the nation.

Behind the news stories there is a private story. For Joe Docks has a life beyond the piers and the headlines. He lives in tenements fringing the waterfront from Brooklyn to Hoboken. There is a wife, in most cases, and a flock of children. If there is an unknown soldier on the waterfront, it is Mrs. Joe Docks, the longshoreman's wife, who faces the challenge of piecing together some sort of stability for her family out of a way of life that has been notoriously precarious.

A longshoreman has no regular employment. He works when a ship is in—if the hiring boss picks him to work that ship. His wife never knows the peace of mind that comes with seeing her husband off for work at eight and having dinner ready for his sure return at six. A dockworker may go down to the pier at seven in the morning, not start work until after lunch, and then work through midnight or later. Or he may find that the ship has been delayed. Or the hiring boss reaches over his shoulder to pick another man. He's left standing on the street. And he needed that day bad. There's no money in the house and no grub in the icebox.

HOUSEHOLD PLANNING IS USELESS

A longshoreman's life runs exactly contrary to a woman's instinctive conservatism. Meals on time, savings for the children, plans for a monthly budget, and all those other estimable domestic aims are rarely possible for Mrs. Joe Docks.

Mrs. Helen "Dolly" Mullins, who lives on Manhattan's West Side, faces these problems the year round. Her husband, Tim, has been working fairly regularly, for the last couple of years at least, on Pier 45, a few blocks away.

Dolly Mullins is a buxom, hearty woman in her middle thirties with a likable moon face under Mamie bangs. Emphatically Irish, she is outgoing and sociable, quick-witted and fun-loving, although the pressure of caring for three children between the ages of seventeen months and four years leaves scant time for recreation or free evenings.

Dolly and her family live on the second floor of a shabby tenement, the kind landlords seem to abandon to their fate. The walls along the stairway and narrow corridors are cracked and stained and scribbled with the random observations of occupants, present and past. The preparation of half a dozen different meals in the beehive apartments creates a warm, sweet, and not unpleasant hallway aroma. You hear impromptu counterpoint: a baby crying, the gunfire of a radio melodrama, a domestic argument, group laughter, a jazz broadcast.

You enter the Mullinses' flat through the small kitchen, beyond which are two small bedrooms and a larger living room looking out on Eleventh Street. The flat is built smack against the wall of the next building, a garage, so there is natural light only in the front room. The first time I called was shortly before Christmas, and Dolly was embarrassed because Tim hadn't had a chance to finish his traditional holiday wallpapering, repainting, and general redecorating. One of the small bedrooms was nearly repapered in a floral design, and Tim was determined to get through before Christmas. He had come home from work about one that morning and then painted until dawn. Pretty tiring after a long stretch on the dock, he admitted, but easier than painting during the day when Dink and Tommy, his four- and three-year-old sons, insisted on helping him by getting their hands in the paint and throwing it up at the ceiling.

THEIR LAST FLAT HAD RATS

The wallpaper and linoleum of the other rooms were dirty and worn. While acknowledging that the place was a little small, and that with no doors between the rooms it was easy for parents and "the wild Indians" to get on each other's nerves, still Dolly cheerily preferred this to their last place, a few blocks away. There the rent was somewhat lower ($19.60 a month as compared with $26.30 here), and they had almost twice as much room, but the flat was overrun with rats so large and so bold that the cat Tim brought in to cope with them was bitten to death.

"After that, I was ready to move, no matter how much room we had. We may be a little crowded here, but at least the rats aren't sharing the place with us. Biggest animal I've seen here is a cockroach. At least they don't bite."

Besides the new wallpaper and linoleum, Dolly is looking forward to a new living-room set. They have been saving toward a down payment. Dolly is patient. A congenital optimism peppered with a healthy cynicism gives Dolly Mullins a positive attitude toward—if not resignation to—things as they are.

One reason for this may be that she was brought up in this neighborhood and belongs to an old respected waterfront family, the Barrys. Her father was a cooper (a cargo repairman), and one of the founders of the coopers' union in New York. Dolly remembers he once ran for alderman, although he was barely able to read and write. "But he was smart as a whip, remembered everything he heard. He could really tell you something about this waterfront. A wonderful man." Her brother Eddie Barry, also a leader of the coopers, has been in the forefront of the present struggle to pry the waterfront unions free from racketeer control. Two other brothers are waterfront workers with strong convictions about cleaning up the harbor. Tim himself has four brothers on the docks. One of them, Jackie, is safety man on Pier 45.

My visits with Dolly and Tim invariably took place in the small kitchen, which serves as entranceway and improvised sitting room, since Tommy and Dink sleep in bunk beds in the little room opening out on the kitchen, and the baby's crib is in the other bedroom. While Tim and I sat around the kitchen table, Dolly—called "Skinny" by her husband as a family joke—would perch on the lid covering the bathtub next to the sink.

Before that, she had run down for a handful of cigars for me, and also some beer and cold cuts. As we talked and ate and smoked and drank, Dink, Tommy, and Dale, a doll-like, robust colleen of seventeen months, wandered in and out, strumming on toy ukuleles, wrestling, climbing in and out of our laps, and snacking from the table.

DOLLY'S USED TO DISTRACTIONS

Dolly is used to these distractions. She would pour me another beer, keep on talking, fondle Dale and hand her a pretzel to keep her quiet, referee a bit of fisticuffs between the two boys and banish them from the kitchen, temporarily, "so we can hear ourselves think." It was all accomplished with good-humored patience.

Dolly Mullins is no waterfront Pollyanna, however. With a longshoreman's life, she says, "it's either a feast or a famine." There are times when Tim "gets his three or four days a week and come Friday we've got seventy, eighty dollars and everything is lovely." But there have been weeks when he only "grabs a day or two." And Dolly remembers with bitterness the long, hungry weeks when Tim was on strike for benefits she feels most American workmen won years ago and longshoremen were denied because crooked ILA leaders consistently sold them out. "When I hear *strike*, I get shudders, no kiddin'." Dolly said. "The '51 strike, I'll never forget it. You can't get an unemployment check until you've been out of work seven weeks, so just when you need it most you're SOL. If our grocery man hadn't carried us, I don't know what we'd've done. He was an Armenian fellow, and he let us run up a bill so at least we kept eating. But I felt nervous all the time, thinkin' how long it'd take us to pay it off. Strikes, I been through 'em and I hate 'em. Sure, I come from a labor family, and I know the strike is the only power you got. But it's no picnic for the housewife, believe me. I know what it is to try and get by on nothin' a week. And I sure don't want to make a habit of it." Dolly laughed heartily. "Not the way this family eats."

Tim, tall and wiry, with unruly dark hair, grinned, pulled his cap over one eye, and spoke in that rapid way of the West Side. "You should talk, the way you pack it away." Dolly accepted this good-naturedly. "I admit it. I like to eat." Then she added, half joking, "What other fun do I get out of life these days?"

When he was courting her, Tim recalled, just after he got out of the Army, he took her to an Italian place and she ate two full helpings of spaghetti. The whole evening set him back around $9.50. Dolly enjoyed talking about that date, back in the days when they knew what it was to have an evening to themselves. She was slender in those days, she said, regarding her present figure with disarming candor. "I must've gained forty pounds. But I tell Tim, at least there's no danger of losing me in the dark." She grinned saucy and Irish.

She went on talking about food. "You know where most of our money goes? Right here on the table. I figure first things first, and the kids got to eat well." She figures her food bill runs at least thirty dollars a week, excluding meat, which she shops around for and often buys at Hearns Department Store at cut-rate prices. ("You can get three pounds of hamburger for a dollar.") Tim brings home around three hundred dollars a month, and, from Dolly's estimate, nearly half of that "goes on the table."

Was the violent '51 strike the hungriest time the Mullinses had known? No, Dolly said, the real bad time, the worst, was back in 1948, when Alcoa pulled its ships out to another part of the harbor. This move shut down two piers where Tim's local was favored. Tim had to roam the waterfront "taking the leavings, grabbing a day here and a day there. But not enough to feed us. And I was eatin' for two; I was carryin' Dink. I got so I was dreamin' of hamburgers. Finally, it got so bad I went to the church and asked for food tickets. Only I didn't have the nerve to tell Tim. You know, he's got that Irish pride. I'm Irish, too, but the eating comes first, the pride can come after. Well, anyway, it just happens that the next day Tim gets eight hours and he comes home with a big steak and a carton of beer. We're just sittin' down to it when the Father comes in with my five-dollar food ticket. He sees the steak and the beer—the first we had in Lord knows when—and I'm afraid he thinks I'm lyin'. And now Tim knows about me goin' to the church and he's got his Irish up. 'Why no, Father, we don't need any help. You see how we're doin', steak and beer.' I felt like hitting him right in the head." Pier 45 finally went back into operation, just about the time Dink was born. Since that time, Tim has become part of a "regular gang" employed whenever a ship is in. On days when there's no work at Pier 45, he tries to pick up extra work at other piers. Dink was Dolly's smallest baby, and she feels sure there is a direct connection between that fact and the closing of those two piers.

In times like those, Dolly says, it is the individual kindness of neighbors that pulls you through. When, as an aftereffect of childbirth, she hemorrhaged and had to return to the hospital, her neighborhood doctor refused to take any money. "I know your husband isn't working right now, so don't worry about it," he assured her. The name of this doctor, Hayunga, is a household institution throughout the neighborhood. His father, now in his eighties, is said to have delivered at least 70 percent of all the babies born in this section for the past fifty years. His son is still referred to as a "two-dollar doctor" because he has never wished to make medical expenses a burden to people who work so hard for a living.

"WE HELP EACH OTHER OUT"

"It's still two dollars," Dolly says, "and if you haven't got the two dollars that's all right, too. Wonderful people, the Hayungas. A lot of people down here would be dead without 'em. There are some good people in this world. We've got some right here in this building. We help each other, borrow back and forth [a little girl had just knocked on the door to ask for aspirin for her sick sisters]. I like people to be kindhearted and generous." And then she added, "And yet some of them turn out to be such stinkers."

Second in importance to getting good meals on the table is keeping the children well clothed. This calls for painstaking shopping, for after the rent and eating money has been deducted there is only about $125 left for everything else. Tim's needs are simple, limited chiefly to cigarettes and beers. His work clothes, consisting of old brown trousers, a wool shirt, a windbreaker, and a ski cap, are worn on all but the most solemn occasions. Dolly would like a few more dresses, and the fur coat she has is a hand-me-down in the family. But, like Tim, she dotes on her kids, despite frequent complaints about what nuisances they are, and she is proud of the clothes she manages to find for them at bargain prices.

HOW SHE STRETCHES A DOLLAR

"You can spend your whole afternoon trying to stretch a dollar," Dolly says. She knows what it is to hike up and down Fourteenth Street pricing comparable articles until she finds one a little cheaper than the rest. One afternoon, for instance, Dolly saw a brown pants-and-shirt ensemble she wanted for Dink, but it ran a few dollars over what she could afford. She shopped for hours until she found a pair of pants in one store and a shirt in another, close enough in color to pass as a set. This saved her over a dollar.

While Tim's average, in recent years, of about $4,200 gross income does not compare unfavorably with workers in other industries, Dolly thinks the unevenness of the income and the uncertainty of the future make them feel as if they are always poor. "You never seem to catch up. You have some bad weeks or a slow season and you owe the grocer, and the doctor, and everybody else, and then when you have a good week, like, say, maybe Tim brings home as much as ninety dollars, you never feel 'in the money' because it goes out so fast to pay the back bills. A strike or a shutdown pier or an upheaval like the one that's going on now can set you back so far you spend the next two years trying to catch up."

ALWAYS READY FOR THE WORST

This is one reason the Mullinses keep their rent under a dollar a day. Ordinarily, an annual wage like Tim's could finance better housing than their narrow railroad flat. But the specter of a shutdown pier and the resultant rat race for survival always hangs over Tim and Dolly. They have to be ready to cut down to the bone when the going gets tough.

Feeding on this insecurity are the loan sharks, or *shylocks*, as they are commonly known on the docks. Every pier has them, and the Mullinses, like nearly every other longshore family, has had to fall

Budd Schulberg is the son of P. B. Schulberg, a famous Hollywood director. Schulberg's first big successes came as a novelist, whose instant classics included *What Makes Sammy Run?* and *The Harder They Fall.* *On the Waterfront* was eventually nominated for eleven Academy Awards, winning eight, including Best Picture, Best Director, Best Adapted Screenplay, Best Actor for Marlon Brando, and Best Supporting Actress for Eva Marie Saint. It also won Schulberg an Oscar for Best Screenplay.

back on them when Tim failed to grab enough days. A loan shark is glad to loan you fifty dollars, at rates of five dollars each week. If it takes you ten weeks to repay the principal, the interest has mounted to 100 percent! These loan sharks are bankrolled by the mobs that are still clinging tenaciously to a majority of the piers.

The men on the pier where Timmy works today, Pier 45, scored a spectacular victory over agents of the Dunn-McGrath mob, which used to terrorize all the Greenwich Village piers. It took a series of running battles over a period of years, but they won. The shop steward, chosen democratically by the membership of Tim's local, William (Pete) Loughran, is scrupulously honest about the voluntary welfare contributions that come in from the men each week for the relief of the injured and the needy. "Pete runs the most honest box on the waterfront," Dolly says. "He'll walk in to a family where the man is laid up and can't work and say, 'Here's a hundred.' He could just as well say, 'Here's thirty, or forty,' and keep the rest, like a lot of them do. But not Pete. He was a regular longshoreman for too many years. He feels for the men." On too many other piers, Dolly thinks, the welfare box has been just another racket swelling the pockets of racketeers.

Dolly was raised in the stronghold of the Dunn-McGrath mob, and today she knows many of the West Side muscle boys by sight. She thinks she speaks for nearly all the waterfront wives when she curses out the racketeers as leeches who have kept honest longshoremen from getting the kind of protection they deserve.

THE DOCKERS' CODE OF SILENCE

As the showdown between the criminal group on the docks and the AFL reform crusaders grows more desperate, Dolly knows a number of friends and relatives prominent in the AFL whose lives and families have been threatened. Her brother Eddie was one of the first to testify publicly against the waterfront rackets, out of his conviction that only by getting the facts to the public would the underworld's perversion of unionism be checked. This marked a break with a long-established waterfront code of silence and refusal to give information to the police or government officials. Dolly has known longshoremen who refused to testify against the very hoodlums who assaulted them or hijacked their local. She has her own very strong ideas on this subject. "'You talk about ratting,' I tell them. 'How dopey can you get? Is it ratting when you do what Eddie did, telling the truth in order to get the mob off your backs? Boy, if that's ratting, and I had a chance to rat, would I rat!'"

At this point, I couldn't resist telling Dolly that the waterfront movie I had been working on for the past year with director Elia Kazan (*On the Waterfront*, starring Marlon Brando, and soon to be released by Columbia) was based on exactly that issue. "Well, we never go to the movies," she said, "but if that's what your movie is about we'll have to figure out a way to see it."

DOLLY VERSUS THE SALOON

This business of adhering to an outmoded code isn't Dolly's only criticism of longshoremen. She is equally frank in telling you that she doesn't like the longshoreman's habit of stopping off in a bar and spending too much of his money and his time away from home. This is a traditional skirmish in the war between men and women particularly familiar to Irish dockworker families. The old saw of "Father, dear Father, come home with me now" is not entirely anachronistic on the streets near the river. Timmy is not a hard drinker, and he is known as a good family man, but it is in his blood to stop off for a few beers. Occasionally, Dolly will send someone looking for him, as a gentle reminder for him to come home.

"Once in a while, he fools me and tries a new place," Dolly says, having carefully charted all of Tim's favorite haunts. It is a kind of half-joking, half-serious issue in the Mullins family, although Dolly, like most longshoremen's wives, is resigned to the fact that lifting a few with the boys is as much a part of a longshoreman's life as swinging a cargo hook. For one thing, their homes are too small to encourage much company, so the bars become a kind of overflow living room for men only, where the longshoreman can enjoy a bit of surcease both from his work and his home life. As a result, there tends to be a barrier between the life of the men, flowing in a natural cycle from pier to bar to home and back to work again, and the life of their womenfolk, limited almost entirely to their few small rooms and the hour-to-hour needs of their families. On this subject, as on all others relating to the waterfront, Dolly Mullins is consistently direct.

"I never get a chance to get out. I'm cooped up with the kids all the time, especially in winter when it's too cold for them to stay out on the street very long. So I figure if Timmy wants to drink, he can just come home and drink with me." Tim listens to this and grins good-naturedly. For in this home, as in many another Irish working-class household, the mother is a tough-minded matriarch.

On Friday night, when Tim has his week's pay in his pocket, Dolly gives him an hour's grace. Then, if he isn't home, she goes on the prowl for him. Longshoremen have been known to drink up a week's pay in a night's drinking, or lose it all in a tossing game. Dolly has had too many longshoremen in her family to risk that.

At the end of a long, hard day when the children finally have fallen asleep, Dolly relaxes—in her fashion. Sometimes she watches TV, for a good laugh at Sam Levenson or Jimmy Durante, though the baby sleeps in the same room with her and she must keep the sound down. Sometimes she reads a comic or a murder mystery. Her taste in comics runs to horror stories. "It gets my mind off what I've been doing all day," she said.

The large-screen TV set in the bedroom has become the focal point of Dolly's home. When Dink and Tommy, his freckled-faced younger brother, tie themselves into a tearful knot or drown out all talk with their toy ukuleles ("I must've been out of my mind when I bought 'em those things!"), the invariable last resort is, "Go in and watch the television."

THE CHILDREN STAY UP LATE

Since Dink and Tommy have not reached school age, and since any conversation in the kitchen clearly carries through the adjacent rooms, the children are allowed to stay up until they fall asleep naturally. "They are good sleepers, like all the Mullinses," Dolly says. Dink has begun to venture down into the street by himself, often in pursuit of candy from Benny's grocery store, and Dolly naturally worries about him whenever he is out alone. Yet it is impossible to keep him penned up in a small apartment all the time, and she is reconciled to, but none too happy about, the prospect of Dink's having to take his chances on so tough a block at so tender an age. Bigger boys grab his toys away, and there is the constant danger of trucks speeding toward the docks.

The high point of Dolly's year, and perhaps the one time when she is really content, is summer, when the Mullinses take a bungalow at Highland Beach on the Jersey shore. "Dink gets brown as an Indian, and both boys just live in the water, like a couple of fish." Timmy joins the family there from Friday until Monday. Highland Beach is a place Dolly knew as a child, and she loves the idea of being there again. The rent for the summer is $325, and, no matter what else they do without, the Mullinses make sure of having that golden sum ready for their summer landlord. The uncomfortable winter months are always made more bearable by counting the days until they are ready to pack off to Highland Beach.

Much of what I learned about Dolly Mullins and her life poured out on Friday evenings, which have a special place on the Mullinses' calendar. Friday is their social evening. They sit up drinking beer in the kitchen, and sometimes, if they have guests, a nip or two of something stronger. Sometimes Dolly brightens the occasions by playing old records on a small phonograph on the kitchen table. She likes to sing in a hearty jazz style, and she is not inhibited about chiming right in with the Mills Brothers, Bing Crosby, or anyone else if they're singing one of the old, sentimental ballads she is especially fond of. The music and the singing and the laughter in the kitchen may even disturb the children. But Dolly feels she has worked like a dog all week, there has been little or no time for her own self-expression, and Friday night is the one time when she can indulge herself. The responsibilities of being a longshoreman's wife keep her cooking, scrubbing, shopping, darning, caring for the baby, and constantly scrimping to get by, so her Friday-night beer-and-song party is a necessary hair-letting-down session for her.

Less placid and less easily satisfied than Tim, who is able to live a freer life and who prefers the outdoor work of a longshoreman to any confining factory job, Dolly Mullins may blow off a lot of steam on a Friday night. But by Monday she is ready to cope with life as she finds it, whether Timmy pulls down four days work that coming week or only a single day, whether he is pulled out on strike or winds up in the pier's first-aid room.

"Somehow we always make out," Dolly says, "but lots of days I've wondered how the devil we did it."

The Saturday Evening Post, September 7, 1963

The Waterfront Revisited

Noted author Budd Schulberg returns to the scene of his prizewinning movie On the Waterfront *for an up-to-date report on the rackets and racketeers still contaminating the docks of our leading seaport.*

Civil war was raging through New York harbor ten years ago, when director Elia Kazan and I were there to film *On the Waterfront*. Insurgent longshoremen, backed by the American Federation of Labor, were battling the mob-infested International Longshoremen's Association (ILA), just expelled from the AFL, in a bitterly fought election campaign to determine which union would bargain for the forty thousand men who move $6.5 billion worth of cargo through the port every year. We didn't know how to end our picture because no one could predict how the real-life waterfront struggle would end. In the final scene of my script, the hoodlum dock boss, Johnny Friendly, facing jail, hollers, "I'll be back—and I'll remember every last one of yuz!"

Now that ten years have passed, I recently asked New York Port Authority director Austin J. Tobin what had become of men like Johnny Friendly. "His threat was true then," Tobin said, "and unfortunately it's still true today. Actually, the hoodlums never went away."

I had first entered this crime-ridden world with the help of the Reverend John Corridan, the celebrated "waterfront priest." A tall, intense man who spoke the gritty language of the dockworkers, Father John really believed that all men were brothers in Christ. "Some people think the Crucifixion took place only on Calvary," he had begun one memorable sermon on the docks, going on to preach in terms the dockers understood—of "Christ in the shape-up."

Father John ticked off for me the various mobs controlling different sections of the harbor, named the hiring bosses with criminal records, and described the evils of the shape-up hiring system. He gave me chapter and verse on the wholesale pilferage from ships' cargoes and explained how ILA hoodlums extorted payoffs from the shipping companies, highly vulnerable to threats of work stoppages since idle ships earn no money. He sketched other dockside rackets—narcotics, gambling, loan-sharking—and he introduced me to a sawed-off longshoreman called Brownie who would guide me for a look at harbor conditions.

That night, Brownie took me on a tour of the bars that face the docks. "Keep ya ears open and ya mouth shut," he warned me. I got a close, hard look at the loan sharks, the bookmakers, and their muscle, who took their bread out of the envelopes of longshoremen. In the neighborhood of the luxury liner berths were the enforcers who had moved in through bank robber Mickey Bowers's notorious "Pistol Local" 824: the reptilian-eyed John Keefe, "Apples" Applegate, and "Sudden Death" Ward. These men may sound like extravagant creations of the late Damon Runyon, but they were there in the flesh—although invisible to the tourists waving happy good-byes from the decks of passenger ships like the *Île de France*, the *Queen Elizabeth*, and the *United States*.

I elbowed close to Danny St. John, hiring boss of Pier 84, who had been arrested twenty times on charges including assault, robbery, and murder. And in Workman's, on West Street, Brownie pointed out Albert Ackalitis, a machine-gun man paroled from Sing Sing at the request of William J. McCormack's stevedore company, to be a hiring boss.

Big Bill McCormack had worked his way up from bully boy on a horse-drawn meat truck before World War I to become a multimillionaire industrialist, a power on the waterfront—*the* power, some say—and a kingmaker at City Hall. Ties between political and waterfront leaders have always been close. To see how close, you had only to study the guest list of an ILA president's testimonial dinner. There prominent city officials and judges sat jowl by jowl with the "labor leaders," shipping executives, stevedore bosses, racketeers, and killers—one big happy family of despoilers gathered together in tribal ceremony, flaunting their power over the harbor and the city it serves and controls.

If Big Bill McCormack was the top, the bottom layer of waterfront corruption was the shape-up. Even after reading Malcolm Johnson's Pulitzer Prize–winning newspaper series—the basis for our film about the waterfront—I was still unprepared for what I saw on a pierhead one bleak, despairing dawn. Five hundred men hoping for work, beating their hands together for warmth, shaped themselves into a huge human horseshoe in front of the hiring boss—nominally, an employee of the stevedoring company that hired the longshoremen but, in actual fact, a man designated by the ILA leaders.

> He who wishes to behold one of the most extraordinary and least-known scenes of this metropolis should go down to the [docks] at half past seven in the morning. . . . It is a sight to sadden the most callous to see thousands of men struggling for only one day's hire, the scuffle being made the fiercer by the knowledge that hundreds out of the number there assembled must be left to idle the day out in want. To look into the faces of that hungry crowd is to see a sight that must be ever remembered. Some are smiling to the foreman to coax him into remembrance of them; others, with their protruding eyes, eager to snatch for the hoped-for pass. For weeks many have gone there, and gone through the same struggle, the same crisis; and have gone away, after all, without the work they had screamed for.

That could be my description of the shape-ups I saw in the early fifties. It happens to be an eyewitness account of a London shape-up ninety years earlier. Outlawed in England before the end of the nineteenth century, and abandoned in nearly all other American ports, this was the barbarous way I saw men still being hired in the modern metropolis of New York. I looked into the faces of men passed over, some because they couldn't get up the two dollars to kick back to the hiring boss, some too old, some too outspoken against this inhuman system. Many stood there staring vacantly, and took a long time turning away. Five hundred men for two hundred jobs. And the same situation at all the pierheads around the harbor: forty thousand men crowding around their hiring bosses begging for less than twenty thousand jobs.

I followed the rejected back to the bars for the long wait till the one o'clock shape. How did they get the bar money? Waiting for them were the shylocks, as they called the loan sharks. Money came easy. Only paying it back was hard. Borrow a double sawbuck today, you'd owe twenty-two a week from today. And that 10 percent could add up until you were paying 100 percent on your lousy double saw. To top the indignity, the shylock, part of the mob that had your dock and your local in its pocket, would insure his investment by pointing you to a couple of days on the pier, collecting your brass-work tab, and cashing it himself.

Week by week, month by month, first visiting, then finally moving into, the railroad flats of longshoremen, I felt I was living my way into the jungle world of the waterfront. The shape-up haunted me. And the brazen pilferage. And the bullying violence, the casual killings. I began to identify myself with the group of longshoremen who had been coming to St. Francis Xavier Labor School after dark for advice from Father Corridan.

"Father John knows the score," had become a popular saying by the time I came to know him well. And as the influence of the Corridan group spread through the harbor, so did the violence. One member of the group, Joey Cuervo, was sitting with his children watching TV when a shot was fired into his parlor. Christy Doran, hiring boss on Pier 42, another member of the cleanup movement, fell to his death from a cliff at a church picnic. "*Fell?* That's a hot one," said Brownie, my guide.

On notorious Pier 32, Michael Brogan, an assistant hiring boss, disappeared shortly after his local, 895, voted 5 to 1 to quit the ILA. Three weeks later, Brogan's body was found floating in the river. He had talked openly of breaking with the old crowd and of his troubles with the gunman Ackalitis. With the federally sponsored union election on its way, most of the West Side Irish rebels interpreted Brogan's death as "a McGrath–Ackalitis election maneuver." Eddie McGrath, an ILA organizer for fifteen years, and a mob leader with a record of twelve arrests for crimes ranging from petty larceny to murder, had fled to Florida after his brother-in-law and gang partner John (Cockeye) Dunn was executed for murder in 1949. But he was reported still to be running the rackets on the Lower West Side piers by remote control from Miami—and one of those piers was Pier 32.

Intimidation, beatings, and murders dominated this whole campaign, for the racketeers were fighting for survival on the waterfront. But on election night, May 26, 1954, the rebels were in a victory mood. With no union hall of their own, thousands of them gathered at the Seafarers International Union Hall in Brooklyn to await the election returns. Paul Hall, the formidable ex-sailor president of the SIU, was the ranking AFL officer in this war against the ILA. Beer was on the house that night for the men who had stood up to danger, ostracism, and starvation in their effort to wrench control of the harbor from the racketeers. Confident of their strength in Brooklyn, on the Lower West Side, on the Jersey shore, dockworkers, who wore their battle stripes on their faces, lifted brews together in premature celebration.

At first, it seemed that the graft-ridden ILA was finally being pried loose, but, by midnight, it was creeping up on the rebels. And by early morning, when the returns were in, the ILA had polled 9,110 votes to 8,791 for the reform movement. A mere 319 votes separated the old order from the new. In Jersey City alone, buses scheduled to carry anti-ILA dockworkers to the polls mysteriously failed to show up. One of the AFL organizers responsible for this transportation was promptly rewarded by the ILA—promoted to hiring boss. That one defection—and there were others—cost this tragic photo-finish defeat.

What happened to the nearly nine thousand longshoremen who gambled their livelihood, and some of their lives, only to blow it by less than 2 percent of the total vote? Scores had to ship out as sailors to escape mob vengeance. Our dock boss in the film had shouted down the rebels as "living dead men," and that's what the stand-up guys of the narrowly defeated movement soon became. Men I had come to know in the battle for the harbor were starved out. Some threw in the sponge and turned to other jobs—a stagehand, a helper on a truck. The demoralized drifted off into alcoholism. But there were diehards strong enough to stick it out on the docks, unsung heroes in the long upward struggle for freedom from degradation, crime, and corruption on the waterfront.

Recently, near the pier where he was lucky enough to be working that day, I joined a coffee break with a representative member of this group, a hardworking Irish longshoreman we'll call Tommy Monohan. He's a hatch foreman, a man who knows and loves his job. That's important to understand about longshoremen. Most of them aren't down there because they're shiftless drifters who like to pick up a couple of days a week to pay the bar bills. The Tommy Monohans are as attracted to their profession as a sailor is to the sea. There is something of the sea about the job, the changing moods of the river and the weather, the sense of working out-of-doors. Tommy speaks for thousands of fellow dock wallopers who will tell you they couldn't stand being cooped up—a humdrum nine-to-five office job would shrivel their souls. They thrive on hard work and long hours, working, say, from 1:00 P.M. until 5:00 the next morning to ready a ship to be turned around—one of the deepwater vessels leaving the great harbor every forty-five minutes.

I tell you this about Tommy Monohan, son of an Irish-born longshoreman, and a deck man for nearly twenty years, because he is his own best answer to the familiar question, "If they're having all that trouble, why don't they look for some other kind of job?" Tough, honest, independent, concerned for his wife and kids, a natural leader among his fellow workers and in his local whenever it is run democratically, Tommy Monohan is determined to make up the ground he lost in the ten lean years.

It has been a long climb back. Not all the way back, because he is still only a member of an extra gang—getting the surplus work behind the regular gangs. But he thought his story was typical of the legitimate longshoremen who had been paying a price for their efforts to clean up the docks.

"After the ILA beat us by an eyelash, the word was out, Don't hire any rebels. There was no place we could shape. They'd pick a one-armed midget before they'd give us a day.

"We were willing to work anywhere, do anything to put food on the table for the kids. Those who wouldn't, who weren't willing to take the leavings, had to get out. Those first five years somehow we managed to keep ourselves together [a blacklisted, occasionally working gang of twenty-one], but a couple of days a week some of us shaped individually, even working in the hold—*bananas*—anything to fill out a week's pay."

When Tommy Monohan's voice underlined *bananas*, he was indicating how low he had fallen in the longshore status system. The early Irish immigrants, like the wave of Italians after them, then the Negroes and, lately, the Puerto Ricans, would take anything. Today, only the Puerto Ricans handle bananas.

"From '54 to '59, it was steady abuse," Tommy went on. "After that, the fellas who'd been against us started to come around. Fellas we'd grown up with and gone to school with, but who hadn't talked to us in maybe six years, started saying a couple of words to us. My own brother stuck with the ILA, and we didn't talk for three years. Of course, the feeling will always be there, it went so deep, but we decided to test it by running for local office. We lost, but only by a handful of votes, and because of our strength we've been able to work out a deal where two rebels are taken back into the local each month. So I guess you could say the old reform movement isn't quite dead."

There have been other indications of reform in the longshoreman's union since I left the waterfront ten years ago. Some of this has come from within the ILA; some has been forced on it from outside. The biggest outside force has been the bistate (New York and New Jersey) Waterfront Commission, set up in 1953 after the New York State Crime Commission declared that waterfront crime was so widespread that it threatened the supremacy of the Port of New York. The bistate commission has authority over all phases of harbor activity, from supervision of hiring to forcing convicted criminals from union office to cracking down on the individual longshoreman who still feels himself entitled to a bottle of Scotch or a can of tuna "so long as it's for home consumption."

One main reform by the commission has been the elimination of the archaic shape-up. Instead, employment information centers—fourteen of them around the harbor—serve as hiring halls, in which only men registered with the commission can be certified for work. Most longshoremen belong to work gangs of about twenty men, and, today, these gangs are usually hired a day ahead of time. Gangs and individuals—"casuals"—without work assignments go to the centers. And a man can be removed from the register—"decasualized"—for seeking work less than eight days a month, or for criminal activities. In this way, over the years, the commission has brought the size of the workforce more into line with the port's labor requirements.

"The big change over the past is the hiring," Tommy Monohan told me. "A hundred percent improved. Well, let's settle for eighty. A

A later photograph of Joseph P. Ryan (*right*), head of the International Longshoremen's Association, and well-known rackets boss Anthony Anastasio (*left*), the brother and right-hand man of Albert Anastasia. Photograph copyright © Bettmann/CORBIS.

lot of the men bitch about the Waterfront Commission, but you gotta give the commish credit for their information centers. Now the stevedore company agents come to the men at the centers instead of the men going to the piers. At the pierhead, you were helpless. If you got passed over, you didn't know where to turn. The hiring boss had you. That's why he could force the kickbacks on you. You bought your job or you went hungry."

Reform from within the longshoremen's union has been less spectacular, but there have been hopeful signs. After the Crime Commission issued its report ten years ago, ILA president Joseph P. Ryan, who died last June, was indicted on fifty-one counts of misusing union funds, and replaced in office by tugboat Captain William V. Bradley, also a McCormack man but clean enough to lend a cloak of respectability to the organization. Bradley has been described in the cruel wit of the waterfront as "all fat from his ankles up." In recent years Thomas (Teddy) Gleason, who beat out Bradley for the presidency last July, has been "the man to see at Fourteenth Street," ILA headquarters. And while Gleason has a record of consorting with gangsters, he has recently shown signs of developing an interest in trade unionism.

"At Fourteenth Street," Tommy Monohan said, "the same faces are still there, and the same tough guys dropping up or phoning in, but this year, for the first time, they seem to be thinking about the membership. This last strike [December 23, 1962, through January 26, 1963] was the first time they didn't try to sell us out to the shippers. This time I gotta give Teddy Gleason credit; he did a good job.

"In the Bowers's section"—the redolent "Pistol Local" controlling the luxury liner piers—"it's a hulluva lot different from when you were here before. Mickey's son Johnny is doing a job for the men. Oh, sure, he gave soft jobs to the old pistoleros like Wards and Keefie because they were pals of his old man. But Johnny isn't running the local just to fill his own pocket. He's one of the best leaders to come along on the West Side." Bowers, in fact, became executive vice president of the international in the July elections.

The most dramatic—and the most hopeful—instance of reform from within has been the redemption of Anthony (Tough Tony) Anastasio, boss of the Brooklyn docks until his death last March. Tony had climbed the ladder of American success from lowly shipjumper to mob-backed hiring boss to union leader. He consolidated the six "Camarda locals," Mafia fiefdoms named for one family of dockside overlords, into one mighty local that gave him control of the entire Brooklyn waterfront. If you wanted a job, you went to see Tony. If you had a beef, you went to see Tony. Tony's beachmaster bellow could be heard from Red Hook to the Erie Basin.

No one knows all the reasons for the transformation of "Tough Tony" to "Tender Tony," but he was undoubtedly influenced by the barbershop execution of his brother Albert Anastasia, Lord High Executioner for Murder, Inc. (the brothers spelled the family name differently), and by a heart condition that must have turned his mind to his own impending death. In the mid-fifties, Paul Hall, his neighbor in Brooklyn as president of the Seafarers Union, helped persuade the aging tyrant of the docks that there was still time for the padrone respected through fear and hatred to become one respected through gratitude and affection.

So well did he succeed that, as Tough Tony's $25,000 funeral procession paraded past all the pier heads of Brooklyn, I saw even Irish longshoremen—for generations enemies of the Italians—bow their heads. "We lost a good man," they said. "We lost a damn good labor leader."

Reform on the Brooklyn docks did not end with Tough Tony's death, for one of his cleanest breaks with the past was his choice as son-in-law a man outside the Mafia aristocracy. Tony Scotto, who inherited the leadership of Anastasio's huge local, was born a few blocks from the union hall, the son of an immigrant longshoreman, and himself a part-time longshoreman as he worked his way through Brooklyn College.

Tonys I and II are classic examples of the Americanization process. The accent of the Italian peninsula was strong in the guttural speech of Tony I. Tony II speaks smoothly in phrases that would become a college sociology instructor. Discussing the Italian–Irish rivalry in the harbor, he says, "The ethnic problem, unfortunately, continues. But I look forward to working in cooperation with Johnny Bowers and the other West Side officers for the common good of the membership. If they will only outgrow their prejudice and meet us halfway."

Only twenty-eight, although active in the local's activities for the past nine years, Tony Scotto is the kind of enlightened trade unionist who could not have existed on the waterfront in the dark ages when an ILA leader carried the charter in his hat and the treasury in his pocket. Scotto is proud of the contrast and credits his gravel-voiced father-in-law for making the jump from primitive extortion to trade unionism. "The cookie jar days are gone forever," he says, referring to former ILA treasurers who admitted under oath that union funds were kept in cookie jars at home and dipped into at personal whim. "We account for every cent now with IBM machines."

Unlike many ILA officers, Scotto is too sophisticated to blast the Waterfront Commission as a totalitarian abomination. While the labor movement is officially opposed to any government supervision of union activities, Scotto will concede that some of the reforms around the harbor could be credited to the bistate commission. But he believes many of these would have happened even without the commission, through the natural evolution of the waterfront.

"Ten years ago, seven out of ten Italian longshoremen couldn't speak English. Many of them were bewildered immigrants not yet oriented to the new world. They had no rights where they came from and didn't expect any here. Some of them were ship jumpers, and the dock boss could always threaten to turn them in if they didn't accept whatever he handed out to them. They had no self-respect; they had a peon psychology; they were the ready-made victims of extortion."

Today, Scotto points out, seven out of ten Italian longshoremen do speak English. "They are able to express themselves and we encourage them to. When you first came to the waterfront, there were no union meetings—just henchmen getting together once in a while. Now we educate members to attend meetings.

"We're a good union because we had to be," Scotto admits. "The rebel rivalry and the closeness of the election forced us to toe the mark. As a result, more has been done for the men in the past ten years than in all the previous years put together. Our $2 million medical-and-dental clinic, the Tony Anastasio Memorial, is making waterfront history."

THE POWER OF THE MAFIA

Modern, intelligent, forward-looking, leader of the largest local of longshoremen in the world, Tony Scotto is a refreshing change from the Mafia that held these Brooklyn docks at gunpoint when I first came in. Still, it would be foolish to say that organized crime has departed from the Brooklyn docks. Despite the social gains and hope for the future that Scotto represents, the Mafia still has its tentacles entwined around the piers.

During the reign of Tough Tony Anastasio, the earlier alliance between the Mafia dons and the union became a truce. Tony ran his union without their interference, and the boys ran their rackets without his. Tony Scotto may have the desire but hardly the power to take on the mob. His approach seems to be one of passive resistance, to win by patience and attrition what he could lose through precipitous opposition. He is looking to the future, to the influence of education and prosperity, when people no longer tied to the old world will not have to resort to crime and secret organizations as an answer to insecurity.

While the old guard Mafia perseveres despite death, deportation, or imprisonment, a "young Turk" Mafia symbolized by the Gallo brothers has been making old-fashioned music in Brooklyn. They have dared to upset the fraternal understanding with which syndicate business has been conducted around the harbor, and they have showed an appetite for violence in their grab for a bigger slice of the pie. One prime target is control of dockside rackets, and Gallo's defiance of clean-cut Tony Scotto is both vocal and violent. "With Tough Tony out of the way," says one of them, "little Tony [Scotto is six foot one, weight 218] is nothin'. We spit on Tony."

One of the most highly placed enforcement officers on the waterfront is concerned that mobsters—whether Gallo mavericks or senior underworld—will move in on Local 1814 now that the prestige of Tough Tony is no longer there to hold them at bay. "I hope this surprisingly healthy local will not be pieced off and redivided like Charlemagne's empire after the great emperor's death," he said to me. "Scotto's on the ball, and he's tougher than he sounds, with his college vocabulary, but I'm not sure he's strong enough to hold it."

Scotto has a powerful ally in Paul Hall of the SIU. And Hall—though his union is cleanly run, with classes to teach shop stewards democratic and progressive union procedures—has long boasted that he has the best muscle on the waterfront. When hoodlums tried to move in on his outfit years ago, he took them into a back room and beat the whey out of them. Once, fighting fire with fire, he held a mobster by his legs over a window sill and threatened to drop him unless he promised never to darken their union hall again.

In my return to the waterfront this year, I found myself back in the same roomy, book-lined, leather-chaired office of Hall's where we had waited out the election returns nine years ago. Now a vice president of the AFL-CIO, Hall was still the dominant figure I had known. We mentioned some of the mob celebrities who still have their fingers in the pie but about whom Paul prefers not to talk for publication. "Not that I'm afraid, but I still have to live in this jungle. It's still the *arm*. The man who stands the tallest calls the shots."

Paul Hall opened a large humidor on his desk, reached for two thick, expensive cigars, and tossed me one. This powerhouse of a man was warming to one of his favorite subjects—anti-Hoffaism, closely related to the future of the harbor because trucks driven by Jimmy Hoffa's teamsters pick up where longshoremen leave off—11,400 trucks moving cargo in and out of the port every day.

One of the major reasons for the continuation of graft and pilferage in the harbor lies in the Teamsters power play on the docks. Two years ago, Jimmy Hoffa, driving toward his master plan of one big transportation union, signed up Joe Curran of the National Maritime Union and Captain Bradley of the ILA. With Harry Bridges's West Coast longshoremen also in tow, Hoffa's goal seemed to be within reach. But a mighty bellow from the late Tony Anastasio, whose Brooklyn local of fifteen thousand longshoremen represents half the working force of the port, forced Bradley to withdraw.

Waterfront experts saw in Bradley's hasty about-face signs of a future struggle for control of the harbor: on one side, Hoffa plus Joe Curran plus the unreconstructed ILA racketeers who run most Jersey docks as if the Waterfront Commission never existed; on the other, Anastasio's longshoremen, now led by Tony Scotto, allied with tough, gruff, wily, dangerous Paul Hall. Now that Teddy Gleason has replaced Bradley as ILA president, it remains to be seen which side the international will back.

When Hall takes on Jimmy Hoffa and his "Teamos," as the ex-sailor contemptuously calls them, the repercussions can be felt from Maine to Galveston—not to mention San Juan, lately the scene of a jurisdictional battle between the two unions. "Hoffa's union dropped a million and a quarter fighting us in Puerto Rico." Paul Hall punched his words through the cigar smoke. "Gin gorillas were hired for two bits to four bits a day [in square talk, goons who draw their courage from bottles and assault Teamster enemies for fees of twenty-five to fifty dollars a day]. But guys ain't gonna die for fifty bucks a day. They can't stand up against the amateurs who believe in what they're doing. Lousy two-bit and four-bit gin gorillas," he muttered.

Hoffa protested to the NLRB that the sailors in San Juan were "resorting to violence to solve a labor dispute." Paul Hall grunted a sailor's oath. "That's typical Hoffa. If his guys had sent our guys to the hospital instead of the other way 'round, you think I'd go crying to the NLRB? I'd say we need stronger troops and we'd wipe up the docks with those Teamos before we got through."

The head-on, rough-and-tumble, do-it-yourself approach is typical Hall. In his fight against Hoffa, and the syndicate, and the West Side mob, he doesn't welcome any help from the government. He doesn't support Attorney General Bobby Kennedy in his efforts to bring Hoffa and his battalion of Teamster racketeers to justice. He believes these problems should be solved by labor itself, fighting to clean its own house. In the Chicago cabdriver revolt against the rule of Teamster hoodlum Joey Glimco a year ago, Paul Hall went out to the Hub himself and offered the victorious insurgent hackies a charter with his SIU. When Joey Glimco tried to interfere, Hall flattened him. "On the way down maybe Glimco was still a gangster, but when he got up he was just another little fella," Paul Hall explained.

"The legitimate labor movement can handle Hoffa if they've got the guts. Hoffa has been running the biggest 'sandy' [fo'c'sle word for *bluff*] in the history of the labor movement. He thinks he can divide the house of labor that expelled him and piece off the AFL-CIO transportation unions by pulling them into his national transportation setup. Curran followed him like a sheep, which is a funny way for an AFL-CIO leader to act. But you saw how Captain Bradley dropped that pact like a hot potato as soon as Tony A. shouted, 'No sale.'"

The battle to keep Jimmy Hoffa from grabbing control of the docks is far from won. Future developments in this battle, as in Tony

Scotto's imminent struggle with the Mafia racketeers, will bear watching. But there is still another major fight going on on the waterfront, and it may be the most important of the three. This is Teddy Gleason's continuing campaign against the Waterfront Commission.

Gleason, the new ILA president, is a mercurial figure known around the harbor as having "a mind like a ferryboat—and he doesn't have to turn around to move forward or backward." At one time, for example, he flirted with Father Corridan's reform group. Yet the New York State Crime Commission found him implicated with mobsters ten years ago. According to the commission's report:

> Control of operations in the section on the North River below the Bowers domain was taken over by Edward J. McGrath and his brother-in-law, John (Cockeye) Dunn, with the assistance of Andrew (Squint) Sheridan, Thomas (Teddy) Gleason, and Cornelius (Connie) Noonan. This group also organized the platform workers into ILA Local 1730, of which Gleason and Noonan are still officers. Daniel Gentile, who at various times worked for the group, described in detail gambling operations and other illegal activities which were operated from the offices of Local 1730. McGrath, Gleason, and Noonan refused on constitutional grounds to answer any questions concerning these operations.

Teddy Gleason is today not only a highly successful labor leader but, taking a page from Jimmy Hoffa's book, a prosperous businessman as well. While Teddy was drawing salaries as president of one ILA local, financial secretary of a second, business agent of a third, and an organizer for the international, he was also a business partner of Connie Noonan, in a deckful of deals frequently and flagrantly dependent on their influence as waterfront labor leaders.

He has also been looking ahead. Containerization, an operation in which huge cargo containers are hoisted from a ship's hold by giant cranes, dropped onto waiting wheels, and tractored away, has begun to revolutionize the longshore operation. It conjures up the specter of automation, with one ten-man crew perhaps able to do the work of six twenty-one-man gangs; and this threat to longshoremen's jobs looms as the next major crisis on the nation's docks. Meanwhile, however, one of Gleason's sons, John, and Eugene Burke, brother-in-law of his other son, Thomas Jr., are, respectively, secretary-treasurer and president of a company selling cargo containers and related equipment in New York. No matter how the longshoremen make out in this dispute, the Gleason family will do all right.

Teddy Gleason is known as the waterfront's champion nonstop talker, and his favorite subject right now is the Waterfront Commission. "I don't think any union in America could survive too long under the kind of control the commission is putting on us," he told me. "In the first few years, there might have been some justification for it, but the situation has been steadily improving. Our members are a hundred percent better off than they were when you were doing that movie. You won't see any bodies floating down the river anymore. You don't think we could have gotten back in the AFL-CIO if we were as bad as they said we was ten years ago?

"The Waterfront Commission tries to take credit for the progress we made. But the credit belongs to the men themselves and to collective bargaining. Now that the old shape-up is gone, ninety percent of the hiring is set up the day before. We were coming to that without the commission. The commission centers only hire the extra men to fill in for absentees. What right has the state got to be supervising that? It's quasi-socialism, that's what it is. Our contract calls for every man to be hired by three o'clock the day before he reports to the pier. *We* won that by negotiations.

"What do we need the commission for," Teddy raced on, "when we already have the Landrum-Griffin Bill, which is the greatest guarantee for all unions? It's already a law that you can't hold union office for five years after committing a crime. Under Landrum-Griffin, this so-called criminal element that everybody keeps talking about is unable to operate in a union. I'm willing to obey the law, but this Waterfront Commission is a threat to democracy.

"In the commission centers, the hiring agent is still picking the extra men he wants. If the hiring boss wanted a kickback, he could get it just as easy as before—who knows what goes on when they're alone? It's the same difference, only now it's under a roof. So what've they accomplished—except to make jobs for a lot of political hacks?

"They can't stay in business, they lose their good-paying jobs unless they keep finding something wrong with the waterfront. A man who gets out of prison must work somewhere, otherwise you might as well set up concentration camps. A lot of them gravitate to the waterfront, and they need help. I think we have rehabilitated a great many more men than have come back and gone wrong."

Teddy had a lot more to say about the commission—all bad. Nevertheless, the things I saw and heard and learned on my revisit to the waterfront convinced me that conditions on the docks would be as chaotic today as they were ten years ago if it were not for the commission's regulations and employment centers.

Ten years ago, forty thousand longshoremen averaged less than \$2,500 a year. I visited the homes of many men living a borderline existence—eat today and starve tomorrow—on a haphazard income of \$2,000: a railroad flat in a condemned building, one toilet in the dingy outside hallway for two large families, two bleak bedrooms, and a rat-infested kitchen where a sink also served as a bathtub for the kids. No wonder the husbands preferred the bars. No wonder the wives got drunk on Saturday nights and shouted down the screaming kids over the blast of the unpaid-for television set.

Today, about fifteen thousand men—slightly more than half the present labor force—are earning \$5,000 or more. Teddy Gleason will tell you that collective bargaining and better contracts have made the difference. Yet the ILA condoned the archaic shape-up and opposed decasualization, and the shipping and stevedoring companies have a history of cupidity and disregard for human welfare.

In this brotherhood of corruption, union officials and company executives were drawn together. A surplus of manpower at each pierhead was good for the labor bosses. The companies wanted to hold at their pierhead the five hundred or six hundred men they could use at their peak periods. The extra bodies swelled the membership of the union, paid dues, and were more pliable and kickback-able because they were desperate. So it was a nice thing all around—except for the men.

Most—unfortunately, not all—uncertainty is gone now. Those fifteen thousand dock wallopers and checkers averaging their hundred bucks a week are reasonably sure of steady employment; for the first time, they can estimate their yearly income. If they belong to a regular gang, or a regular extra gang, or if they are checkers carried on the company lists, they no longer have to live close to the docks so as to be within call of the hiring whistle, since now they know a day ahead of time if, when, and where they'll be working tomorrow. The difference between the old way and the new way is the difference between living in a firetrap you share with rats and cockroaches and having a small house in the suburbs.

Of course, for thousands of outsiders, either half blacklisted like the Tommy Monohans or men who simply never had the luck to work their way into a gang hired as a unit, the work is still iffy. They suffer some of the economic insecurity a majority faced ten years ago.

One morning last winter, I dressed in the dark and hurried out into a frozen dawn to meet a commission investigator who was taking me to a hiring session in one of the centers. It was held in a remodeled garage near the docks, and about three hundred hopefuls were already there when I arrived. At 7:30 A.M., the men looked little changed from the ones I used to see outdoors at the pierheads. Old men, middle-aged, a few in their twenties; some short, some tall, but nearly all heavy-muscled, beefy; the oldsters with faces lined and bejowled, and with potbellies, but hard ones; the young men hard-faced, like members of a semipro team unsoftened by college. All of them in a variety of windbreakers and caps of every description, Irish pea caps, heavy ski caps, baseball caps, Marine fatigue caps. In the old days, they would have been beating their hands around a blazing fire in a big metal barrel. Here, indoors, it was still so cold that you could see your breath.

But now there was no crowding forward and jockeying for position, none of the imminent violence of the early fifties. The hiring agent, who must also be approved by the Waterfront Commission, mounted a small stand so he could look down on the men, and then picked them individually by pointing at them. The chosen went over to the desk to show credentials proving they were in good standing with the commission—occasionally, men are temporarily suspended for infractions of the rules, for pilferage on the docks, or for committing some crime away from the docks. By the time hiring agents for four different shipping lines had made their picks, about a hundred men were left. They also went over to the desk and presented their credentials, receiving "show" slips to prove they were there, ready and willing, that morning, so they would not be lopped off the lists. These show slips are also helpful at the unemployment office.

One of the keys to the information center is the telephone, to keep the thirteen centers in constant touch with one another so that one center with a light day can find out where the demand is heavier and send its men there. Thus, the labor force becomes fluid and is able to flow wherever it is needed. Throughout the day, moreover, individual longshoremen can call in to the centers to find out where they can get a day's work tomorrow. Or they can come to the center and read off a large wall board the job situation around the harbor for the next few days, the number of ships arriving and departing, and the number of men that will be required to turn them around.

At least, that's how it's supposed to work. Unfortunately, it doesn't always; and while hiring procedures have been greatly improved since ten years ago, enough abuses still exist to qualify this as one of the principal continuing troubles on the waterfront.

A few days after my first look at a new-style shape-up, I made an unauthorized visit to another hiring center where an old waterfront hand who had been on the management side but whose sympathies were with the men gave me a disillusioning picture of the employment information centers as he knew them on the working level around the harbor.

"Only a few of the centers are doing their job," this outspoken hiring hall director told me. "We're supposed to *help* the men, not police them. Too many of the center directors are men of low caliber who got there through their political connections. Too many managers stay in their office when the men shape. This is a human job. You're working with men who are struggling to make a living in a tough world. You can't do it by the book. Sometimes we find ourselves in direct conflict with Park Row [the commission headquarters]. An investigator catches a man stealing a bottle. Well, hell. That isn't the biggest crime on the waterfront. A hardworking man with a family, a good man, may get suspended for critical weeks when the kids need food on the table. Too many of these investigators are retired detectives who have the small-minded cop psychology. The men feel someone is looking over their shoulder ready to yank their work card away.

"In this center, we've got the confidence of the men, and they come to us with their problems. We loan them a deuce or a pound [five dollars], if things are slow. They don't go to their union delegates with their beefs because they don't trust 'em. You won't find any of this in the Waterfront Commission charter. We play it by ear, in an area where the shipping companies never have felt any responsibility to their employees, and where the union is still tainted with the same old tough-guy psychology.

"I think one trouble with Park Row is that they're in an ivory tower. They never drop in and see what's really going on. That's one reason they don't realize how unpopular the Waterfront Commission really is. Not just with Teddy Gleason, who boasts that he's going to knock the commission out of the box, but with the ordinary Joe. They've got to stop harassing these men individually, concentrate more on the criminal element that's either back in or trying to get back in, make the hiring centers more comfortable, and give more personal service."

I asked him if, feeling as he did about the employment centers, he thought the Waterfront Commission should be abolished. "The waterfront is a jungle that's far from being cleared," he said. "Without the commission, even working imperfectly and sometimes stupidly, the jungle would grow back to what it was when you first came in."

Watching the new, roofed-over shape-ups, I noticed something else that's still wrong with the hiring system. It showed in the haphazard way the hiring agents made their individual choices: older men, obviously veterans of the docks, were often passed over for younger men.

Myles Ambrose, executive director of the Waterfront Commission, confirmed my suspicions. "Seniority is more honored in the breach then in the observance," he said, going on to enumerate a dozen ways in which the seniority regulations are circumvented. "This should be a labor–management problem resolved through collective bargaining and then enforced by the union and accepted by the shippers. But studies over a number of years have convinced us that the ILA, no matter what it writes into the contract, simply doesn't want seniority. Neither do the shippers."

As a result, the commission last spring issued new seniority regulations, with penalties for infractions. But the ILA, with shippers' support, is still resisting, and a court test in the near future is likely. Meanwhile, there are other sore spots on the waterfront besides the remaining abuses in hiring.

MORNINGS IN A SALOON

Tommy Monohan, the hatch foreman who told me about the rebel longshoremen's lean years, mentioned one. "We still got too many locals," he told me. "Ours is $10,000 in debt. A local of five hundred men just isn't large enough to pay all the local's salaries, the rent, the phone, et cetera. The whole West Side should be one big local. Instead of the storefronts with no accommodations for the men, we should have a setup like Paul Hall has for his sailors in Brooklyn. He built them a beautiful waiting room where they can watch TV, read papers, drink coffee or beer, and bull the time away. Here, if the orders are changed from 8:00 to 1:00 P.M., where can you go to wait? A saloon. What else can you do with four hours in the morning? The bar is the only recreation hall we've got on the West Side—or the East River, Staten Island, or Jersey, for that matter. We still don't *look* like a union. Only, in Brooklyn they do. He did a lot of wrong things, but I gotta give Tony Anastasio credit."

Another major headache on the docks is the unabated pilferage. I happened to be at Waterfront Commission headquarters when the daily papers broke a waterfront story that sounded like a TV writer's dream. On the Lower East Side, an unobtrusive little store that called itself the A & R Trading Company had been receiving illicit goods from the piers around the harbor, not individual articles but in wholesale lots, huge packing cases and enormous bales brought in by the truckload and "fenced" for a fraction of their value. But the sneaker was that instead of being fed into the black market that milks the government and the taxpayers of countless millions of dollars, the hijacked cargo was going to a secret vault in the Waterfront Commission offices. For the A & R Trading Company was a fence unlike any other that ever existed in the harbor. It had been set up by the investigating arm of the commission itself, not primarily to arrest big-time pilferers but to dramatize the incredible extent to which pilferage continues to be a flourishing industry.

The A & R Trading Company alone, a comparatively small operation, fenced half a million dollars' worth of goods in the six months of its unique operation. I walked through the secret display, which looked like a well-stocked section of a pier after the unloading of a richly laden freighter. There were bales of Japanese silk, cases of tape recorders from Japan, a crate of incongruous bassoons for symphony orchestras, boxes of baseball gloves, bolts of expensive linen from Belgium, Japanese transistors, Swill typewriters—and scores of crates still unopened, their destinations neatly imprinted, addressed to consignees who had been trying to trace their whereabouts for months.

This fortune in stolen goods came from every section of the port, the product of teamwork among truck drivers, checkers—who are supposed to check each bill of lading—and hi-lo drivers, whose forklifts mechanically hoist cargo from the pier to the trucks' tailgates. Scores of men arrested for their part in the A & R caper will go on trial this fall, but the commission is not yet sure whether these pilferage teams were independent operators hijacking on their own or cogs in the kind of mob-dominated pilferage operations that methodically looted the docks ten years ago. Either way, the results are the same: Ten years after the sensational revelations of the New York State Crime Commission, pilferage is the same going concern it has always been. Even with criminals no longer visible on the piers, this racket may be draining from the regular flow of commerce even more millions of dollars than in the days when mobsters like Mike Clemente, Eddie McGrath, and "Machine Gun" Campbell were right there in front of you.

"The piers of the port are like supermarkets with no checkout counters," Commissioner David Thompson of New Jersey said drily when I expressed amazement at the fantastic array of pilfered cargo two undercover agents for the commission had pretended to "fence" from June to January.

"If they could siphon off half a million in half a year, think what fifty more could do, bigger and better established," added Commissioner Joseph Kaitz of New York, who is unusually qualified for his position since he had been an able counsel for the original Crime Commission. Speculative arithmetic suggests $50 million a year, a sum ultimately tacked on to the prices paid by consumers and thus stolen from nobody except you and me.

A contributing factor to the pilferage racket has been the passivity, if not the complicity, of the port watchmen. In the old days, the Watchman's Union was run by a pair of Joe Ryan's boys, Charley Spencer and Ike Gannon. A watchman having the temerity to report pilferage was called to account by Ike Gannon and told that the right thing to do on the waterfront was to keep your nose clean. It still is. "Play D 'n' D [deaf and dumb]," is the watchman motto. "The port watchman is the most tragic figure on the piers," the Crime Commission reported ten years ago. A veteran watchman testified that in all his experience no one stealing property was ever arrested, explaining, "If you have some trouble with any of the pilferers, a beating may not happen on the dock, but it may happen on the outside."

It hasn't changed. The Waterfront Commission has urged port watchmen to carry out their responsibilities, but most of these men are old and tired, and it's safer to follow the old waterfront code of D 'n' D. "Our main function is to warn longshoremen not to smoke," a watchman admitted sheepishly. "And if you get the wrong fella, he won't even mind you on that."

A fourth major evil on the waterfront is the loading racket. Ten years ago, the New York State Crime Commission wrote, " 'Public loading' has come to mean the moving or lifting of cargo from a pier and stacking it in a truck and also the reverse operation. . . . With few exceptions, the loading at each pier or group of piers is controlled by a group of loaders whom the truckmen must employ and pay . . . regardless of whether the loaders do any work." If a truck was loaded directly by the stevedore company—using the longshoremen it had hired—the boss loader still got his regular fee. To heighten the scandal, the boss loader was frequently an ILA power, theoretically representing the interests of longshoremen but here doubling as an employer of longshoremen. Mickey Bowers on the West Side, Mike Clemente on the East River—all around the harbor, union officials were also public loaders. Loading wasn't a service but a shakedown.

So imagine my shock when I visited Hugh Sheridan, head of the Trucking Authority, an unofficial association of trucking companies in the New York area, and heard this grizzly, blunt trucker with fifty years of waterfront experience, say, "Hell, I wish we had the public loaders back!"

"But it can't be worse than it was before?" I asked.

"It's a helluva lot worse. With the loader, we could get a trailer loaded in an hour and a half, and the rate was about five cents per hundred pounds. Now it takes eight hours from the time a truck enters the pier until it gets its load off the pier and the rate is thirty-one cents per hundred. The loader used to work by the tonnage, pieceload. Now the stevedores charge us by the hour, and the longshoremen they pick up are the bottom of the barrel. Guys with pressed pants and their shoes polished. Ten years ago, we loaded from the dock to the truck without much mechanical help. Just backed a truck into a pile and tossed from the top. Now everything's palletized and loaded by hi-loes. But waiting for a hi-lo driver can tie you up. And there's a shortage of checkers; that's another tie-up.

"An experienced loader ten years ago could make a million a year and not charge nearly the rates they're charging now. It takes four hours just to get onto the docks. From Eighteenth Street, you can see it yourself, there's a double line of trucks backed up as far as Thirty-eighth Street waiting to get into Pier 57. We used to get two loads a day out of the trucks. Now it sometimes takes as long as two days to get rid of just a single load."

Bottlenecks, six- to eight-hour delays, frustration on the part of the truckers as they see money-consuming hours wasted, have inevitably foisted a new racket in the harbor. Where it used to be a one-man shakedown, with the boss loader "doing lovely," as they say on the docks, now it's become a more democratic shakedown, if the spread of extortion money can be so described. "You tip the pier boss to get a higher priority number to get your rig onto the pier. If you want the hi-lo driver to get to you first, you slip him a pound. You have to get the checker to your truck at the same time, so you also slip the checker a deuce or a pound. And so it goes, day in and day out, all the way around the harbor. If it was ever added up, I think the shakedown runs us higher than it did before."

Hugh Sheridan showed me six hundred detailed answers from local trucking companies in response to a confidential questionnaire on malpractices in the port. Nine out of ten attacked the costly six- to eight-hour delays, and wound up with the plea to bring back the public loaders. "The bad old days begin to look pretty good," one trucking executive wrote. On the subject of kickbacks and shakedowns, they were practically unanimous. "A truckman would be out of business if he didn't knuckle under and pay right down the line," wrote one. And another: "This port is being choked to death by the opportunists, by the terrible nepotism, which foists gangsters, incompetents and trash on the back of our community." "Payoffs all the way down the line," another trucker confessed. "The Port of New York is dying as a result of it." One truckman spelled out the exact amounts he had instructed his driver to peel off, including twenty dollars for the dock boss. Truckers were being shaken down in fives and tens to a total of $50,000 a day, he estimated.

"And the Waterfront Commission hasn't done a damn thing about it," Sheridan insisted bitterly. "Why don't they get busy and move in on this racket?"

At the Waterfront Commission, I put Sheridan's question to Myles Ambrose and the commission counsel, William P. Sirignano.

"We're aware of what's going on, but when it's spread in fives and tens among a lot of people it's more difficult to root out than if it's concentrated in one crooked boss loader," Ambrose said.

And Sirignano added, "We've been urging them to report the shakedowns. The only way we can help them is if they tell us what's going on under the table. They complain about it to you, but they don't report it to us."

Ambrose nodded. "We'd love to take action on those cases, but they've got to cooperate with us," he said.

So loading remains a trouble spot on the waterfront, along with pilferage, the fragmentation of the union into too many small, store-front locals, and the abuses still rampant in the hiring procedure. But all of these are secondary to the real source of continuing evil on the waterfront: mobster influence. And it is in this area that the Waterfront Commission finds its strongest arguments against the efforts of the ILA to free itself of regulation by the commission.

Just how thorough a job the ILA would make of cleaning out waterfront criminals if left to its own devices was indicated two years ago in the course of hearings concerning expansion of the commission's powers. Opposing the commission were such unlikely allies as Teddy Gleason and Paul Hall, Captain Bradley and Tony Scotto, and Archdeacon A. Edward Saunders, Episcopal chaplain of the Port of Brooklyn, a social-minded religious leader to whom Scotto points with pride as "our waterfront priest." From motives white to black, they all supported Archdeacon Saunders's position that "bureaucratic control of our way and manner of living . . . constitutes a grave danger to our free and democratic form of government."

Against the resounding arguments of the anticommission forces, the commission fired back with some startling ammunition. Notorious waterfront criminals supposedly barred from the docks by the commission regulations of 1953 were still solidly entrenched and holding union office and lucrative jobs, thanks to the kind of legal loopholes the ILA has always been quick to exploit. For example, the regulations covered only longshoremen, stevedores, pier superintendents, hiring agents, and port watchmen; other waterfront workers were excluded. And the regulations barred criminals only from office, not from membership, in the ILA locals covered, and did not cover jobs with union welfare funds.

The existence of these and other loopholes permitted a rogues' gallery of hoodlums to remain on the waterfront. Among them were:

John Keefe, formerly vice president of the now regulated "Pistol Local" 824, convicted for assault with intent to kill, who could no longer hold union office because of his criminal record. When this was called to the attention of the ILA, that organization solved its problem by removing him as a union officer and giving him a job as a "clerk" at a raise from $9,200 a year to $12,000.

Douglas Rago and *James Vanderwyde* applied for and received a charter from the ILA giving them the power to form a new local, 1826, for *chenangos*, the men who perform the same work as the longshoremen only from railroad lighters, and who were not covered by commission regulations. The odd name chenango clings to these men from a century ago when itinerant pickers in the apple orchards of New York's Chenango Valley would drift down to find jobs on the city riverfront in the off season. Rago and Vanderwyde's qualifications for union leadership seemed to be their extensive criminal records: Rago convicted for assault, robbery, bookmaking, and perjury; and Vanderwyde for robbery, assault, and possession of a pistol. Rago went from New Jersey State Prison to his new job as secretary-treasurer of 1826, while Vanderwyde became business agent and investigator for its welfare fund. Another business agent was *Frank Gagliardi*, whose business activities included conviction for unlawful entry, policy, bookmaking, and theft from interstate commerce.

David Roche, president of Local 205 when I was making my rounds ten years ago, did four years for waterfront extortion. As soon as he was released, the ILA, panting for readmission into the AFL-CIO, made Roche a legislative assistant in Washington, D.C.

Frank James (Machine Gun) Campbell, a hiring boss on Pier 18 for the McGrath mob in the caveman period, was ruled by the Waterfront Commission as ineligible to hold a position of trust on the docks, since he had been convicted for assault, robbery, using dangerous weapons, and, fairly recently, of conspiracy to bribe police in Manhattan. This did not prevent Machine Gun from becoming president and business agent of ILA Local 1478, and an acknowledged power in Local 1823, both representing warehouse workers—not regulated.

In the spring of 1962, Campbell was indicted for extorting money from meat truck drivers and went into hiding. He was on the lam until last April, when FBI agents apprehended him in Detroit, and he is now out on bail. A longtime lieutenant of Eddie McGrath, Campbell was a frequent visitor to ILA headquarters before his sudden disappearance. Said Myles Ambrose, in his plea for greater legislative power to cover the chenangos and other waterfront workers outside the commission jurisdiction, "Campbell is an excellent example of the species of bistate hoodlum [living on Long Island, bossing Jersey locals, wheeling and dealing on Fourteenth Street] with whom we have to deal. . . . He is both feared and hated throughout the port, and is the driving force of the criminal element."

Tony (Cheese) Marchitto was the Jersey City ILA local boss taking orders for Ackalitis while "Acky" was doing time in Dannemora. An official of the Pittston Stevedoring Corporation testified at the Crime Commission hearings that he was in the habit of paying off Tony Cheese for favors rendered. Despite his underworld ties, Marchitto was appointed by President Bradley in the late fifties as trustee for ILA locals 1823 and 1478, although the hapless tugboat captain admitted to commission investigators that Tony Cheese was "the last guy I would have put anyplace, but I had nobody else." No membership meetings were held under the regime of Campbell and Marchitto, and although dues were checked off by the employers every week no accounting was ever made as to how the locals' treasuries were used. The frequently arrested Tony Cheese has persistently—in fact, defiantly—refused to answer any embarrassing questions on the ground that an honest answer would tend to degrade and incriminate him. The AFL-CIO Ethical Practices Committee is on record that any union official refusing to answer questions under oath concerning union activities on the ground of possible self-incrimination should be expelled. A noble sentiment, with a ringing sound. Two years ago, at the most recent hearings on ILA malpractices, eighty separate violations of the Ethical Practices Code were cited, and the Fifth Amendment was invoked no less than five hundred times by ILA officers.

The evidence of underworld influence dredged up from the harbor muck by the investigating arm of the Waterfront Commission seems unmistakable. The ILA was only as good as the Waterfront Commission forced it to be. In areas beyond reach of the commission, you found the same old faces doing business at the same old stand. If Captain Bradley, Teddy Gleason and "Fourteenth Street" could countenance such union officers as Frankie Campbell in the sixties, who could doubt that total retrogression would set in if it were not for the restraining influence of the Waterfront Commission?

Austin Tobin, executive director of the Port Authority, believes that $2 million—the Waterfront Commission's annual budget—is a bargain price for the service the commission is rendering to the harbor. "Remember, there are 400,000 people who earn a living directly from the port," he told me. "I haven't the slightest doubt but that, without the commission, the situation would revert immediately to the jungle it was before."

In his forceful attack on the Waterfront Commission's request for wider power to plug the loopholes exampled above, my old friend Paul Hall chided the commission for boasting of the notable progress the waterfront has made under the commission's direction, and then asking for still broader powers. The commission was inconsistent, Paul suggested, in pointing to the improved moral climate of the harbor while at the same time asking for enlarged powers to police it. But there may be even greater inconsistency in the position of Paul Hall's mentor, the admirable George Meany, president of the AFL-CIO.

Speaking out against readmission of the ILA to the House of Labor in 1956, Meany said, "The ILA is a disgrace to the good name of organized labor. . . . The ILA, by its very nature, is in trouble and always will be in trouble."

Yet only a little over two years later that same ILA—with the hoodlum freight listed above—was taken back into the AFL-CIO on probation. And two years ago, it again became a full-fledged member of the parent organization.

George Meany's reputation for honesty cannot be questioned. But his opposition to the Waterfront Commission, and his forgiveness toward the ILA he righteously damned a few years earlier, raise a pointed question of motive. And that question has a one-word answer: Hoffa. For an ILA outside the AFL-CIO would surely be gobbled up by the Napoleon of the labor movement, the frequently arrested Teamsters president, James Riddle Hoffa. Neither indictments of Hoffa nor convictions of key Teamster officials seem to curtail the growth of Jimmy's outlawed Brotherhood. And the fear that a union chastised by the House of Labor will swell that growth has virtually paralyzed the AFL-CIO Ethical Practices Committee. The very presence of Joe Curran on this committee at the same time that he is photographed arm in arm with Hoffa poses a Gilbert and Sullivan–type question: If this Ethical Practices Committee contains such men as Mr. C., just how ethical can the Ethical Practices Committee be?

How closely entwined are the activities of Jimmy Hoffa and the old guard of the ILA was recently dramatized when Buster Bell was indicted as one of those involved in the $75,000 jury fixing in the Hoffa–Test Fleet case in Nashville. Bell, although he has been convicted of extortion, remains a power in the ILA—president of Local 1804 and a vice president of the international—and the fact that he is involved in the Nashville scandal comes as no surprise to close observers of the waterfront jungle. Hoffa's union is the great pipeline through which the mob sewers into the labor movement, and since through the good graces of ministers without portfolio like Eddie McGrath it is all one happy family, the Buster Bells will always be glad to be of service to Jimmy Hoffa, and vice versa.

A VIEW OF THE HARBOR

One morning near the end of my revisit to the waterfront, I climbed the 168 circular steps to the top of the Statue of Liberty. Looking out through the crown, I had a Liberty-eye's view of the harbor that had delighted its original European discoverer, Verrazano. I watched the broad rivers washing both sides of the arrowhead island, the Narrows providing a God-given channel between the upper and the lower bays; the great oceangoing ships plowing broad and limpid furrows on the sparkling sea. Sightseeing boats, ferryboats, pleasure boats, coastal freighters, busy tugboats pulling barges, sailboats, and work-day railroad lighters; boat whistles and the cries of water birds—I felt a sense of elation, of patriotic phrases surging, "O Columbia, the gem of the ocean . . ."

And then my thoughts turned from Verrazano to Provenzano, "Tony Pro," the Jersey Teamster boss just convicted for extortion. And to Tony Cheese. And Ackalitis put out to pasture with the operating engineers. And the Black Hands of Brooklyn. And Eddie McGrath, rising for a luxurious late breakfast in his apartment on Treasure Island on the causeway to Miami Beach.

From the top of Miss Liberty I asked myself: From 1953 to 1963, has the New York waterfront improved? Yes, particularly in the daily lives of longshoremen. Do racketeers still control the docks? Yes, although *control* shades down to *influence*, less obvious than ten years ago, more sophisticated, more subtle, perhaps even more dangerous. Pilferage remains a prosperous industry, virtually institutionalized, measured in the tens of millions. Murder, Inc., too vulgar for

Rod Steiger and Marlon Brando in a scene from *On the Waterfront*.

the sophisticated sixties, has been replaced by its more abstract but no less dangerous successor, Apathy, Inc., shrugging off bribery, graft, extortion, and shakedowns: business as usual.

In the black and white of the early fifties, I didn't need a compass to find my way. There were the bad guys and the good guys. The old days were like climbing into the ring with a fighter who had only two hands. Now it's like squaring off with an octopus. A film with the simple thrust of *On the Waterfront* is already a museum piece. The waterfront has changed. "It's a hell of a lot better," said my old friend, Father Phil Carey, an overworked pixie whose sleep is troubled by the daily problems of the workers he serves. Then, typically, he added, "But it still has a hell of a ways to go. The commission may be as necessary as castor oil in the springtime, but it's not palatable, and needs a lot of sarsaparilla."

Father John Corridan, considered by old harbor hands the father of the Waterfront Commission, now teaching theology at St. Peter's College in Jersey City, says with a flash of his old rebellion: "Not until we can bring the spirit of Almighty God into our daily economic, political, and social lives can our city prosper. We have a longer and harder fight here than the fight against communism. Communism is just the Russian version of materialism. On the waterfront, we've got the American version."

Breakfasting with Attorney General Bobby Kennedy recently, I discussed with him the theme of his book *The Enemy Within*, which I had been adapting for the screen. Kennedy has aptly defined that enemy as the corruptive forces among businessmen and labor leaders alike that are eating at the roots of integrity and idealism on which our country depends for growth. "Nowhere is this 'enemy within' more deeply entrenched, more difficult to root out, than in the harbor of New York," the attorney general said to me. "I understand [U.S. Attorney Robert] Morganthau told you it is not a problem that can be solved by law enforcement alone. That's been my experience also. It must be our job to keep the pressure on, but the only way to check rampant racketeering is with the cooperation of an aroused rank and file and a public that cares."

If waterfront "Mr. Bigs" like Eddie McGrath can live like millionaires, who's picking up those hefty tabs? If those multimillions funneled out of legitimate commerce through the pilferage and loading rackets are tacked on to the retail price, who's paying for the flourishing business of waterfront crime? Only the public. Only you, the consumer.

The waterfront will remain—with its better life for Joe Docks, with its trigger boys no longer rattling their hardware on the piers, with the bistate commission able to justify its contribution to "the substantially improved moral climate"—but still rotten to the core.

Vale atque Ave—Father John M. Corridan, S.J.

(Excerpts)

On the eve of the Fourth of July, 1984, when firecrackers and the bottles of imported wine already had begun to pop in the Hamptons, and escapist New Yorkers were working their furious logistics to squeeze in yet another cocktail party, I had a phone call from *The New York Times*.

The Reverend John M. Corridan, S.J., was gone at seventy-three. Did I have any comment?

I must have been thinking the answer for so long that it seemed to flow out of its own accord:

"Father John? 'Pete,' as his old friends called him. He was the closest I ever came to personally feeling what true Christianity was about."

Driving through the hard rain to the chapel here at Fordham for the funeral mass, I thought the nasty weather and the inconvenient date were appropriate symbols for Pete's sendoff as the "waterfront priest." Not just the soul but the guts of the New York waterfront in the tough forties and fifties, he had chosen a dangerous road to Christian service, taking to heart and mind the challenge of Jesus: "If you do it to the least of mine, you do it to me."

Waiting for the mass to begin, I looked around in sadness at the pitiful turnout for this finale. The only celebrants were brother "Jezzies" with whom Pete had lived in his later years of obscurity, a few family members, and a smattering of friends who remembered him from his days as a mover and shaker on the waterfront. A fearless enemy of the corrupt syndicate that ran the harbor of New York, and a voice for social justice, he was determined—despite opposition that reached all the way up to the archdiocese—to put into practice the teachings of Christ as he saw them. He fought for drastic reforms to free longshoremen from the inhuman shape-up and all the other humiliations practiced on them by the racket-ridden International Longshoremen's Association and their unholy allies, the corrupt stevedore and shipping companies.

If the infamous shape-up is now a relic of the past, if there is now a bistate Waterfront Commission responsible for policing a Brooklyn-to-Hoboken waterfront still preyed upon by organized crime, these changes for the better can be largely attributed to one man: Father John Corridan.

Had he died thirty years ago at the height of his influence, instead of the handful who have come to this unheralded funeral mass there would have been thousands: They would have packed St. Patrick's and then some. For *On the Waterfront*, with Karl Malden winning an Oscar nomination for his gritty impersonation of Father John, had made this fearless waterfront priest something of a national celebrity.

Father John put words into action by calling strategy meetings in the basement of the Church of St. Francis Xavier on the Lower West Side, where he counseled his "insoigents" on how to fight against the brutal dictatorship of the ILA and for union democracy. He agitated for a Waterfront Crime Commission that would hold hearings on dock abuses, and he drew on his moral persuasiveness and political savvy to counter the doubts and fears of men who knew they were victims of a rotten system but who were afraid, if they spoke their piece in public, that they would be starved off the docks at best, or sent to the bottom of the river like scores of stand-up guys before them.

When the NLRB finally called a vote between the entrenched ILA and the democratic opposition, Father John was in the middle of it, helping direct the election campaign that saw the old guard winning by the thinnest of margins, thanks to some strong-arm election tactics that reminded waterfronters of the worst days of Tammany rule.

Through those bitter years, Father John's commitment drew plenty of criticism from conservative Catholics who questioned the right of a priest to move so deeply into secular affairs. But Father John stood his ground.

"What hurts me," he said to me over a beer in a waterfront bar in Hell's Kitchen, "is that those Sunday Catholics think nothing of treating their fellow human beings like dirt every day in the week. They seem to forget that every man is precious in the eyes of Our Lord and that He died for all of us, as brothers in Christ Jesus, and not just for the privileged few."

The real boss of the waterfront, I learned from Corridan, was not Joe Ryan, the crafty and grafty president of the ILA. It was Mr. Respectable, Mr. Big: William J. McCormack, who had worked his way up from teenage wagon driver to a monopoly of the stevedoring business for the Pennsylvania Railroad. His cement company paved the city's streets. He sold the city its oil and gas. Tugboats, sand dredging companies, you name it and chances were Big Bill McCormack owned it, dredging up millions of dollars for himself every month. Joe Ryan was his messenger boy, and so was the mayor, Impellitiere, who dropped everything and came running every time Big Bill called City Hall.

Big Bill was also a prodigious donor to the Church, one of those Sunday Catholics against whom Father John railed. So when our waterfront priest heard that "Mr. Big" was up for the Order of St. Gregory (the highest honor available to Catholic laymen), he blew his cork.

It happened that Elia Kazan, the director of our film, was with me for this Vesuvius. I had described Father John to him as "far-out," but this day, given the provocation, Corridan outdid himself.

"That goddamn powerhouse! That Spellman! Who the hell does he think he is, giving the Saint G. to an SOB like Mr. Big? Hell, McCormack's a murderer! Maybe not with his own hands. But he gets the Ackalitises and the Cockeye Dunns [infamous executioners on the docks] to do his dirty work. I'm gonna stop that award if it's the last thing I ever do!"

Retreating to a corner saloon between Xavier and the docks, I asked a shaken Kazan, "Well, Gadge, what do you think now?"

"God Almighty!" he said. "Are you sure he's a priest?"

"Come on, Gadge, you think he rented the cassock and turned-around collar from Brooks Costume? He sure as hell *is* a priest. In fact, if there were more like him I think I might start going to mass."

Father John's outspoken opposition to the ceremonializing of Mr. Big's Catholicity led to a classic confrontation between the lowly but combative waterfront priest and the New York Prince of the Church. The pro-Spellman view is that the cardinal was ready to throw the book (and not necessarily the Good Book) at Father John but relented, acted in mercy, and decided to table the honor to Bill McCormack. The truth was that Father John, drawing on his thorough and damaging file on Mr. Big, presented such an embarrassment of incriminating evidence on McCormack's illegal waterfront activities that the cardinal saw that discretion—at least, for the moment—was the better part of valor.

Father John had won a historic, little-known, and now forgotten battle. But when his longshore rebels got shafted in that tough election, his days were numbered on the waterfront. Both in the *Times* obit and in the moving and unusually personal homily delivered by Father Thomas Brady, it was said that Father John asked to be transferred to Syracuse because he felt his work on the docks was finished. I was with him at the time of his transfer, and, believe me, make no mistake, Syracuse was the last place he wanted to go. What was done to him broke his spirit, his heart, and, almost, his faith.

One time when he was complaining over a beer about hierarchical injustices, I asked him if he had ever thought about quitting the Church. He paused and thought and sipped his beer. "Oh sure, every once in a while. But it would break my mother's heart." Then his fist came down hard on the table. "And, goddamn it, I'm a Catholic!"

Father Corridan was a human encyclopedia of waterfront crime and a moral weather vane pointing to waterfront reform. In the end, as we must acknowledge here at the funeral mass, he paid a terrible price for bringing Christ to the shape-up.

But what he accomplished in those explosive years of the waterfront fifties can never be undone. His superior, Father Philip Carey, as dedicated as, if wisely more prudent than Father John, continues the good work to this day—somewhat like a salmon swimming upstream. But there will never be another Father John (Pete) Corridan. He brought the story of the Crucifixion from Calvary to the piers of the "Pistol Local." And right now I can see him there, not resting in peace but giving hell to the Bill McCormacks, the Joe Ryans, and even some of those all too accommodating monsignors and cardinals who messed up what he considered the true obligations of his Church.

Vale atque Ave, Father Pete.

This photo from the 1940s shows New York City, with hundreds of piers, at the height of the waterfront's extent and power. This single series of interconnected piers was the richest in the world. At the time, the International Longshoremen's Union membership was at an all-time high of more than forty thousand strong. Today, its membership is between three thousand and four thousand members.
Photograph copyright © CORBIS.

About the Authors

Malcolm Johnson was a reporter for *The New York Sun*. He won the Pulitzer Prize in 1949 for his series of articles about crime on the New York waterfront. He died in 1976.

Budd Schulberg is an Academy Award–winning screenwriter and the best-selling author of *What Makes Sammy Run?* and *The Disenchanted*. He cofounded the Douglass House Watts Writers Workshop in Los Angeles in the 1960s and New York's Frederick Douglass Creative Arts Center in 1971. He lives on eastern Long Island.

Haynes Johnson is a best-selling author, a Pulitzer Prize–winning journalist, and a national television commentator. His most recent book, *The Best of Times: America in the Clinton Years*, was a national best-seller and a *New York Times* Notable Book. He lives in Washington, D.C.

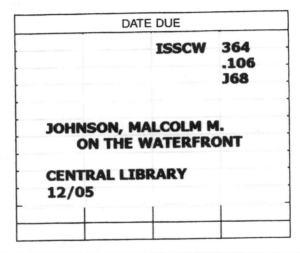